P9-DXI-901

Also by Craig Pittman

The Scent of Scandal:
Greed, Betrayal, and the World's Most Beautiful Orchid

Manatee Insanity:
Inside the War over Florida's Most Famous Endangered Species

Paving Paradise:
Florida's Vanishing Wetlands and the Failure of No Net Loss
(coauthor)

WITHDRAWN

Oh, Florida!

How America's Weirdest State Influences the Rest of the Country

Craig Pittman

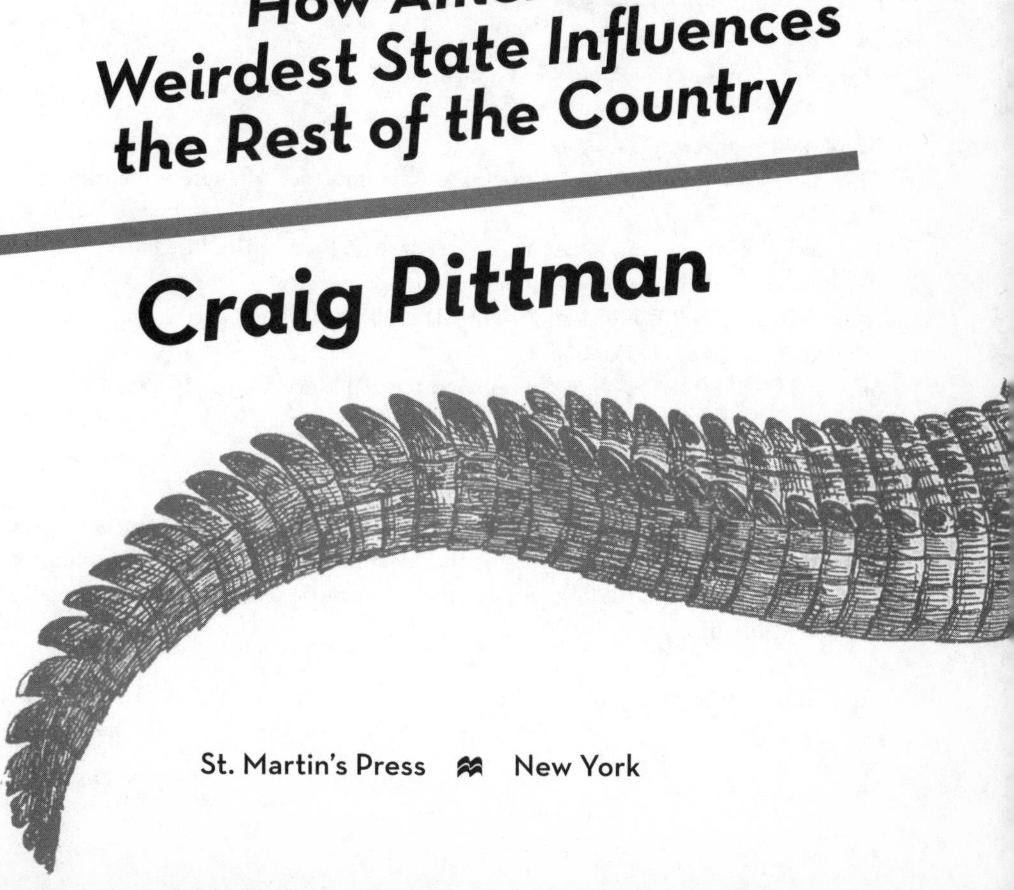

St. Martin's Press ❧ New York

OH, FLORIDA! Copyright © 2016 by Craig Pittman. All rights reserved. Printed in the United States of America. For information, address St. Martin's Press, 175 Fifth Avenue, New York, N.Y. 10010.

www.stmartins.com

Designed by Steven Seighman

Library of Congress Cataloging-in-Publication Data

Names: Pittman, Craig, author.
Title: Oh Florida! : how America's weirdest state influences the rest of the country / Craig Pittman.
Description: First edition. | New York : St. Martin's Press, 2016. | Includes bibliographical references and index.
Identifiers: LCCN 2016003225| ISBN 9781250071200 (hardcover) | ISBN 9781466882171 (e-book)
Subjects: LCSH: Florida—Description and travel. | Florida—Civilization.
Classification: LCC F316.2 .P57 2016 | DDC 975.9—dc23
LC record available at http://lccn.loc.gov/2016003225

Our books may be purchased in bulk for promotional, educational, or business use. Please contact your local bookseller or the Macmillan Corporate and Premium Sales Department at 1-800-221-7945, extension 5442, or by e-mail at MacmillanSpecialMarkets@macmillan.com.

First Edition: July 2016

10 9 8 7 6 5 4 3 2 1

This book is dedicated to the folks who made it possible: the twenty million people who live in Florida and the nearly one hundred million tourists who visit each year. You are the greatest comedy writers in history.

Contents

The notes for the material cited in this book are available at the book's website, www.oh-florida.com

Acknowledgments

In 19mumblemumble, a *St. Petersburg Times* reporter named Tom Zucco, who was both one of the funniest people I ever met and one of the tallest, invited me to help him with an annual New Year's feature that the paper called "The Sour Orange Awards." Modeled on *Esquire*'s "Dubious Achievement Awards," the Sour Oranges collected some of the sickest, stupidest stories that had occurred in Florida in that year. I had always chuckled about weird Florida stories before, but thanks to Zucco I started collecting them, and for that I have to thank him. I should mention, by the way, that Tom was once married to a Weeki Wachee mermaid, so he's got that going for him.

When I joined Twitter, I naturally began posting weird Florida stories, and they always got a great response, so I posted more. In 2013, one of my Twitter followers, a *Slate* editor named Laura Helmuth, contacted me to say she enjoyed those items a lot, and would I please write a blog for *Slate* about Florida? That blog became the genesis for this book. Thanks, Laura!

Thank you to my agent, Andrew Stuart, and to Paul Starobin, who both believed strongly in this project and found it a good home, and to Daniella Rapp at St. Martin's, whose great ideas and enthusiasm were inspiring.

Conversations with historians Gary Mormino and Jim Clark helped me map out the path this book would take. Many of my friends contributed through conversations in person and on Facebook, particularly Caryn Baird, Cynthia Barnett, Bill Cooke, Eric Deggans, George Bowers, Larry Kahn, Barbara Hijek, Brendan Farrington, Ron Matus, William McKeen, and Craig Waters. Caryn and Bill helped me with some particularly important research, as well.

Also I must thank the folks who allowed me to inflict my first draft chapters on them so they could check them for accuracy: Jim Clark, Anna Phillips,

Craig Waters, Gary Mormino, and Kathleen McGrory. If you still find errors in the manuscript, that's my fault.

My wife, Sherry Robinson, deserves the biggest thanks of all. She not only put up with the massive pile of books scattered on both floors of our house and the long hours I spent tap-tap-tapping away on various keyboards. She also read the whole thing first and made some big improvements in the prose—so you should thank her too.

Florida is a study in abnormal psychology, useful in signaling the . . . hidden derangements of the national mood.

—Lawrence P. Lessing, "State of Florida," *Fortune*, February 1948

When the going gets weird, the weird turn pro.

—Hunter S. Thompson, who launched his gonzo journalism career at Eglin Air Force Base, near Fort Walton Beach, Florida

A woman floats in the crystal clear waters of Weeki Wachee Springs, 1947. Florida has more first-magnitude springs than anywhere else on Earth. Photo by Toni Frissell. Photo courtesy of Library of Congress.

Prologue: The Punch Line State

Florida is a strange place. I love it here, and I love how nothing makes sense.
—Author Roxane Gay, whose parents live in Florida

One warm June afternoon, my friend Shannon called me looking for help. She said her women's group was putting on a luncheon for some folks visiting from another country. Each member of her group was supposed to sit at a table full of the visitors from, I don't know, Shteyngartistan or something, and somebody came up with the idea of arming the ladies with Fun Facts About Florida as icebreakers.

The problem, she said, was that the facts they'd compiled about Florida so far weren't all that fun. Leading industries, form of government, so forth. She said, "I was wondering if you—"

"You got a pen?" I asked, wiping sweat from my face. "Take this down. In 1845, when Florida became a state, the first state flag that flew over the capital bore the slogan 'Let Us Alone.'"

She chuckled, aware of how ironic that sounded for a state where the economy depends on bringing in a constant flow of new residents.

I told her about Ochopee, the town with the nation's smallest post office (formerly a toolshed) and Carrabelle, home of the world's smallest police station (a phone booth), and Cassadaga, which has so many crystal balls per capita that it's known as the Psychic Capital of the World. I made sure to mention Sweetwater, the town founded by a troupe of Russian circus midgets whose bus broke down. More recently it's been a haven for Nicaraguan refugees.

I reeled off a dozen oddball bits of Floridiana but avoided the *really* weird stuff—the nude bikers, the Wiccan Klan members, the convocations of furries who throw beach parties in full costume. I didn't mention that families in the little town of Vernon became so dependent on insurance money paid out for lost limbs that people started shooting them off, which is how it became known as "Nub City." I didn't bring up the allegations that both Donald Duck and Tigger groped female visitors to Walt Disney World. And I *definitely* did not recount for her the tale of Carl Tanzler, aka "Count Carl von Cosel," a Key West X-ray technician who in 1930 fell in love with a tuberculosis patient named Maria Elena Milagro de Hoyos. His love transcended death, by which I mean that when she died, he dug up her body and slept with the corpse for nine years, until her sister found out. Put on trial for grave robbing, he was exonerated—because the statute of limitations had expired.

No, some Florida tales are not fit for use as an icebreaker. They might have the opposite effect.

Shannon jotted down what I told her, giggling, then thanked me. "I knew I could count on you," she said, hanging up.

About the time Shannon called looking for Fun Florida Facts, the fine folks at the e-zine *Slate* approached me with a somewhat similar request. They wanted me to blog about Florida, to explain how it can be both the Land of Flowers and the Land of Face-Eating Zombies. They picked me because I highlight both sides in my Twitter feed, @craigtimes, usually tagged as "Oh #Florida!" (It wasn't a conscious nod to Wallace Stevens's poem "O Florida, Venereal Soil," but it works that way too.)

So in the summer of 2013, the Season of "Stand Your Ground," I spent a month detailing the many ways Florida fed the national obsession with oddities. My blog was called "Oh #Florida!" The hard part wasn't filling a month of blog entries. The hard part was finding room to squeeze in all our outrageousness in only thirty days.

As that line on the first state flag demonstrates, Florida's residents have been weird and contradictory and muleheaded for a long time. In 1948, a writer for *Forbes* observed that there's "something in Florida's humid, languorous air" that attracts "pirates, derelicts, remittance men, thieves, madams, gamblers, blue-sky promoters, moneybags, exhausted noblemen, black-market operators, profiteers [and] all the infections of Western life."

That list can still stand today, although I'd add more categories: avid nudists, uniformed Scientologists, professional python wranglers, voodoo priests, spam kings, monkey breeders, circus freaks, retired spies, and strip-club moguls.

And to think, we've got twenty-nine votes in the electoral college! This motley crew of Florida men and Florida women just might choose the next president—again.

Heck, Florida even fielded the most candidates for the 2016 Republican nomination: Jeb Bush, Marco Rubio, Dr. Ben Carson, and Mike Huckabee are all Florida residents, and Donald Trump is a part-timer. You can easily tell they're Florida men: constantly committing gaffes, trying to explain their unsavory associates, doing their best to avoid questions about their finances, struggling to put on a hoodie the wrong way, hitting kids in the face with a football. The rest of America was amazed. Floridians just shrugged.

Oh, Florida! That name. That combination of sounds. Three simple syllables, and yet packing so many mixed messages. Florida offers an abundance of natural beauty—gin-clear springs, sugar-sand beaches, cotton-candy sunsets—and oodles of odd behavior. There was the burglar in Silver Spring Shores who snorted containers of human and canine ashes, thinking they were mind-altering substances. Or the man dressed as a pirate, complete with a sword and two knives, who stood on a bridge in the Keys firing blanks from his black-powder pistols, unaware that he was scaring the bejeezus out of the tourists driving by. Or the wannabe mermaid who got in hot water with her Tampa area homeowners' association for wearing her costume in the community pool. It violated the "no fins" policy.

To me, that combination of beauty and the bizarro makes Florida the most fascinating state of the fifty. Reading the news here regularly produces gasps of astonishment and guffaws of guilty laughter. Sure, weird news pops up everywhere there are humans, but Florida seems to produce more of it than anywhere else, and our news tends to be weirder. For instance, in one seven-day period in December 2014, the news carried stories about Floridians who

1. faked a heart attack in Walmart to steal Barbie toys
2. kidnapped a seventy-pound giant African land tortoise and made taunting phone calls to the owner
3. slapped a grandmother for refusing to accept a Facebook friend request
4. tried to hire a hit man by giving him title to a pizza delivery van and saying, "Have fun!"
5. violated probation by possessing meth while visiting the probation office
6. got into a brother-vs.-brother sword fight
7. tore down a holiday display at the state Capitol that was put up by the Satanic Temple—but did not touch the Festivus pole

Carl Hiaasen, the *Miami Herald* columnist renowned for his wacky Florida crime novels, says he gets plenty of material from his daily paper. "My big problem has been being ahead of the curve of weirdness with the novels," he said. "It's hard to write something that won't come true in Florida. Time and again, I've thought I'd come up with the most revolting and twisted scenario only to have it trumped by something in the *Herald* days later."

Our reputation has gone international. When my friend Katie visited Japan in 2015, one of her interpreters described an area of Osaka this way: "This area used to be really dirty and have crazy people. Many Florida Man."

Florida is a place where tragedy often wears the mask of comedy. This is the state where a Miami man confessed on Facebook to killing his wife, and then turned out to be the author of a book titled *How I Saved Someone's Life and Marriage and Family Problems Thru Communication.*

Part of Florida's appeal is that it's the Land of a Thousand Chances, the place where people go who have screwed up elsewhere and need to start over. In the 1920s, after Carlo Ponzi was busted in Boston for running the original Ponzi scheme, he fled to Florida. He was then caught running a real estate scam.

Nothing in Florida is ever quite what it seems. Visitors to Key West drive over the Seven-Mile Bridge, which isn't that long; and marvel at the six-toed cats proudly featured at Ernest Hemingway's house, even though Papa didn't own any cats; and snap selfies at the Southernmost Point in the United States, which isn't.

In Florida, the crimes tend to be weirder and the scams bigger. Other places have con men, but only in Florida would you have the West Palm Beach con artists who raked in $1 million by convincing elderly people to buy "special" toilet paper. Other places have thieves, but only in Florida do you find the Gainesville paleontology enthusiast accused of swiping an entire dinosaur skeleton from Mongolia (it's been returned). Other places have drug smugglers, but only in Florida do you find the crew who dumped cocaine from their plane, only for it to land in the middle of a Homestead crime watch meeting, narrowly missing the police chief's head.

Florida is really something, folks. Not necessarily something good, mind you. We are regularly ranked as the nation's mortgage fraud capital, the tax fraud capital, the identity theft capital, the pill mill kingdom, not to mention a hotbed of Fix-A-Flat butt enhancers. As one news report noted in 2015, we've got "fake Jamaican lotteries, false marriages for immigration purposes, mediocre seafood marketed as better seafood, . . . even foreign substandard cheese passed off as domestic top shelf."

In our tropical heat, tempers boil faster and a machete or some other odd weapon tends to be in easy reach. The mosquitoes are bloodthirstier than any *Twilight* vampire. Sharks lurk just offshore, ready to chomp on your leg while you're shuffling around to avoid the stingrays. Alligators show up at your picnic to eat your burgers, then go off to bite a police cruiser's bumper. And without any warning, the ground is liable to swallow you up.

I always tell people: Live here and you'll never be bored. And you'll never suffer an irony deficiency. This is the place where

- a wrecking crew that was supposed to demolish a historic house in Miami mistakenly rammed their bulldozer into the house next door—the headquarters of the group that had been trying to preserve the historic home
- a Gainesville man trying to steal a car accidentally locked himself inside it
- a state wildlife commissioner from Davie got in trouble with the wildlife commission because he illegally wrestled an alligator (and nearly lost)

Florida produces so much weird news that, as I write this in 2015, at least three blogs and four Twitter accounts pump this precious resource to the outside world, not unlike offshore rigs extracting crude from beneath the Gulf of Mexico. All the major news aggregators—*Gawker,* BuzzFeed, *Huffington Post,* etc.—recognize Florida stories as major click bait and spread the wildest stories far and wide.

My one concern about this is that once we've turned the Sunshine State into the Punch Line State, nobody will take Florida seriously. That, my friend, is a major mistake. No matter how hard you may laugh at Florida, the fact is it's constantly influencing all the other states. They just don't notice it.

If you live in Florida for a while, you learn to follow the news in a certain way. When big news happens in other states, people say, "Oh, my goodness!" or "What the—?"

But we Floridians will scan a story or click over to CNN or Fox and mutter to ourselves, "Okay, where's the Florida connection?"

We do this because we know that any big story is likely to have a link to America's strangest state. A guy lands a gyrocopter at the Capitol to protest campaign finance laws? He's a Floridian. A Major League Baseball doping scandal? The clinic was in Florida. The 9/11 hijackers got their flight training here. When the planes hit the Twin Towers, President George W. Bush was reading a story about a heroic goat to Florida schoolchildren. Who gave special prosecutor Ken Starr permission to dig into President Bill Clinton's affair with an intern? Attorney General Janet Reno, a Florida native. Remember the 1972 Watergate break-in that brought down Richard Nixon? Guess where the burglars were from. And don't forget that Florida decided who would be the Leader of the Free World in 2000, guaranteeing no one would name a child Chad for at least fifty years.

Go back in American history, and you'll discover many of the major events have a Florida angle. Take Abraham Lincoln's assassination. One of John Wilkes Booth's conspirators was a Florida man named Lewis Powell. He bluffed his way into Secretary of State William Seward's house, pulled a gun that misfired, then pulled a knife and stabbed Seward. Seward recovered. Powell was caught and hanged, shortly after posing for a precursor of the modern mug shot.

These days, everywhere you turn, you see Florida, but you may not know it. Former Florida high school students pop up as stars: television (Barbara Walters, Miami Beach High, 1947 graduate); movies (Johnny Depp dropped out of Miramar High when he was sixteen to play in a band); and magazine covers (*Sports Illustrated* swimsuit star Kate Upton dropped out of Holy Trinity Episcopal Academy in Melbourne to focus on modeling). If you bought merchandise online or even used a computer, you can thank Florida. If you gawked at a supermarket tabloid or skimmed through *USA Today,* that was Florida calling you. If you ever gambled at an Indian casino or needed help from a public defender, you've been touched by Florida. If you saw a once endangered species that's been saved, or visited a national wildlife refuge, thank Florida.

To live in Florida is to live with change. We've survived the most wrenching demographic alteration in America. We went from being the least-populated Southern state in 1940, with 1.8 million residents, to 20 million now. This human tsunami brought in the young, the old, whites, blacks, Asians, Hispanics, and a host of other census classifications, all bumping up against each other, ramming into each other's cars, shouting at each other in various languages, objecting to whatever weird thing their neighbors are doing.

Florida recently passed New York as the third most-populous state. Contemplate that for a moment. Despite (or perhaps because of?) all the reports about weird behavior here, millions of people moved to Florida anyway, figuring it was the ideal place to create their future. Tourism hasn't suffered, either. In 2014, it surged to more than ninety-seven million. Experts say the number will soon hit one hundred million.

I love it here. I'm a native Floridian, married to another native Floridian. My ancestors arrived in 1850, no doubt looking for a good deal on waterfront condos.

I grew up hunting in Florida's forests, fishing in its lakes, canoeing its rivers. I have battled its sandspurs and no-see-ums. I have savored the sweet scent of a grove full of orange blossoms and gagged on the stench of a pulp mill. I have dined on every type of Florida cuisine, from Apalachicola oysters (surprisingly sweet) to fried gator tail (chewy) to the Cuban sandwiches of both Tampa and Miami (Tampa's are better). I've zoomed through the Everglades on an airboat and braved the deli line at Publix. I've even pondered some of Florida's greatest mysteries—for instance, why mullet suddenly leap from the water. Some scientists say it's to evade predators, others say it's to clean their scales of parasites. I think it's due to fish flatulence.

Since 1989, I've worked as a reporter for Florida's largest newspaper, the *Tampa Bay Times* (formerly the *St. Petersburg Times*). I've chatted with death row inmates, survived hurricanes and wildfires, and followed the state's most popular politician into a restroom to ask him a question he didn't like. I've rooted around in the attic of Florida history and written books about wetland fillers, manatee killers, and orchid smugglers.

What I hope to do with this book is explain my favorite state to you. I want to tell you why it's so awful and awesome, so darkly weird and wonderful all at the same time. I also want to make you see how Florida and Floridians have already altered life in the rest of America and the world at large, and how they're continuing to influence the future.

This is not a history of Florida, although I'll be recounting some of our twisted backstory. This is not a memoir, although I'll sprinkle in a few personal anecdotes to make a point. This is not one of those books that consists entirely of a bunch of wacky stories, although I'll spin some of those yarns as well. My goal is to make you see Florida the way I see it, to appreciate Florida the way we natives do, to relish its fantastic flavors and wild variety. Think of me as your tour guide on a journey of exploration, a cross between squint-eyed Rod Serling and one of those patter-drunk boat captains on Disney's Jungle Cruise.

For starters, here's the best story I know to give you a sense of what it's like here:

When I was twelve, I was camping with my Boy Scout troop down by a river. While crossing the deepest part of the river I lost my footing and the current pulled me under. I remember the rippling water closing over me, the pitiless blue sky above. Even now, years later, I sometimes dream about this, struck by the beauty of what seemed like the last thing I'd ever see. Just before the river claimed me for good, I grabbed hold of a rope that was strung across one end of the swim area.

To me this sums up life in Florida: surrounded by dangerous beauty, in way over our heads, pulled along by powerful forces, desperately grabbing for any lifeline.

Children run through the surf at St. Petersburg Beach, 1948. For those of us who grew up in Florida, the smell of cocoa butter is our madeleine. Photo courtesy of State Archives of Florida.

1

Growing Up Floridian

> I have an unusual hobby: I collect pictures of people I don't know. It started when I was a kid growing up in South Florida, the land of junk stores, garage sales, and flea markets, as a kind of coping mechanism.
>
> —Ransom Riggs, author of *Miss Peregrine's Home for Peculiar Children*

My wife and I were talking to our kids one day about what it was like growing up in Florida way back in the long-time-ago. At one point I said rather casually, "I remember back when there was no Disney World."

I have now seen what it looks like when a child's mind is blown.

They couldn't picture it. A Florida without Disney? How could that be? Could Florida exist without Disney?

Well, sure. Florida muddled along for several centuries without Uncle Walt and his Happiest Place on Earth. We drew tourists with our healing springs, our beautiful beaches, our tropical breezes. We pulled them in with our cheesy roadside attractions, our gator rassling, and our fresh-squeezed orange juice samples.

Those of us who grew up in Florida remember what it was like. We remember the old tourist traps, like Six Gun Territory, the Cypress Knee Museum, and the Atomic Tunnel. We have an abiding affection for the ones still hanging on by their fingernails, like Everglades Wonder Gardens.

You might think Florida kids would all be beach bum slackers. It is true that we tend to love the beach. My friend Connie, who grew up in Fort Lauderdale, says that until she was twenty-five she virtually lived in a bikini.

But don't assume all Florida kids are underachievers. John Atanasoff became fascinated with the slide rule that his engineer father used at a Polk County phosphate mine. He graduated early from Mulberry High School, then earned a degree in electrical engineering from the University of Florida in 1926. While a professor in Iowa in 1941, he invented the first working computer.

Then there's Jeff Bezos, 1982 senior class valedictorian and class president at Miami Palmetto High School. That summer Bezos started his first business, a summer camp. That same entrepreneurial spirit would eventually lead him to launch Amazon.com, making a profitable use of Professor Atanasoff's invention.

So don't underestimate what Florida kids can do. Still, I wonder sometimes what today's Florida kids will remember about this place they call home. Memories may be the main thing they have left. To grow up in Florida is to see things nobody else sees but you, says veteran war correspondent Dexter Filkins, who hails from Cape Canaveral.

"You grow up watching everything you know being destroyed, and it leaves you with this kind of haunted feeling," he explained to me one day.

It's like being the kid in *The Sixth Sense*: You're always seeing things no one else sees, because you remember what existed before everything changed.

The truth is, there aren't that many of us Florida-born Floridians to begin with. Florida has the second-fewest natives of any state (number one: Nevada). The 2010 census says only about a third of Florida's nineteen million residents are natives. Some of those six million—nobody knows how many—are kids born in the last decade.

It's never been easy to be a kid, with all the learning and growing you have to deal with. I would argue that it's tougher than ever to be a kid in Florida because it's such a crazy place. Every time you turn around, grown-ups are leaving you to sit in a hot car while they party at a Lil Wayne concert, hit a bar for a few hours, or visit a strip club. In 2013, so many dads left their kids alone to hang out in strip joints that a newspaper suggested that such establishments should co-locate with day care centers. Even babies have it rough. In 2013, a woman caught shoplifting tried to avoid arrest by hurling her baby at a cop.

Still, growing up in Florida has its perks. You can expect at least one class field trip to see the rocks and rockets at Cape Canaveral. You can play outdoor sports year-round. If your family can afford it (a big if, given how prices have gone up), you can count on at least one vacation trip to a theme park—Disney World, SeaWorld, Busch Gardens, Legoland, the Wizarding World of Harry Potter, you name it. They're all within driving distance of the state's major population centers and open nearly all the time, ready to take every-one's money. There's even a theme park called the Holy Land Experience that recreates Jesus's crucifixion six days a week.

We here in Florida are so used to having these giant fantasy generators just down the road from our daily reality that it *can* be hard to picture what Florida was like BW (Before Walt). When I was a kid, Walt was just some guy with a Sunday night TV show. The closest we got to Fantasyland was the Goofy Golf place on the beach.

I grew up on a red clay road on the edge of a town named Pensacola in the farthest western part of the Panhandle. The sky was filled with Navy train-ing planes by day and blinking fireflies at night—except when the mosquito-control truck drove by spewing a billowing cloud of bug spray. Some kids pedaled their bikes along behind it, taking in big lungfuls of the stuff, trying to get high. I believe they all grew up to become members of our legislature.

Summer vacation meant trips to the beach, particularly Fort Pickens, a relic from before the Civil War, surrounded by glistening white sand dunes and sea oats that swayed in the breeze from the Gulf of Mexico. Or my family would go fishing, reeling in our catch from a lake full of bream. Or we'd stand on the beach casting our lines out into the surf, hoping to snag a pompano.

Or we'd go camping. I remember one vacation where my parents tried to drive a pop-up camper to every state park we could hit in a week. At one point we stopped by the famous Suwannee River, the one that's featured in Flori-da's state song (written by Stephen Foster, who never actually set foot in Florida, and how very Florida is that?). While my parents cooked on a Cole-man stove, I tried to cross the shallow, burbling water on some slippery stones. Halfway there I slid off and fell in. Back then I was mortified because my pants got wet, but now I look back on my Suwannee baptism with pride.

In those days there was no *Gawker*, BuzzFeed, or *Huffington Post* to label our state as weird based on the news we produced. Yet my parents, devoted readers of the morning and afternoon papers, frequently pointed out to me the oddball stories they saw: the funny crimes, the stupid things politicians did. Back then we thought California was the weird state. That's the one the comedians made fun of.

To someone growing up in Florida back then, things that other people might consider weird didn't seem like anything out of the ordinary. Didn't everybody have elected officials who called themselves "the He-Coon" and "the Banty Rooster"? Didn't everyone occasionally wear a swimsuit and flip-flops to the mall, the grocery store, even church? Didn't every beach town have a house shaped like a flying saucer? I mean, didn't *every* state have an economy that relied on drunken sailors, horny college kids, and speculative home building?

In school we had to learn the names and locations of all of Florida's sixty-seven counties, but that was about it. Meanwhile, thanks to the Cuban missile crisis ninety miles off the Florida coast, we had to take a course in our senior year called "Americanism vs. Communism." Our legislators feared that in case of an invasion we'd bow down to Fidel Castro as our *El Jefe* unless we made a close study of J. Edgar Hoover's *Masters of Deceit*.

I wish instead they had required the schools to tutor us on the tenets of Florida-ism—the worship of sun, sand, and surf. I wish they had drilled us on our geography (flatter than Kansas!) and geology (the beach sand is made of quartz!). I wish they had talked a bit about our folkways and culture (Jimmy Buffett, driving barefoot, eating hush puppies). I wish they'd taught us some Florida basics, such as the best way to remove sand spurs (lick your fingers); how to avoid burning your thighs on a hot car seat; and why the best parking spot isn't the closest one to the store but the one in the shade.

I wish my teachers had spent some time on our checkered five-hundred-year history, the way the schools in Virginia and Indiana and other states do. Our teachers could have explained how Pensacola got its nickname of "The City of Five Flags." Our mayor—a Pontiac dealer and John Birch Society member known for wearing a plaid jacket and a million-watt smile—always said the phrase proudly, then went on to call us "the Western Gate to the Sunshine State, where thousands live like millions wish they could." In fact, although a bunch of countries thought our port was important, nobody—not the Spanish, not the British, not the French or the Confederates—could hold on to it for long. We were the municipal equivalent of a football fumblerooski.

The teachers did tell us about Juan Ponce de León discovering Florida during the spring of 1513. They mentioned that he named the place "La Florida," not because that's Spanish for "Whoa, look at the size of those cockroaches!" but because of the profusion of flowers and the fact that he first sighted land six days after Easter, *Pascua Florida*.

They also mentioned his search for the fabled Fountain of Youth, a story we now know was concocted by one of his enemies to belittle him. Back when I was a kid, though, it was considered just as factual as the story of George Washington and the cherry tree. Like every other tin-hatted Spaniard, he was actually after gold, something Florida could not provide. Any natives they saw sporting gold necklaces or rings had scavenged their bling from the beach, the detritus of shipwrecks bearing treasure from other Spanish conquests.

Our teachers didn't mention that on a subsequent visit to another part of Florida, our great discoverer was mortally wounded by a poison-tipped arrow fired by the Calusa. Nor did they mention that the native inhabitants might disagree with anyone claiming Ponce de León "discovered" their home-land. In fact, I don't recall hearing one word about our original aboriginals, builders of vast shell mounds and hewers of sleek dugout canoes. To listen to our teachers, it was as if the Spanish had found the land empty, an Eden await-ing all their armored Adams.

That wasn't all they left out. They could have told us about how in 1559, long before Jamestown or the Pilgrims, the Spanish landed in the Panhandle. Don Tristán de Luna y Arellano and fifteen hundred soldiers came ashore in the vicinity of what is now Pensacola, only to lose most of their supplies to a hurricane. De Luna, laid low by fever, defeated in every attempt to find food (while never trying to grow any), eventually slunk back to Havana.

They also never mentioned Fort Caroline, which the French built at the mouth of the St. Johns River in 1564. Imagine how different Florida would look—and sound—had that settlement lasted. Instead, Spanish soldiers marched through a hurricane to slaughter all the inhabitants for being the wrong religion. The killer in charge of that bloody foray, Pedro Menéndez de Avilés, founded his own settlement in 1565—the town of St. Augustine.

That's why St. Augustine can boast that it's the "oldest permanently oc-cupied European settlement" in the United States. And that's why St. Augus-tine's current inhabitants turn quite a tidy profit from the school groups that come to gawk at the history on display. Their colony stuck. Pensacola's got blown away.

The teachers could have told us about how Pensacola had eventually been revived and became the capital of the Spanish West Florida colony, the yin to St. Augustine's East Florida yang. Then future president and $20 bill fig-urehead Andrew Jackson entered the picture. He invaded Pensacola in 1814 as part of the War of 1812, then again in 1818 at the start of the First Semi-nole War, hanging Indians and anyone else who crossed him. He also dis-patched a crew that blew up an old British fort that served as a refuge for escaped slaves, killing 270 of them. Fortunately, genocide is a path to the White House that is seldom followed these days.

We did learn, in passing, that in 1821 Jackson returned to Pensacola one last time to oversee Florida's transition from Spanish colony to American ter-ritory. We didn't hear about how he wore the title of territorial governor as if it were the mantle of a god, or that he locked his Spanish predecessor in the hoosegow. Nor were we told that his wife, Rachel, found Pensacola to be "filthy and disgusting," describing it in a letter as "a vast howling wilderness." Can you imagine what she'd say now, with all the garish billboards and adults-only establishments?

At her urging, Jackson shut down all drinking and dancing on Sunday, which made him less than popular among his new subjects. Luckily for them, these Jacksons soon moonwalked back to the more comfortable confines of the Hermitage in Tennessee. Once they were gone, the Sunday drinking and dancing returned. You can still find a dignified bust of Jackson on display in downtown Pensacola as if he were the city's favorite homicidal son. When I was growing up there, it was just a short walk from the Jackson bust to the town's most famous hangout for Navy fliers, Trader Jon's, where the strippers would show you a different kind of bust. One would sometimes bounce hers on the patrons' heads as if she were playing the bongos.

Another thing our teachers could have told us is that the Civil War nearly started at Fort Pickens in 1861. Yankee forces controlled the fort. Confederates surrounded it. The Confederates planned an attack—but then, as often happens in Florida, the weather changed. They postponed their assault until the rain stopped. While they were waiting for the skies to clear, Confederate soldiers in South Carolina fired on Fort Sumter, and Pensacola was again a historical also-ran.

But no, we heard none of this. We didn't learn that the first free black colony in the continental United States was Fort Mose, near St. Augustine, or that the Underground Railroad ran south in Florida, down to Key Biscayne and over the water to the Bahamas.

We didn't learn about the rogues and rascals who ran the state for their own profit, like David Levy Yulee, our first U.S. senator. Born David Levy, he rejected his Jewish heritage, changed his name, married a Presbyterian hottie, and began claiming he was descended from Moroccan royalty (he wasn't). He also turned his back on his father's crusade to abolish slavery. In 1845, the senator was an ardent advocate of Florida joining the Union. Fifteen years later, he was an ardent advocate of Florida seceding from the Union. This is why his nickname was "the Florida Fire-Eater," and not "the Senator Who Takes Logically Consistent Positions." His one great accomplishment was building Florida's first cross-state railroad—and funneling federal mail contracts to it, thus lining his own pockets.

We didn't even learn about the tough-as-leather settlers who built thatched-roof huts for shelter, ate gopher tortoises and manatee stew, suffered through malaria and yellow fever, and cut down entire forests without ever thinking to plant a single acorn. We didn't hear about how their attitude toward the hot and unforgiving Florida landscape could be gauged by the names they gave its various features: Lake Hell n' Blazes, Tate's Hell Swamp, the Devil's Millhopper.

This devilish description of a place the marketers now call paradise is completely understandable. After all, not only were the gators, bears, panthers, snakes, mosquitoes, and the brutal heat all out to kill them, but it often seemed like the plants were too. In marshes, they faced the fearsome sawgrass, its fronds edged with sharp teeth that could cut your hands if you handled it wrong. In the forests, they contended with the plant known as Spanish bayonet, named because it had a sharp point like a knife. And in some places they even had to deal with manchineel (*manzanilla de la muerte* in Spanish, "little apple of death"), the most poisonous tree in America. One bite of its tangerine-size fruit could set your mouth on fire and lead to excruciating internal pain. The sap was so deadly that the Calusa dipped their arrow points in it (ask Ponce de León about that). Even a sip of the rainwater dripping off its leaves could put you six feet under.

Perhaps living so close to death explains why many of Florida's settlers had a somewhat cavalier attitude toward the law. Some made their money stealing timber off government forest preserves. Some poached gators for their hides and meat, or slaughtered whole rookeries of egrets and spoonbills for the feathers, used in fashionable ladies' hats up north. Some lured ships onto the rocks so they could strip the wreckage of supplies. Hey, it was a living.

We didn't learn about any of these things because one of the basic principles of life in Florida is: Don't pay attention to the past—unless you can get money from the tourists for it.

For instance, every year for the past century Tampa has thrown a huge party called Gasparilla, or more formally, Ye Mystic Krewe of Gasparilla Invasion and Parade of the Pirates, which attracts five hundred thousand people to town to drink heavily, stagger around, urinate in public, and flash their private parts in exchange for beads. This is all done in the name of an eighteenth-century pirate named José Gaspar, the "last of the buccaneers." There's an elaborate story about Gaspar's life and death, and it's all bunk. Gaspar's story was invented to promote one of Florida's early resort hotels. Keeping the story going keeps the money flowing, though, so no one objects to celebrating such fakery.

Still, sometimes the reality is greater than legend. I grew up at a time when John Wayne and Clint Eastwood were twirling six-shooters on movie screens, so I wish even one of my teachers mentioned that Florida had cowboys too.

I would argue that Florida's cowboys were tougher than either Clint or the Duke. Instead of herding cattle through wide-open prairies, they had to find them hiding deep amid the swamps. They weren't known as cowboys. They were called cow *hunters*.

In 1895, long after the Western frontier had been tamed, *Harper's New Monthly Magazine* dispatched Western artist Frederic Remington to assess the Florida cowmen. He landed in Arcadia, a Central Florida town smack in the middle of a range war. For six years, Florida's ranchers rustled cattle, burned homes, and ambushed each other. Some of the cattle barons brought in hired killers from out west to shoot it out with the crafty Florida cowpokes. Passions ran hot, and vengeance overtook justice in popularity. At one point, a posse pursued three rustlers across the state, shot two of them dead, then hanged the third from a cypress tree. No sheriff objected.

Standing outside a store on Arcadia's main street, Remington got his first glimpse of Florida's cowboys. He did not like what he saw.

"Two very emaciated Texas ponies pattered down the street, bearing wild-looking individuals, whose hanging hair and drooping hats and generally bedraggled appearance would remind you at once of the Spanish-moss which hangs so quietly and helplessly to the limbs of the oaks out in the swamps," Remington wrote. "The only things they did which were conventional were to tie their ponies up by the head in brutal disregard, and then get drunk in about fifteen minutes."

Remington was even less impressed by the cattle the cowboys were fighting over. He was amazed at these "low-browed cow-folks" who would "shoot and stab each other for the possession of scrawny creatures not fit for a pointer-dog to mess on."

Oh, if only someone had told me about the low-browed cow-folks! I would've recognized them straightaway as fellow Floridians. I knew these guys. They sounded a lot like the cousins I met at a family funeral who got into a drunken brawl in the limousine heading to the cemetery. Or they could have been the mullet-haired snuff dippers who worked with me on a survey crew one summer and who took great delight in finding and stomping snakes for fun.

Still, even without the help of my teachers, I learned a lot on my own about Florida. I learned key survival skills, as all Florida kids do, while collecting sunburns and skeeter bites the way I collected baseball cards. I soon learned that the best route to follow when walking anywhere wasn't the straightest one but the one that kept you out of the sun. I learned that there are two kinds of mosquitoes in Florida—the kind that merely annoy you with their buzzing, and the kind that silently slip up and suck your blood and leave you with itchy welts. And I learned to love dragonflies because they eat mosquitoes. My grandmother used to call them "skeeter hawks."

My wife, who grew up in Sarasota, learned that backyard fruit tastes better than what comes from the store. She remembers her family driving across the state every summer to visit her aunt, who had succulent mangoes growing behind her house. She also remembers her dad taking the family to the Pittsburgh Pirates' spring-training games in Bradenton, where they'd get autographs from Willie Stargell and Manny Sanguillen. They'd wave frantically at Roberto Clemente, but he was too shy to talk to them.

My friend Cynthia said she grew up loving "the fairy tale experience of climbing a banyan tree in South Florida. The warm Atlantic Ocean. The cold springs. Braking for hot-boiled peanuts on the side of the road. And watermelon when it gets down to $2 on Fourth of July week."

Back then, when the only TV shows for kids were the Saturday morning cartoons, we had to find a way to entertain ourselves. I spent a lot of time climbing trees and wandering around in the woods pretending to hunt squirrels. Cynthia had more exotic hobbies.

"I made condominiums for the cockroaches," Cynthia said. "I put out cardboard boxes with wee doors and windows cut out and drew them little flower boxes. I think you can't be afraid of roaches and be a Florida kid." (My wife strongly disagrees with that statement.)

Boston University journalism school dean William McKeen spent some time growing up on the Air Force base in Homestead, south of Miami. He remembers the Cuban missile crisis as the time he and his friends were allowed by the base commander exactly thirty minutes to go trick-or-treating.

A few years ago, McKeen edited a fascinating book called *Homegrown in Florida*. It features essays from thriller writer Michael Connelly, rocker Tom Petty, and other folks who grew up here, reminiscing about their childhood and how it shaped their futures.

Petty met Elvis while the King was filming the movie *Follow That Dream* in Ocala and environs, and it spurred Petty's interest in music. Connelly, while working as a teenage dishwasher at a Fort Lauderdale hotel, witnessed a crime and got hauled into the police station, where he was questioned by cops who didn't trust his story. He started reading the crime reports in the local paper, checking to see if the robbery was ever solved. (It wasn't.) That led to his fascination with what cops do.

McKeen contends that childhood isn't as much fun these days as it was back when he was a Florida young'un. He blames Little Leagues, gymnastics, and the other scheduled activities kids get locked into these days.

"It seems that when I grew up in South Florida, all the stuff we did was organic," McKeen told me. "We could have a great day just messing around in the canals, riding our bikes around the fields, or going down to the upper Keys to fish with my dad on a whim . . . Living there was an adventure. Now it seems more like an endurance test."

But when I asked my kids what they like about growing up in Florida, the list they rattled off made me think things haven't changed so much. Sure, they enjoy the theme parks and the roller coasters. But they also like camping out, tubing down a spring-fed river, and going to the beach—especially the one at Fort De Soto, a nineteenth-century relic surrounded by glistening white dunes and sea oats that sway in the breeze.

They said they like collecting tangerines from our backyard tree. And they like taking school field trips to Cape Canaveral and the Sea Camp on Big Pine Key. They like spring-training baseball and having warm weather most of the year.

My older son said that as far as he could tell, there's only one downside to growing up in Florida: "No snow days."

We do have something a little like those, though: hurricane days.

Miami News reporter Milt Sosin phones in a story about a hurricane as it slams into Jacksonville, 1964. Florida is hit by more hurricanes than any other state. In one year, 2004, four of them made landfall here. Photo courtesy of *Tampa Bay Times*.

2

Flirting with Disaster

Where in the hell is the cavalry on this one?
—KATE HALE, DADE COUNTY EMERGENCY DIRECTOR, THREE
DAYS AFTER HURRICANE ANDREW HIT FLORIDA IN 1992. HER
PLAINTIVE WAIL ON LIVE TV STUNG THE GEORGE H. W.
BUSH ADMINISTRATION INTO AT LAST PROVIDING FEDERAL
ASSISTANCE, FORESHADOWING A SIMILAR DELAY AFTER HURRI-
CANE KATRINA HIT NEW ORLEANS DURING HIS SON'S ADMIN-
ISTRATION THIRTEEN YEARS LATER.

In 2014, a real estate blog called *Estately* announced that, according to its highly scientific calculations, the scariest state in the Union is Florida. Why? Because of our hurricanes. And our shark attacks. And our tornadoes. And our lightning strikes.

"The most dangerous state in America is the most likely place to experience a real life Sharknado," the blog noted.

Of course, as a Floridian, I was incensed by this. They forgot about our sinkholes!

It's true that Florida can be a scary place. For a state that's notoriously flat, we're constantly teetering on the brink of calamity. Honestly, instead of "Old Folks at Home," our state song ought to be "Flirtin' with Disaster," the 1979 hit by the Jacksonville-based band Molly Hatchet.

Think about it. Hurricanes swirl in and wash away buildings and beaches. Sinkholes pop open and swallow cars, houses, the occasional person. Funnel clouds sprout up and suck in everything in their path, making you wonder, "Whatever happened to Florida being the 'Sunshine State'?"

As with many things about Florida, that nickname is a bit of tourism hyperbole. Through repetition and legislation, it's become accepted fact. The truth is that other states get more sunshine than we do: Arizona is first, then California, Nevada, New Mexico, and Texas.

Yet Florida inmates have been printing SUNSHINE STATE on license plates since 1949. I'm sure it was just a coincidence that this new slogan was added a year after a devastating hurricane hit South Florida, killing three people and causing $21 million in damage, and two years after a pair of them caused what's known as the Great South Florida Flood, which put four feet of water in the streets of Miami and turned Broward County into a vast lake.

Then, in 1970, the legislature approved it as Florida's official nickname. The year before this momentous legislative decision happened to be the year that the most tropical storm systems in recorded history slammed into us. One dropped twenty-three inches of rain on the Panhandle town of Havana, near Tallahassee. Is this what convinced lawmakers of the need for a sunny nickname? Alas, the official record is silent.

A more accurate nickname would be "The Soggy State." The tourism brochures never mention that several of our cities get more rain a year on average than famously gloomy Seattle—Miami (61 inches), Tallahassee (59), and Tampa (46) compared to Seattle's 36. My hometown of Pensacola is the wettest city in the state, with an annual average of 65 inches a year. Think about that—that's more than 5 *feet* of rain a year.

Why do we get so many of what my grandmother used to call "gully-washers" and "toad-frog stranglers"? Blame our peninsular geography. Low-pressure systems passing over from the east suck in moist air from the Atlantic Ocean. Low-pressure systems passing from the west do the same from the Gulf of Mexico, "and where the two air masses converge the air rises," Morton Winsberg of the Florida Climate Center explains. "If the air masses are large enough, and they rise to a high enough altitude for the water vapor within them to condense, they are capable of producing prodigious amounts of rain in a short period."

"Prodigious" is putting it mildly. The typical afternoon thunderstorm can dump enough water to make Noah nervous. Veteran Floridians know to keep an umbrella or rain jacket handy, and possibly some snorkel gear. Yet the rainfall can be spotty. Every Floridian has a story about seeing a drizzle in the front yard but not the back, or on one side of the road and not the other. Even a dry day may contain so much humidity that stepping outdoors is like walking into a wet blanket. My friend George contends that the constant damp is what's behind all the odd behavior here—too many people suffering from brain rot.

Sometimes we get more than just rain. On Labor Day 1969, residents of Punta Gorda were stunned when their regular afternoon shower dropped dozens of golf balls on their town. *Popular Mechanics* theorized that a water spout had slurped up the contents of a golf course water hazard and deposited all those Titleists in a more urban location.

In a land so flat, the sky looms large, and towering nimbus clouds become the Florida version of the purple mountains' majesty. But when all you can see is a single sheet of gray from sky to sea, it can be hard to remember why you came to Florida.

Sometimes this can have dire consequences for the economy. Look at what happened in the Roaring Twenties.

Starting around 1920, people flocked to Florida not just for the gentle sea breezes but also because the real estate market had gone berserk. A dusty lot recently scraped out of the scrub might, on paper, be worth more than a family could live on for a year. Word spread and people pursuing the easy dollar came flooding into the state, including, as one historian noted, "movie stars, professional and top amateur athletes, major crime figures, petty criminals, preachers, teachers and titled Europeans," all of them hustling after a piece of the action.

But then the railroads heading to Florida became so overloaded with construction materials that they halted shipments, stalling the building of new houses. A ship being refurbished as a floating casino sank in Miami's harbor, blocking anything from coming in by boat. Then the weather changed. A national investment bankers' convention gathered in St. Petersburg in December 1925, expecting fun in what local promoters called "the Sunshine City." To their chagrin, the conventioneers saw only drizzle every day for a week. No one could go golfing. No one could go fishing. No one could go ogle women on the beach. With nothing else to do but get down to business, the disgruntled bankers started asking hard questions about the real estate market, getting answers they didn't like.

The boom sputtered, then ground to a halt. In September 1926, a hurricane slammed into South Florida with 150 mph winds and a twelve-foot storm surge. It blew away or damaged most of the buildings that had just been put up and killed hundreds—many of them new arrivals who had had no clue that this tropical paradise might be subject to tropical storms.

Florida's sogginess can even have a national impact. A group of researchers concluded recently that had our skies on Election Day 2000 been clear and not stormy, Al Gore would have easily won, without the need to check any-one's chad.

In 2014 a financial analysis company called CoreLogic rated Florida as the state facing the highest risk of losses from natural hazards. Each state was as-signed a score from 0 to 100 based on the level of risk from hurricanes, tor-nadoes, earthquakes, and so forth. Florida earned a score of 94.5. The No. 2 state, Rhode Island, scored below 80.

People who live here generally react to this sense of constant peril in one of two ways:

1. Prepare, prepare, prepare.
2. Par-TAAAAAAY!

My mom has always been in the first camp. When I was growing up, every year on June 1 she tucked a fresh hurricane-tracking map behind the radio in the kitchen. For the next six months, whenever the radio blared an alert, she'd pull out her map and chart the movements. She watched every storm that might roll up through the Gulf like a bowling ball to flatten our green cinder-block house and do a seven-ten split on our pine trees. By November 30, the end of hurricane season, her map was covered with dashes and jots, but we were still safe. I wondered if her constant mapping of the storms was what kept them away from our door.

I have friends who fall squarely in the second camp. They don't track diddley-squat. They don't binge-watch the Weather Channel to see if that daredevil Jim Cantore might turn up on their front porch (generally a bad sign). Unless it's a Really Big Monster Storm, they don't see the point of evac-uation. To them a hurricane is both a drink and an excuse to drink, nothing more.

Is this a responsible attitude? No. But I can see where they're coming from: As the early settlers figured out, Florida is out to kill us. So why not enjoy the time we have left?

How is Florida trying to kill us? Let me count the ways:

1. Florida is the Lightning Capital of the Western Hemisphere. Around the world, only Rwanda gets more lightning strikes than we do. Other states have to wait for the Fourth of July to see fireworks. In Florida we get a daz-zling flash-bang production nearly every summer afternoon. That means we

frequently lead the nation in deaths and injuries from lightning, and scientists recently found what they called "rogue antimatter" in Florida thunderclouds. Still, what a show!

Storms are not like this in the Panhandle, where I grew up. The first time I saw a real Florida lightning storm, I was driving on Interstate 75 near Sarasota, dodging eighteen-wheelers and monster trucks and Beemer convertibles all going 90 mph. Suddenly I realized that the sky had filled with a flotilla of thunderclouds, so thick and menacing that I wondered if this was a run-through for the Apocalypse. Just then, multiple lightning bolts started zapping this way and that, one right on top of the other, jagged streaks of blinding brightness followed by a bone-rattling boom. I was so awestruck I had to pull over to the side of the road and watch it for a good five minutes. Later, I tried telling a friend about what I'd witnessed. He just snorted. "That's a normal storm around here," he said.

2. Florida is the Shark Bite Capital of the World. (Cue *Jaws* theme.) According to the International Shark Attack File—a repository of reports on shark encounters, which is, of course, located at the University of Florida—in 2012, shark attacks in the United States hit their highest level in more than a decade with fifty-four bites. Half of those—twenty-seven—were reported in Florida. Most occurred along the beaches of just two Atlantic coast counties, Volusia and Brevard, and generally involved surfers whose dangling appendages were mistaken for fish.

Why do sharks nibble on so many people in Florida? Shark biologists say the second half of that equation is the key part. Nearly one hundred million tourists visit Florida every year, and a lot of them join us residents in splashing around in either the ocean or the gulf, which happens to be where the sharks are swimming. Thanks to our climate, people visit the beach for a longer season than anywhere else too. Thus there are more people (and arms and legs) dangling in the water more often, tempting a confused shark to nosh on human flesh.

You have to remember that sharks—several species of which are now considered endangered thanks to what *we* do to *them*—don't like the taste of people. They prefer turtles or fish. When they bite a human, it's by accident. Shark biologists have asked that the term "shark attack" be dropped in favor of something more neutral, like "encounter." That's about as likely as a real Sharknado.

3. Florida reigns supreme among the states on the number of reported sinkholes that open up and swallow everything on the surface. Florida's landscape may seem solid, but it's not. What's down below is not thick, unyielding

rock but something about as solid as Swiss cheese. Geologists call it karst—limestone caverns that easily crumble, prompting a cave-in of whatever's on top of it.

Archie Carr, in his book *A Naturalist in Florida,* recalled the time a sinkhole near Gainesville made a brand-new 1931 Buick disappear: "The owner telephoned Tarpon Springs for Greek sponge divers who could come up and fasten chains on it so that it could be hauled out. The divers went down but soon came back up, intimidated by the depth and darkness of the cluttered hole. So the Buick is down there yet."

In the documentary *Water's Journey: The Hidden Rivers of Florida,* a pair of divers equipped with a tracking device plunged into a Florida sinkhole to explore the underground channels connecting to it. Meanwhile, a pair of researchers tromped around on the surface, meandering through forests and fields following their radio signals. Thus you get to see the divers squeezing through the narrow passageways deep belowground, while the guys up top blithely stroll through backyards and past the salad bar at a Sonny's BBQ.

When a sinkhole yawns, it can be a voracious and indiscriminate consumer of whatever was perched above it. In 1981 in Winter Park, a sinkhole opened that was so huge that, as the *Orlando Sentinel* reported, it "gulped down 250,000 cubic yards of soil, five Porsches from a foreign car repair shop, the deep end of an Olympic-size swimming pool, chunks of two streets and a three-bedroom home." So long, suburban sprawl! Talk about conspicuous consumption!

In 1994, at a phosphate mine near Mulberry, a sinkhole that measured 110 feet in diameter and 200 feet deep split the ground apart under one of the mine's toxic waste piles, known as gypsum stacks. Wags dubbed it Disney's new attraction, "Journey to the Center of the Earth." The fact that pumps around the property were slurping eight million gallons of water a day out of the ground for use in processing the phosphate might possibly perhaps have had something to do with the ground's collapse. Atop the stack was a pond of acidic water, the contents of which fell into the hole and thus into the aquifer, the source of our drinking water. Hey, just think of it as "flavoring."

A sinkhole doesn't have to be big to be dangerous. In March 2013, Jeremy Bush (no relation to our ex-governor) woke up to what sounded like a car crashing into the house in Seffner that he shared with his brother Jeffrey (ditto). Then he heard Jeffrey screaming for help. He ran to his brother's bedroom, arriving just in time to see his brother's mattress disappearing into the earth. Jeffrey Bush was never seen again. The sinkhole that swallowed him was just thirty feet wide. Two years later it opened again and had to be sealed up.

My favorite sinkhole story has a happier ending. In 2011, Carla Chapman of Plant City fell into a sinkhole in her backyard. She had her cell phone, so she dialed 911 and screamed, "Help me, I'm in the grooooouuund!" Half an hour later a police officer found her and pulled her out.

The best part: This wasn't the first time Ms. Chapman had been eaten by the earth. A year earlier she had been swallowed by a sinkhole in that same backyard. She'd been stuck there for two hours until her screams finally brought a neighbor running.

I don't know why Ms. Chapman fell into two different sinkholes in her backyard in successive years. If it were me, I would've moved—or at least quit going into the backyard.

4. Florida gets hit by more hurricanes than any other state. Nobody likes to mention this fact to new residents. If it were up to me, though, everyone who moves to Florida would be handed a pamphlet listing all the hurricanes that have hit us, plus showing local flood zones and evacuation routes. On the back would be a tutorial on hurricane terminology: "Spaghetti models" do not pose for the cover of Italian *Vogue*. "The cone of uncertainty" is not a horcrux sought by Harry Potter. "Saffir Simpson" is not Homer's brother.

Why does Florida get so many hurricanes? Because we are the chin that a combative North American continent sticks out into the Caribbean, just daring the big storms to hit it. Often, they do. In 2004, we were clobbered by four hurricanes in a two-month period. People who were living here then can still rattle off the names in order: Charley, Frances, Ivan, and Jeanne.

That 2004 string was part of a line of nine hurricanes that stomped through Florida during Jeb Bush's term as governor. Unlike another politician named Bush, Jeb rose to the challenge—creating more shelters, pushing for greater preparedness, visiting devastated areas within twenty-four hours.

His sense of urgency stemmed from personal experience. He was not prepared for Hurricane Andrew, a monster that obliterated much of southern Miami-Dade County in 1992. Instead of evacuating, Bush and his family rode out Andrew's fury huddled in the hallway of a friend's home. At one point, as the wind howled outside, the air pressure changed and the house shook. Everyone was sure it was about to implode. Since Bush did not serve in the military, you could say this was his trial by fire.

"When I talk about this with friends, the fear starts rising, my heart starts pounding," Bush said a decade later. "It's one of the scariest things I've ever lived through."

Those who survived Andrew were plunged into a primitive world with no air-conditioning, no microwaves, no TV to show them what was going on else-where. Sunrise brought the rumble of portable generators, the pounding of hammers, the constant whir of helicopters overhead. Nighttime brought loot-ers. Andrew killed sixty-five people, demolished more than twenty-five thou-sand homes in Florida, and damaged another hundred thousand. More than one hundred thousand Dade residents moved away—although many went no farther than the next county to the north, suggesting they had learned nothing.

Unlike Bush, Florida's promoters have always downplayed the danger of the big blow. In 1937, an especially boosterish guidebook came out called *So This is Florida* (or as I like to call it, "So? This is Florida!"). The authors wrote, "It should be apparent that Florida hurricanes . . . are essentially bugaboos."

Grady Norton knew the truth. Norton grew up on an Alabama farm, learn-ing early to watch the skies for weather affecting the crops. His colleagues later joked that if the boll weevil hadn't wiped out the family's cotton, the lanky six-footer probably would have stayed put.

Norton's glasses and bow ties disguised the fact that he was largely self-taught, able to discourse on literature and philosophy—but his passion was weather. He spent World War I learning meteorology in the Army Signal Corps, and afterward he joined the fledgling National Weather Service. In 1928, he drove down to Florida on vacation to visit relatives and stumbled across something that changed his life: a funeral.

Not just any funeral, either. This was a mass memorial in West Palm Beach for the hundreds of people killed by a horrific hurricane that had swept across Lake Okeechobee and sent floods roaring through the farm towns perched along its rim. Zora Neale Hurston, in her novel *Their Eyes Were Watching God,* compared the lake to a "monstropolous beast" awakened by the storm and sent to walk the earth "with a heavy heel." People had trusted in the dike around the lake to hold it in check. Thousands paid for that misplaced trust with their lives.

Norton overheard someone at the funeral say that if only the forecasters had warned everyone in time, those victims might not have died. The remark stuck in his mind like a fishhook, sharp and gleaming and painful. He swore he would dedicate the rest of his life to preventing such tragedies.

In the early 1930s, the forecasters watching for hurricanes were based in Washington, D.C. They worked twenty-four-hour shifts when they were on call but not in the office. A record number of storms skittered across the Gulf in 1933, and the predictions about their paths proved to be so inaccurate that everyone lost confidence in the Weather Service. The last straw came when a forecast put the entire Texas coast on hurricane watch. Chamber of Commerce officials looked at clear skies overhead and sent a telegram to Washington demanding an explanation from the forecaster. The telegram in response said, "Forecaster not available—on golf course." An uproar ensued.

To quell the criticism, in 1935 the Weather Service decentralized its hurricane forecasting, opening offices in several towns, including Jacksonville. Norton was put in charge of the new Florida office and soon faced his first crisis.

As Labor Day approached, a major hurricane thundered across the Atlantic toward the Florida Keys, where hundreds of out-of-work World War I veterans had been hired to build an overseas highway along what had been a railroad line. Twelve hours before the storm hit, Norton called the office employing the veterans and warned them to get those men out. Bureaucratic fumbling delayed the evacuation. Some four hundred were killed.

The tragedy of the Labor Day storm renewed Norton's determination to do something more to save lives. When hurricanes threatened Florida, he went on the radio to talk about what was about to happen. He would warn people to evacuate but also soothe their fears so they wouldn't panic. His honeyed drawl charmed listeners. They trusted him. They started calling him "Mr. Hurricane."

In 1943, the Weather Service moved from Jacksonville to Miami to take advantage of new World War II military bases. That office has been there ever since, eventually taking the name of the National Hurricane Center and taking charge of hurricane forecasts for the entire Atlantic. In the two decades that Norton oversaw that office, the accuracy of his forecasts and his persuasive abilities on radio combined to lower the average American death toll from hurricanes that made landfall from five hundred to five.

The key to his accuracy was his theory that upper-level winds steered the storms. By using a wartime invention, radar, Norton was able to track the path of balloons released into the upper atmosphere, determining their speed and direction. Thus Norton could give people up and down the coast twenty-four hours' notice of where a hurricane might make landfall, enabling them to be better prepared.

The American faith in technology over nature led to a series of experiments in trying to control hurricanes. In October 1947, a hurricane hit Cape Sable, at the Florida peninsula's southern tip, and dumped so much water on Miami that people navigated the streets in skiffs. Then the storm spun northward again, out into the Atlantic, and stalled.

So three aircraft took off from MacDill Air Force Base in Tampa, flew out to the hurricane, and dropped 180 pounds of dry ice into it. The goal of the experiment, known as Project Cirrus, was to make the storm dump its rain and dissipate. Instead the storm remained still for a day or so, then abruptly turned back to land and hammered Savannah, Georgia. Norton was convinced the artificial seeding had turned the hurricane, but the official weather service verdict was that the experiment had failed. Otherwise, someone might blame the government for the damage done to Savannah. Project Cirrus never flew again.

Norton worked around the clock when a storm approached. He kept up this punishing schedule even after a doctor warned him to stop. In October 1954, Norton put in a twelve-hour day tracking a hurricane headed for North Carolina. Then he told his staff he was tired and went home. That night he suffered a fatal stroke. His colleagues listed him as Hurricane Hazel's first fatality.

One of Norton's successors overseeing the National Hurricane Center was Robert Simpson. In 1969, he got a note from a local engineer named Herbert Saffir outlining a way to classify hurricanes on a scale of 1 to 5. Saffir had worked on Dade County's building codes and had developed his rating system while working on a United Nations project to strengthen buildings around the world in cyclone-prone regions. It occurred to him that he could rank each storm based on the amount of damage it did, and then link that to the corresponding sustained wind speeds that would produce that kind of damage.

Simpson liked Saffir's proposal but thought it needed something else, so he included the size of the projected storm surge. Thus was born the Saffir-Simpson Hurricane Scale, which ranks hurricanes as Category 1 (the weakest one, barely enough to rate a hurricane party) through Category 5 (monster superstorm, such as Hurricane Andrew).

"Now the emergency management people tell me they don't know how they got along without the scale," Saffir said in an interview years later. "They use it as far as Australia, in modified shape."

We bandy these terms around so glibly now, even abbreviating them as Cat 1, Cat 2, and so forth as if they were Dr. Seuss felines. Imagine what it was like for Grady Norton, trying to warn people about big killer storms without being able to tell them, "It's a Category 5, for heaven's sake—run for the hinterlands!"

So put it all together—lightning, sharks, hurricanes, sinkholes—and you can see why we're supposed to be the Scariest State (and I didn't even mention the clown college in Sarasota). Then add in all the other threats to life and limb, such as mosquito-borne diseases, flesh-eating bacteria, and the occasional brain-eating amoebas hiding in warm lakes, and you can see why some folks think Florida is a land for living for today.

That sense of precariousness is part of the reason people in Florida often behave the way they do. You're constantly at risk of being betrayed by the sky, the air, the earth, not to mention most of the politicians and bureaucrats. If the future is so uncertain, why bother worrying about the consequences of your actions? Why not just have your own personal Hurricane Party every single day?

As a reporter here in Florida, I've covered all kinds of disasters—sinkholes, hurricanes, floods, the legislature, you name it. One thing I've learned is that what the rest of the country might see as a disaster, a lot of people in Florida see as an opportunity.

In 1992, Hurricane Andrew's winds were so strong they stripped the instruments off the National Hurricane Center. Not until a decade later were the experts able to figure out that it was indeed a Category 5. After the storm passed, it took less than a day before the first grinning vendors appeared along the highway selling T-shirts in three sizes, four colors, and five styles that said I SURVIVED HURRICANE ANDREW. (Yeah, I bought one.)

The big money, though, is not in T-shirts.

Remember the four hurricanes of 2004? One of them, Frances, slammed into the state on Labor Day just like the 1935 killer 'cane. Frances made landfall near Stuart, on the state's Atlantic coast, juked west across the peninsula, skipped across the Gulf, then made a second landfall in the Panhandle.

At no point did Frances come within a hundred miles of Miami-Dade County. Yet the Federal Emergency Management Agency paid $31 million to people who filed claims there. People got money to buy furniture, clothes, TVs, microwaves, refrigerators. They got checks for new cars and to pay dental bills. FEMA even paid for funerals, although not one single death there was attributed to Frances.

The most recent major disaster to hit Florida was not a hurricane but the 2010 BP oil spill. The Deepwater Horizon rig exploded on April 20, killing eleven crew members, and days later began spewing oil from the wellhead five thousand feet underwater. The first gobs of gooey oil began washing ashore in Florida in early June.

The first Floridian to spot those tar balls was Robert K. Turpin, a fourth-generation native in charge of Escambia County's marine resources department. Turpin is a tall, slender man whose ringtone makes the sound of waves slapping the shore. That day he got up before dawn, put on his county uniform, and at 4:30 A.M. drove out to Fort Pickens, built in 1834 to guard the pass into Pensacola Bay. Turpin said he wanted to see if what he thought of as "the enemy"—the oil—had slipped past the fort.

When he stepped out on the beach, shining in the light from a half-moon, he found his worst fears had come true—globs of black goo littered the white sand.

"It was a beautiful night," he told me. "I walked out on the beach and I started seeing them. Then I started seeing more and more. I took some pictures and then got on my BlackBerry and sent out an alert. They were between an inch and six inches big, and a quarter to half an inch thick, and they averaged about one every linear foot."

By the time BP stopped the flow in late July 2010, mats of oil had tainted the beaches of eight Panhandle counties. Wads of the stuff washed up on beaches I'd played on as a kid. I saw people picking it up with their bare hands, the thick gloop shining in the sun. Soon workers in hazmat suits were tromping all over the beach, scooping up the tar balls and toting them away. The next day, they had to do it all over again. The sight was enough to break your heart.

Afterward, counties and cities all over the state filed million-dollar claims against BP, arguing that so many tourists canceled trips during those few months that it killed their whole season. A businessman from Miami, which saw no oil, filed claims against BP totaling $15 million. Many of them were on behalf of seven hundred or so low-wage workers who paid him $300 each as a "processing fee," according to prosecutors. He was convicted of fraud.

Scamming on a major scale can lead to tragedy. BP handed over millions to the Florida counties hardest hit by the spill, expecting they would use it to rebuild their tourism. But the executive director of Okaloosa County's Tourist Development Council used $800,000 from his county's share to buy a beach home and another $710,000 to buy a yacht.

"I sincerely apologize because I lost your trust, you know, just like that, my fault," he told county commissioners once he was caught. Then he disappeared, leaving behind a suicide note. Three days later, he was dead.

The scams perpetrated after the hurricane and oil spill really amount to peanuts, though, compared to the biggest con of all. Florida has more than 1,260 miles of coastline—more coastline than any other state in the continental United States. Given our vulnerability to hurricanes and flooding, where's the most dangerous place to live? The coast. Yet where do most of us live? The coast. And where's the one place you can get taxpayer-subsidized flood insurance? The coast.

Meanwhile, climate change is making the seas rise up, pushing the storm surges even higher—but our state has no plan to deal with that. In fact, our governor, who has a beachfront mansion in Naples, doesn't even want to talk about it. It's as if he's Scarlett O'Hara and this is something to think about tomorrow.

Before leaving this topic, let me say one more thing about my mom's hurricane fixation. In 2004, the year of the four hurricanes, her darkest nightmare came true. She charted the path of Hurricane Ivan right up through the gulf and down her street.

On the day before the storm was due to make landfall, my dad, in his seventies, boarded up all the windows. I called to see if they would evacuate. No, they would ride the storm out in their own home. When Ivan crashed ashore, my mom stayed up all night crying and praying. My dad slept through it. They came through the storm okay, but Mom was so mad I don't think she spoke to Dad for a week.

Now that you know all the ways Florida is trying to kill us all, you might wonder why people keep on moving here. The answer is simple, really.

It's because we lie to them.

A car drives through the entrance to an unbuilt subdivision near Tampa in 1926, at the end of the Florida land boom. Photo by the Burgert Brothers. Photo courtesy of State Archives of Florida.

3

Getting Stucco

Two boom-time speculators were talking over their experiences. Said one, "The truth about Florida is a lie" and the other agreed, but added,—"though it would be just as true the other way around."

—F. Page Wilson, "Miami: From Frontier to Metropolis, An Appraisal"

In 1528, a Spaniard named Pánfilo de Narváez landed on Florida's west coast with three hundred men. Only four made it back. One of them, Álvar Nuñez de Cabeza de Vaca, wrote an account of their expedition. The tale spun by the man whose name means "cow's head" marks him as Florida's first bona fide huckster.

The book "made one of the best imaginative works ever," a historian concluded four centuries later. "It abounded in glowing descriptions of cities always just a little bit beyond, whose inhabitants wore civilized garments, lived in palaces ornamented with sapphires and turquoises, and possessed gold without end. Usually this gold was in nugget form and scattered about the streets so thickly that walking without a stout pair of shoes was almost prohibitive."

Cowhead's account so fired the imagination of another Spaniard, Hernando de Soto, that in 1539 he set out for Florida with 570 men, 223 horses, a pack of hounds, and 300 hogs. He expected riches galore. He soon learned he had been misinformed. Survivors of his ill-fated trek later reported that Florida was "a land full of bogs and poisonous fruits, barren, and the very worst country that is warmed by the sun."

Along the way, some hogs got loose. Their descendants are now one of the worst pests in the South, using their sharp tusks to rip up the ground so it looks like a drunken plowman wandered by. They are de Soto's lasting legacy.

This pattern repeats itself throughout Florida history, a cycle of buildup and letdown that at times resembles an out-of-control roller coaster. Meanwhile, we do our best to alter the state that we're telling the suckers is so wonderful, trying to make it look like something it's not so it will be more appealing to them. As poet Campbell McGrath observed, Florida is "a place whose history begins and ends / with a sales pitch, / a shill, a wink, and a nudge / . . . and scorched savannas peddled to unwary out-of-towners."

I saw this firsthand one summer while working as tail chainman on a land-surveying crew. We spent weeks wading through hip-deep water in a titi swamp, laying out a development that would be called "Paradise Bay." The part that wasn't swamp was a hog farm, where the water was just as deep but twice as nasty. We joked that the name should be "Paradise Bay of Pigs."

Because I was a dumb college kid, I told one of my coworkers I couldn't see how anyone could build anything out there except a duck blind. He snorted and told me that with enough fill dirt, you could turn any wetland in Florida into something temporarily dry enough to call it a subdivision. Print up some pretty brochures and buyers will believe it's prime real estate—at least until their yard turns into a lake.

Florida has long been known as a haven for hustlers—or, to borrow a line from W. Somerset Maugham, "a sunny place for shady people." In 1843, two years before statehood, one visitor wrote that Florida "is the tip of the top for rascality and knavery. Nowhere this side of Texas can you find so many rascals who live by their wits." Half of the people living in Florida towns were "ruined spendthrifts," he said, while the rest were "rogues and scoundrels."

In 1877, as Reconstruction ended, Florida was the least populous state east of the Mississippi River. Only 250,000 people lived here, scattered through the Panhandle and along the coast. They suffered from the heat, the mosquitoes, and the occasional yellow fever epidemic, which they believed could be cured by shooting off cannons. By 1900, that number had more than doubled, and by 1920 the population was closing in on a million people.

One big reason for that huge gain: hustlers talking up the real estate, painting hog farms and swamps as heaven on earth. We've had some distinguished hucksters pushing Florida real estate over the years—silver-tongued presidential candidate William Jennings Bryan, poet Sidney Lanier, and baseball commentator Joe Garagiola—but it all starts with Harriet Beecher Stowe.

After her antislavery bestseller *Uncle Tom's Cabin* helped touch off the Civil War, Stowe moved down to the St. Johns River in Florida and fell in love with the state. She wrote a series of newspaper articles singing the praises of her new home and urging her fellow Yankees to visit. She invented Florida's tourism industry, now the source of 80 percent of our jobs.

Still, she conceded, "full half of the tourists and travelers that come to Florida return intensely disappointed, and even disgusted." The problem was that people wanted Florida to look like paradise all the time. They "generally come with their heads full of certain romantic ideas of waving palms, orange groves, flowers, and fruit, all bursting forth in tropical abundance; and in consequence they go through Florida with disappointment at every step." Florida isn't like that everywhere every day, she explained.

But Stowe's cautionary note about overhyping Florida has gone unheeded. Hucksters are never confident enough in Florida to promote the state based on what's real. They're constantly promising more.

Consider Ransom E. Olds, whose mass production of the Oldsmobile had made him a wealthy man. He decided the right place to build a town with his name on it was in Florida, so he developed thirty-seven thousand acres just north of Tampa and called the town "Oldsmar." He ran special excursion trains down from Detroit and encouraged his auto workers to buy property. He built a casino that drew customers by the busload.

But that wasn't enough. Olds took it a step further. He spent $100,000 drilling an oil well. When the well produced water instead of black gold, someone tried fooling investors by pouring a little oil into the well every morning. (Successful oil wells in Florida are about as common as cool days in August.)

In the end, he lost $3 million. His town, which he'd hoped would grow to one hundred thousand people, didn't get above two hundred in his lifetime.

In Olds's era, the king of Florida hucksters was Dickie Bolles, the man I suspect is most responsible for inspiring the phrase, "If you believe that, I've got some Florida swampland to sell you." A photo shows a dapper gent in a bowler hat and a dark suit with a long white goatee dangling over his tie. I think people trusted him because when he talked, the goatee flapped around and hypnotized them.

Bolles made and lost several fortunes speculating in stocks, Colorado mining, and questionable Oregon real estate, then decided the time was right to move east and try selling swampland.

Bolles found a willing seller: Florida's government. Gov. Napoleon Broward, who was a former sheriff *and* a former gunrunner, had vowed to drain the Everglades and turn it into farms. He was so determined to dry up the vast marshlands that he cranked up the first dredge personally. But the cost of keeping his dredges running proved to be higher than he expected. To pay the bills, Broward held a fire sale of Florida's wettest property.

Bolles bought hundreds of thousands of acres in the Everglades and created the Florida Fruit Lands Co., cut up into ten-acre lots. He also created (on paper, at least) a town called Progreso. Then, not unlike the Wicked Witch dispatching her flying monkeys, Bolles sent a squadron of salesmen across the country to hawk this property. They were particularly successful with the desperate widows of the Midwest.

The salesmen were armed not just with their own glib tongues but also with brochures that quoted government experts, including the U.S. secretary of agriculture, on how fertile Everglades farmland would be once it was drained, and how smart a buyer would be to snap up one of Bolles's lots immediately. They raved about the land, calling it "a Garden of Eden," a "Tropical Paradise," even "a Promised Land."

A more accurate description would have been "a land of broken promises." Buyers soon learned that not only was the property not surveyed, most of it wasn't even above water. Newspaper exposés, congressional hearings, and criminal indictments followed.

The trials featured testimony from a farmer who declared he had bought land by the acre and land by the foot before, but this was the first time he'd bought "land by the gallon." Another witness, an Illinois schoolteacher, testified that when she tried to visit her plot, she had had to abandon her car and start wading.

"The farther we went, the wetter it got," she said. "Water was everywhere. When it got between a foot and a foot and a half deep, I had to turn back. The farm lay further on more than a mile."

A prosecutor asked how that discovery made her feel. "I felt entirely at sea," she said. It took her a minute to figure out why the jurors were laughing so hard.

A couple of Bolles's copycat competitors went to prison for fraud, but Bolles had the perfect defense: He had relied on the assurances of government officials that the Everglades land would be drained. He was acquitted in one case, then indicted in another. He managed to avoid further legal entanglements by dying, under a cloud of suspicion but still a free man, in 1917.

So to review:

1. Hustlers overhype Florida.
2. The government is complicit.
3. Gullible people are left holding the bag.

Newspaper coverage of Bolles and his ilk hurt Florida's reputation across the nation. You'd think people would be forever wary when the subject of Florida real estate came up. Yet just a few years after Bolles's death, the 1920s Florida land boom cranked up the hype machine all over again.

"Throughout Florida resounded the slogans and hyperboles of boundless confidence," Frederick Lewis Allen wrote in his book *Only Yesterday.* "The advertising columns shrieked with them, those swollen advertising columns which enabled the *Miami Daily News,* one day in the summer of 1925, to print an issue of 504 pages, the largest in newspaper history, and enabled the *Miami Herald* to carry a larger volume of advertising in 1925 than any paper anywhere had ever before carried in a year." One Miami woman joked that she'd like to subscribe to the Sunday paper "but I'm afraid it'll fall on me."

Some of the copy read as if its authors were being paid by the syllable.

"Florida is bathed in passionate caresses of the southern sun," one advertisement read. "It is laved by the limpid waves of the embracing seas, wooed by the glorious Gulf Stream . . . Florida is an emerald kingdom by southern seas, fanned by zephyrs laden with ozone from stately pines, watered by Lethe's copious libation, decked with palm and pine, flower and fern, clothed in perpetual verdure and lapt in the gorgeous folds of the semi-tropical zone."

How did such punch-drunk prose convince people to take another chance on Florida? My theory is that it started with actual drunks.

In 1919, the Volstead Act banned the manufacture and sale of alcoholic beverages. When it took effect in 1920 and Prohibition began, thirsty people turned to Florida.

Geographically, the state was a rumrunner's dream. Its miles of coastline included thousands of places where a savvy sailor with a quiet boat could slip a load of hooch ashore unnoticed. West Palm Beach lay just sixty miles west of the largest settlement on Grand Bahama Island, which had nine liquor warehouses. More alcohol was available in nearby Cuba and Jamaica. As the boats landed in Florida, limos would line up at the wharves to collect the shipments, wrapped neatly in brown paper and labeled "fish."

When the boats couldn't bring in the stuff fast enough, daredevil pilots—many of them veterans of World War I—landed the liquid gold at makeshift airstrips scattered around the state.

Meanwhile, as often happens with an unpopular law, Florida's cops took a lackadaisical approach to enforcing the booze ban. A federal report noted that Florida officials vowed their undying support of Prohibition—but only in the summer, when the tourists had gone home. The rest of the year, whatever the visitors wanted, they got. Some of the lawmen were well paid to turn their heads, or even help get the hooch to its destination without it being hijacked.

As a result, "Florida . . . was the wettest country I've ever known," a British traveler wrote. He wasn't talking about the swamps.

Soon everyone from department store magnate J. C. Penney to New York Yankees owner Jacob Ruppert had bought property in Florida. Chicago gangster in chief Al Capone bought a home for himself on one side of the state and one for his mother on the other.

Florida officials loved all the big-name big spenders bringing big bucks down to their little old state. Gov. Cary Hardee pushed the legislature to approve a pair of constitutional amendments to make Florida even more of a millionaire magnet. The amendments forbade the state to ever collect an income tax or an inheritance tax. Then they revised the law governing incorporation to make it easier than ever to start a company.

Then, having cut the state's taxing ability, they borrowed money to build new roads across the state, and raised the speed limit to 45 mph, the highest in the country. That prompted jokes that Floridians wanted to make sure nothing would "slow down the danged fools bringing money into the state."

As demand grew and land prices climbed, people saw they could turn a tidy profit from quickly selling what they had bought. Crowds of would-be entrepreneurs hawking land clogged the streets of Miami to the point where one journalist wrote, "One might think that a number of interesting and simultaneous murders had just taken place behind the facades of a hundred different business establishments, and that the morbid crowds had assembled to talk them over."

The writer Ben Hecht landed a job shilling for a real estate promoter and created a frenzy with a phony treasure hunt. He said Florida real estate became so crazy nobody wanted to do what you would normally do: "Everybody was trying to get rich in a few days. Nobody went swimming. Nobody sat under the palm trees. Nobody played horseshoes."

The mania spread nationwide. "Everybody is telling stories of Florida and the wonderful real estate developments there," the *New York Times* reported. "Hardly anybody talks of anything but real estate, and one is led to believe that nobody in Florida thinks of anything else in these days when the peninsula is jammed with visitors from end to end and side to side—unless it is a matter of finding a place to sleep."

This was the era when, as modern historian Gary Mormino aptly puts it, "Florida became Florida." The hashtag was implied. This was when Florida first gained a national reputation for wacky behavior.

Not all of it was because so many people were drinking so much and driving so fast and telling outrageous lies. Some of the craziness was carefully planned to promote real estate sales. Carl Fisher, a half-blind daredevil from the Midwest who built the Indianapolis Speedway, dredged up fill from the bottom of Biscayne Bay to turn a bug-infested mangrove island into Miami Beach. He built houses, hotels, golf courses, and polo fields (and a sewer line that ran straight into the bay). But his true genius lay in advertising.

Fisher acquired a baby elephant named Rosie, and when President-elect Warren G. Harding visited Fisher's golf course, Fisher dispatched Rosie to serve as his caddy. Newspapers across the country ran the photo, notifying every American with eyes that in Florida anything could happen.

Fisher was such a diligent stage manager for his development that Will Rogers quipped that he'd "rehearsed the mosquitoes till they wouldn't bite you until after you'd bought." He also pioneered using sex to sell Florida real estate, employing "bathing beauties" to show that they could wear skimpy (for the time) swimsuits when it was too cold up north to go outside.

Charles Green Rodes, a West Virginia coal miner from a family of twelve, applied his knowledge of digging to turn land into water, and vice versa. Along the New River in Fort Lauderdale, Rodes dredged a series of canals, then used the fill to create rows of small peninsulas that stretched into the river as if they were grasping fingers. This way every lot on every street backed up to a canal and thus could be sold as waterfront. The technique, dubbed "finger-islanding," quickly caught on, and it took years before anyone realized that the canals became stagnant cesspools and the development destroyed the habitat of manatees and other wildlife. By the 1980s, the lots began sinking back into the ooze from which they'd been conjured.

Rodes was no genius. Because of the canals, he called his subdivision "Venice," which he pronounced "Venus." Yet he raked in enough money to take his extended family of fifty-four people on a cross-country train trip in 1925.

"How did I make my money?" the fifty-one-year-old dredge-and-filler said to an interviewer in Kansas City. "Fort Lauderdale, sir, and the climate . . . Fifteen months ago I was offering some suburban lots for $150,000 total. Eight months later they sold for $593,000—that goes into my pocket."

How could property prices escalate so fast? The Florida fever spread, wrote Harvard economist John Kenneth Galbraith, because buyers lived in "a world inhabited not by people who needed to be persuaded to believe but by people who wanted an excuse to believe."

The state's bankers were in on the scam. Banking records from the 1920s show that the real estate promoters eagerly sought their own bank charters, which the state's top banking regulator eagerly approved. They could grant themselves all the loans they needed to keep their projects afloat. Then, to ensure silence from their pals in the government, those pals got "loans" that they didn't have to pay back.

Between 1921 and 1929, State Comptroller Ernest Amos—I like to think of him as "Infamous Amos"—approved 129 state bank charters. During that period, 127 state banks failed. Amos's avid support of the expansion of the banking system, and his lack of curiosity about the bank hanky-panky going on, may have had something to do with the fact that he was being loaned money by the banks he regulated. Amos used his connections to beat an indictment and dodge impeachment. The voters finally kicked him out, albeit long after the damage had been done.

By this point the boom had become, as one Florida developer wrote after it was over, "a greedy delirium to acquire riches overnight without benefit of effort, brains, or services rendered."

The land being sold, and the structures on it, became less important than the paper that was flying between buyers and sellers. Each transaction inflated the value, pushing it higher and higher like Icarus and his waxy wings soaring toward the sun. Real estate developers hired "binder boys" to convince the suckers to make a 10 percent payment—a binder—on their property, sight unseen.

"It was only necessary to point carelessly to a mudhole and tell a prospect that there was his fortune," one of Florida's biggest ballyhoo artists, Wilson Mizner, wrote later. It should be noted that Mizner—con man, raconteur, artist's muse, drug addict, and gigolo—is credited by some sources with the saying, "Never give a sucker an even break."

Mizner's brother Addison was busy developing Boca Raton with the aid of such eager partners as the actress Marie Dressler and Delaware Sen. T. Coleman du Pont. Addison Mizner is still remembered today for creating the distinctive Palm Beach architecture described by one biographer as "Bastard-Spanish-Romanesque-Gothic-Renaissance-Bull-Market-Damn-the-Expense style." He kept on his shoulder a monkey named Johnnie Brown that once ran for mayor of Palm Beach. (He lost.) Mizner owned two other monkeys, Ethel and Deuteronomy, but the historical record is silent regarding their political ambitions, if any.

Addison Mizner was more than just an architect, notes historian David Nolan—he was a trendsetter: "When he wore his shirt tails out to cool his great girth in the warm weather, for instance, the sport shirt was born." Mizner was not the most meticulous designer of forty-room mansions, yet Florida's priorities were so screwy that when he forgot a door or a bathroom or a stairway, his wealthy clients would brag about it. Owning a Mizner slip became a status symbol—so much so that buyers who couldn't find a real flaw would invent one.

His brother Wilson was the perfect sales manager. He made it known that he and Addison were setting up a screening committee to ensure that anyone buying property in Boca Raton was truly worthy and not just some social climber. Then he quietly advised the screeners not to turn down anyone with ready money. Snobs who wanted in literally threw the deposits at them. The staff gathered the checks from the floor in wastebaskets.

That same air of rapacious rascality hovered over every development of the day. Salesmen would promise anything to hook a buyer. Did beautiful orchids grow wild in the trees? Promise the suckers anyone could make a fine living harvesting orchids and selling them—even as builders were cutting down the trees. Did they want to hobnob with the high and mighty? Tell them you're representing an exclusive yacht club that's selling memberships with every lot—even though the lots are landlocked. Do they want property near town? Tell them Manhattan Estates is very close to the growing city of Nettie—even though there is no such city.

Northern newspapers began running stories exposing the more outlandish Florida scams. Sen. du Pont and other Mizner investors helped organize a New York event that was supposed to generate more positive press coverage, but it turned into a PR fiasco. Shortly afterward, du Pont resigned from the company and accused the Mizner brothers of mismanagement—a very public, very damaging split that spelled the beginning of the end for them.

The news coverage clearly inspired the playwright George S. Kaufman, who wrote the script for a 1925 Marx Brothers show called *The Cocoanuts*, starring Groucho as a shady Florida land promoter.

"You can have any kind of a home you want," he tells his customers. "You can even get stucco! Ohhhhh, how you can get stuck-o."

By the time the movie version—the Marx Brothers' first film, by the way—hit theaters in 1929, the Florida boom was long over and a lot of people had gotten stuck-o. Farmers who had sold their land to speculators and cursed their luck when the price quadrupled now discovered that, through a series of defaults, they had gotten it back—along with the taxes due on the inflated value. All over Florida, half-built houses stood on unfinished streets behind grand concrete arches that resembled nothing so much as Ozymandias's vast and trunkless legs.

Florida's reputation was, in a word, mud. "The ill feeling against Florida was widespread, though the speculators themselves were at least as much to blame," a historian wrote thirty years later. "A few, knowing when to stop, came out ahead. Many more lost."

So to sum up:

1. Hucksters overhyped Florida.
2. Government was complicit in the scam.
3. Gullible people were left holding the bag.

(This pattern repeats a lot.)

Would I argue that the Florida bust set off the Great Depression? No, I would not. Although it's true that after the boom went bust, foreclosures nationwide mounted each year leading up to Black Friday, the Depression started with the stock market crash on October 31, 1929, and subsequent runs on the banks. That's not Florida's fault. Well, not entirely.

No less an authority than Professor Galbraith contended that the Florida real estate euphoria "was the first indication of the mood of the Twenties and the conviction that God intended the American middle class to be rich"—and that attitude set the stage for the Crash of '29.

Maybe *that* should be our state motto: "Florida: A bad influence on the nation's psyche for nearly a century."

After the Roaring Twenties slid into the Starving Thirties, the Florida hucksters melted away like snow cones on a July afternoon. Wilson Mizner moved to California to write witty movie dialogue and help run the Brown Derby restaurant. Meanwhile, everyone else experienced a strange case of amnesia that allowed no one to learn from what had happened.

Florida continued experiencing cycles of boom and bust. Each one was fueled by hucksters and hype and government complicity. Each turned into a Ponzi scheme that stayed afloat only so long as new suckers could be recruited to toss in more cash. Each one, as it ended, left behind shattered dreams, busted buyers, and the skeletal remains of not-quite-finished condos and homes and stores, waiting to be torn apart by scavengers or covered over by Florida's creeping vines.

Over the decades, the hucksters learned some new techniques, such as flying couples down from up north and putting them up in motels that the salesmen had bugged, so they could listen in on the discussion and better tailor their sales pitches.

What they hadn't learned, though, was how to develop a true community in Florida. They figured that stuff didn't matter as long as the money kept pouring in.

In the 1950s, near Fort Myers, the developers of a community called Lehigh Acres simply stamped out a grid pattern over one hundred thousand acres, marking everything as lots for sale and paying no attention to any need for parks or anything else.

They poured all their resources into convincing people to put $10 down for the lots. In winter, they would find a spot in a snowy Northern town, sweep away the snow, set up a prefab model home, fire up smudge pots around it for warmth, then bring in a squad of bikini-clad women to lounge under potted palm trees. To top it all off, they had an elephant parade around this scene with a sign on its sides that said FLY TO FLORIDA FOR PEANUTS, encouraging the suckers to sign up for a free airplane flight that would, of course, deliver them straight to the salesmen making the hard-core pitch.

The sales were considered the be-all and end-all, and that posed a problem.

"We gave so much thought to selling the land that the normal reservations for commercial properties, schools, all the ancillary things you need in a community, weren't made," one of the developers admitted years later. "We even had canals that ran uphill. I don't know any mistake you could make that we didn't make."

In the 1960s, the General Development Corporation designed a community called Port St. Lucie on the Atlantic coast. I am using the word "designed" very loosely. What the company officials did was to plat thousands of quarter-acre lots, then scatter the sales haphazardly around a maze of roads so full of curlicues that a city map looks like a cross section of the brain. The lots were not hooked to a central water or sewer system. GDC's plans left out schools, commercial districts, even a downtown. Despite what the advertising brochures said, residents had no direct access to the nearby beaches and only two bridges to carry them across the St. Lucie River, which bisects the town. In 1990, GDC pleaded guilty to federal charges that it bilked home buyers, then went bankrupt.

Then there's Cape Coral, a community near Fort Myers that a pair of Baltimore shampoo magnates named Leonard and Julius Rosen developed using Charles Green Rodes's finger-islanding technique. Their Gulf American Land Co. also launched an ambitious development on the edge of the Big Cypress Swamp near Naples, calling it Golden Gate Estates, which they touted as "America's largest subdivision." Soon Gulf American had become the nation's biggest land development company. Its grand edifice was built on a foundation of deception.

The company ran glowing ads in the Midwestern papers boasting about how you could buy an acre of land, subdivide it, sell off the lots, and make a fortune, because of course Florida real estate would always increase in value, right? The Rosens employed a boiler room full of telephone pitchmen—some of them former carnival barkers with criminal records—to persuade people to buy lots sight unseen, usually by lying about where they were and what amenities were built nearby. Sometimes they secretly switched the lots that had been bought for the ones that no one would buy because they were too far inland to be accessible.

The *Wall Street Journal* ran a front-page exposé of Gulf American's shady tactics in 1967, kicking off a grand jury investigation and an order by the state to suspend all sales. Ultimately, the Rosens resigned from the company, which sold all its assets to another developer, which went bankrupt. In the 2000s, state officials spent years tracking down the owners of half of the never-developed Golden Gate lots and buying the property back to restore the Everglades' flow.

Cape Coral stumbled along with its stunted development and stagnant canals until the early 2000s, when suddenly building there boomed all over again. The *New York Times* noted that the city's sudden growth spurt had turned "musty flatlands into a grid of ranch homes painted in vibrant Sun Belt hues: lime green, apricot, and canary yellow." The Internet had made it possible for people in colder climes to see pictures of sunny Florida and click on pictures of homes for sale for what seemed like a cheap price. The pictures sure looked nice—but they didn't show everything.

Meanwhile, the banks allowed for more creative financing than before, allowing lots of people to become "flippers"—buying homes and then quickly reselling them for a higher price. All over the state, another Florida frenzy began as everyone tried to get rich. Houses that had gone for $10,000 sold for ten times as much.

Some of the old and busted developments saw fresh interest. In his 2010 book *Exiles in Eden,* Paul Reyes tells of going to visit a Lehigh Acres lot his father had bought in 1969 but never built on.

"In 1997 my father couldn't have gotten more than $2,000 for this lot," Reyes writes. But then in 2005, the letters began arriving, offering him $23,000, then $35,000, then $40,000. "None of it seemed real to him. He was convinced it was all some kind of a scam." Reyes gazed at the brush-covered lot, baking in the hot sun, and summed it up: "Forty thousand dollars for a sandbox."

His dad was right about the scam. That lot was never hooked up to water or sewer lines, and a veteran real estate salesman told him it probably never would be. To justify the expense of putting in water and sewer, the area would need enough residents—but nobody would move there without water and sewer. It was, Reyes realized, "a public works Catch-22."

Politically, the biggest beneficiary of this boom was Florida's governor at the time, Jeb Bush, who took office in 1999. Soaring real estate sales fueled a thriving economy during his two terms, allowing him to claim credit for leading the state into a prosperous future. The rising tide lifted *his* boat, at least, so that when he announced he was running for president he could boast, "We made Florida number one in job creation and number one in small-business creation . . . That is the record that turned this state around."

Housing prices peaked in mid-2006. By 2007, just as Bush handed the wheel to his unlucky successor, Charlie Crist, the inevitable bust followed, plunging Florida into a recession that wiped out hundreds of thousands of families. The reversal exposed that the boom Bush had bragged about as just another scam. What had been sold and resold and resold again was, just as Reyes's father suspected, never real. Home prices tumbled like a drunk tourist tripping down a cruise ship gangplank. The people who had mortgaged property at far higher values than their land was really worth wound up underwater.

Soon real estate firms and construction companies shut down, leaving their BMW-leasing employees wondering about possible openings at 7-Eleven and McDonald's. Foreclosures became Florida's big real estate business. The courts became swamped, and people who had lost construction jobs found employment on crews cleaning out abandoned homes, battling the stench from mold, dog poop, and the occasional snake that had slithered up inside the fridge. In Cape Coral, the city laid off eighteen of its building inspectors and used the savings to hire landscapers to go around mowing the lawns of the empty homes.

Reyes quoted his Lehigh Acres salesman taking the long view of the latest bust. "It only feels different because you're not remembering the last one, or the one before that, or the one before that," he said.

But it *was* different, in some ways. In Tampa, a *St. Petersburg Times* investigation uncovered the fact that the biggest flipper in the region, a former tattoo artist with a taste for exotic cars, had been making millions by committing a massive mortgage fraud. He was using thumb-on-the-scale appraisals and phony documents and straw buyers to inflate the value of worthless hovels. He did so well because, it turns out, flipping was a nifty way to launder drug money and make a big profit. The flipper went to prison, but not the mortgage brokers, title insurers, and bankers who knew what was happening and made the scams work so they could get their cut.

"Is Florida the Sunset State?" *Time* magazine asked in midmeltdown, i.e., July 2008. "We've got a water crisis, insurance crisis, environmental crisis and budget crisis to go with our housing crisis." Savvy hucksters organized foreclosure tours, taking European and Asian buyers around in buses to show the half-built places they could now buy cheap.

Riding the wave of booms and busts could leave anyone feeling jittery and unsettled—not unlike living in a land full of sinkholes. The landscape changes over and over, buildings being torn down and rebuilt or left vacant until the next boom. Roads are constantly widened or rebuilt or redirected or vacated. Nothing's the same. Everything changes. See that forest? We're cutting it down and planting orange trees. See that orange grove? We're cutting it down to build a strip mall. See that strip mall? We're knocking that down to build apartments. See those apartments? We're knocking those down for a parking lot. And so on.

In a place where the landscape can change so quickly, it's easy to feel unanchored, adrift. Fortunately, when you're feeling unsettled in the suburbs, Florida offers plenty of calming natural wonders.

Although you should be aware that nobody's renting out saddles for the manatees.

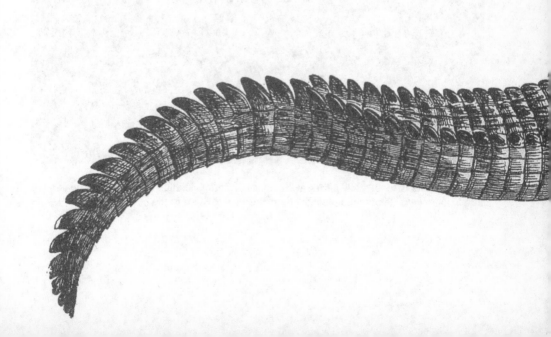

A woman tosses food to alligators at Homosassa Springs, 1960s. Animal attractions have drawn tourists to Florida for decades. Photo courtesy of State Archives of Florida.

4

Trading Gators for Beer

The strange quality of the light upon this habitat, the stillness
of it all, the sense of waiting, brought me halfway to a kind of
ecstasy.

—*ANNIHILATION,* THE FIRST BOOK IN THE SOUTHERN REACH
TRILOGY BY JEFF VANDERMEER, WHO LIVES IN TALLAHASSEE

Florida's most widely recognized piece of architecture is a big house that
nobody lives in, Cinderella's Castle at Walt Disney World. This is an apt
symbol of a state full of recent arrivals where we tend to focus on surface
flash. It's also a shame, because Florida contains far more interesting buildings than Mr. Disney's flight of fancy.

On the campus of Florida Southern College in Lakeland are ten buildings designed by Frank Lloyd Wright, the most of the master's work collected
in one spot. Architects rave about Miami Beach's iconic Fontainebleau Hotel
with its famous curve, the palm-in-the-hole Atlantis condo in Miami, and
the tin-roof cool of the Panhandle town of Seaside.

I prefer our quirkier structures: the mysterious Coral Castle south of
Miami, built by a lovelorn man using techniques no one has figured out; the
kitschy arrangement of half-buried trailers outside Tampa that's known as
"Airstream Ranch"; and "Betsy," the thirty-foot-tall, forty-foot-long spiny lob-
ster that stands guard in Islamorada. And who could forget the twenty-eight-
foot concrete brachiosaur looming by I-4, startling drivers who hadn't noticed
the signs for Dinosaur World?

In prehistoric times, mammoths, mastodons, and saber-toothed cats rum-
bled through the jungles of Florida. They left behind plenty of fossils, many

of them uncovered when phosphate miners churned up the ground for fertilizer ingredients. But Florida held no actual dinosaurs, roaring their terrible roars and gnashing their terrible teeth. These days, though, we've got enough to stock three *Jurassic World* sequels. In addition to Dinosaur World's 150 or so, there are dinosaurs adorning a Panama City Beach Goofy Golf course, serving as a Spring Hill gas station, and attracting camera-toting tourists at Palm Beach County's Lion Country Safari. I have no proof, but I am convinced that Florida contains more faux dinosaurs than any other state.

Still, fake dinosaurs and fake castles aren't what make Florida special. For that, you've got to check out the state parks.

Florida's 171 state parks offer amazing views, from the soaring dunes of Topsail Hill Preserve State Park in the Panhandle to the lush and mysterious depths of the Devil's Millhopper Geological State Park just outside Gainesville. There are ghost orchids hidden in the swamps of the Fakahatchee Strand State Preserve and black bears snuffling through the woods at Wekiwa Springs State Park and a four-thousand-pound underwater Jesus statue amid the sponges and corals at John Pennekamp Coral Reef State Park, the first undersea park in the United States. The parks boost the state's economy too, drawing more than twenty-seven million visitors in 2014.

Some Florida state parks are, shall we say, more "Florida" than others. Paynes Prairie Preserve State Park has a rambunctious herd of bison imported from out west in the 1970s because Florida had bison until the early settlers wiped them out. Being a home where the buffalo roam has turned into a headache for park officials. The critters regard fences as a mere suggestion and escape to wander through the nearby suburbs. Even when they stay in the park, they sometimes block hiking paths and charge rangers. One woman was trapped in a felled tree by a herd. Instead of being trampled, she wound up covered with what an official report referred to as "buffalo snot."

I interviewed Buffalo Snot Lady, who showed the spirit of a true Floridian. The whole time smelly beasts were painting her with mucus, she said, her one thought was, "I am going to die today, but isn't this *awesome*?"

Even more Florida is Torreya State Park, and the adjacent Apalachicola Bluffs and Ravine Preserve, which is owned by the Nature Conservancy. I have hiked through here and can attest to the fact that the view from the bluffs is one of the prettiest in the state. Some people think it's downright heavenly. In the 1950s, a lawyer and former gubernatorial candidate named Elvy Edison Callaway contended that, based on the river formation and other evidence, this was the site of the Garden of Eden. For just $1.10 a head, he'd allow you to walk where Adam and Eve strolled around naked.

The most Florida of all of Florida's state parks, though, is Weeki Wachee

Springs State Park. It's the only government operation in the world where the list of jobs includes "mermaid."

To understand this, you have to understand Florida's karst geology. Deep beneath the suburban sprawl is an underground river that supplies most of the state's drinking water. As the aquifer rushes through the Swiss cheese caverns, it sometimes bubbles up to the surface in one of our one thousand springs—the greatest concentration of springs on Earth.

Florida's springs have been dazzling visitors for centuries. When the pioneering naturalist William Bartram peered into the depths of Florida's springs in the 1700s, he described them as "enchanting and amazing crystal fountains." Scholars credit Bartram's depiction of Florida's springs as the inspiration for Samuel Taylor Coleridge's feverish poem "Kubla Khan" whose stately pleasure dome was built "where Alph, the sacred river, ran through caverns measureless to man down to a sunless sea."

The springs were Florida's first tourist attraction, drawing visitors who believed that the water must have healing properties. White Springs, now a sleepy hamlet north of Gainesville, once needed fourteen hotels for all the Yankees flocking in, including Teddy Roosevelt and William Howard Taft.

In 1947, a visionary named Newton Perry figured out that the way to boost the tourists' interest in visiting a spring was to add the element of sex.

A heavyset man with curly hair and a tinkerer's eternal curiosity, Perry had been a Navy frogman during World War II. He bought Weeki Wachee Springs and hid air tubes around its main boil. He built a theater with glass windows looking into the heart of the spring, and then hired nubile young women to swim around waving at the audience, holding their breath until they could slip a bit of air from a tube. The water was so clear it was like peering into a strange dreamscape where weightless beauties performed a languorous ballet.

To promote the attraction, Perry snapped photos of his cast in all sorts of unlikely underwater poses—having a picnic, hanging out with a seahorse, hugging Santa—and sent the pictures to papers around the country. When his employees donned mermaid costumes, a kitschy tradition was born.

Tourists became hooked on Perry's aquatic erotica. In 1966, Weeki Wachee incorporated as a tiny city—population: six—just to get on Florida road maps. By then, the choreographed mermaid shows were attracting half a million visitors a year. Since 1991 the shows have featured a lip-synched rendition of the mermaids' theme song, "We've Got the World by the Tail": "We're not like other women / We don't have to clean an oven / And we never will grow old / We've got the world by the tail!"

Soon, though, profits from the mermaid shows began tailing off, so to speak. By 2008, the place was on the verge of closing, so the state park system assumed control. That put the mermaids on the government payroll and led to some interesting conversations about charging the taxpayers for bikini tops and waterproof makeup.

As you might expect from a group whose members pull on a sixty-pound prosthetic fish tail every day for work, the mermaids are a dedicated bunch. A *New York Times* story on the park quoted one of the women who worked at Weeki Wachee and left, but was drawn back like a sailor captivated by a siren's song: "I spent about a year and a half trying not to be a mermaid, and it was just like, 'Well, I am.'"

The irony of this mermaid cosplay is that Florida already has thousands of the original "mermaids"—better known as manatees. The first person to record a sighting of manatees was Christopher Columbus, who noted that mermaids were not as attractive as he had been led to believe.

Given their shape and size, you can't blame Columbus for his put-down. Florida's early settlers, though, found the manatee to be less a myth and more a tasty meal—finer than Tennessee beef, according to one diner.

Then gun-toting tourists began showing up, blasting away at manatees, Florida panthers, alligators, black bears, and anything else that struck their fancy. Florida's wildlife seemed so abundant, surely the supply could never run out.

One tourist was different. In 1867, a man in his twenties with a thick red beard tramped across the state, following the railroad tracks from Fernandina to Cedar Key. As John Muir finished a thousand-mile walk from Indiana to the Gulf of Mexico, he eagerly drank in the amazing sights around him. Normally, Muir would have made his own path through the forest, but in Florida, the razor-edged Spanish bayonet and thorny vines proved too daunting. He was also reluctant to get near any alligators.

There were other, less obvious, hazards. At some point as he strolled along enjoying all the delights of nature, one of nature's less delightful creatures, a mosquito, bit him. Not long afterward, he fell ill with malaria. The future founder of the Sierra Club, the man who would someday lead the fight to protect the Grand Canyon and Yosemite Valley, lay sprawled senseless for several days before a kindly Floridian nursed him back to health.

Rather than keep moving the way he preferred, Muir was forced to stay close to one spot for several months. He had already spent some time working in one of Cedar Key's factories, turning cedar trees into pencil blanks for the Eberhard Faber pencil company. Now, as he just watched the birds flit through the trees and thought about everything he had seen in Florida, he experienced an epiphany that became the basis of the American environmental movement.

Maybe, Muir reasoned, not everything in nature was designed to fulfill mankind's needs and desires. Maybe there were things in nature that didn't relate to humans at all. Maybe there were things in nature that tried to repel humans, such as bayonet plants, or tried to kill them, such as mosquitoes and alligators.

"Nature's object in making animals and plants might possibly be first of all the happiness of each one of them, not the creation of all for the happiness of one," he wrote. "Why should man value himself as more than a small part of the one great unit of creation? And what creature of all that the Lord has taken the pains to make is not essential to the completeness of that unit— the cosmos? . . . Man claimed the earth was made for him, and I was going to say that venomous beasts, thorny plants, and deadly diseases of certain parts of the earth prove that the whole world was not made for him."

Such a notion seemed revolutionary at a time when thousands of stately Florida cedars were being cut to make pencils (when the supply ran out in 1890, the factories closed). But the idea slowly caught on, shaping the country's future direction.

At the Cedar Key Museum is a plaque commemorating Muir's visit, with his epiphany getting only a passing mention. If I were the Sierra Club, I would erect a massive monument to Muir's mosquito, not unlike the famous Boll Weevil Monument in Enterprise, Alabama. Without that skeeter bite, I'm not sure Muir would have slowed down enough to make his discovery.

Not long after Muir's epiphany, some people started thinking about another revolutionary idea: setting aside land that would be protected from people, to benefit wildlife. In 1903—the same year Muir took him camping for three days in Yosemite—Teddy Roosevelt designated a Florida bird colony, Pelican Island, as the first-ever national wildlife refuge.

Roosevelt did this because of a campaign by Paul Kroegel, a German immigrant who lived across the Indian River from the island. Kroegel had been horrified by all the hunters who trekked to the island to slaughter the pelicans to get their feathers. Milliners used plumes from Florida's pelicans, herons, and egrets on fashionable ladies' hats. Such was the demand that at that time a pound of feathers was worth as much as a pound of gold.

Kroegel became America's first wildlife refuge manager, protecting pelicans and their habitat with a badge, a shotgun, and a small sailboat. He earned a salary of $1 a month—paid by the Florida Audubon Society, not the government, because Congress hadn't budgeted for refuges.

Kroegel's noble effort came to a classic Florida end. Twenty years after Pelican Island became a sanctuary, a hurricane swept through and the pelicans moved to a different island. With no pelicans on Pelican Island, Kroegel's bosses saw no need for a refuge manager. He was fired. Then, of course, the pelicans came back.

Still, the concept caught on. There are now more than 560 federal wildlife refuges from the Caribbean to the Pacific, and other countries are copying the refuge idea.

Seventy years later, Congress took John Muir's idea to its logical conclusion, in large part because of the work of Nathaniel Reed. Reed is tall and slender, with an aristocratic bearing. He reminds me of a wading bird so much, I always halfway expect to see him standing on one leg. Reed owes his keen interest in nature to his upbringing on Florida's Jupiter Island.

"I lived on the Indian River and the barbless backwoods west of Hobe Sound," he told me. "I had an insatiable desire to learn the names of animals, fish, birds, plants, and trees—the whole world that surrounded me."

He learned to appreciate nature's bounty and to worry about its fragility in the face of human encroachment. "To me, the imperative of protecting creatures and plants that cannot testify in their own behalf is a major test of humanity," he said. "Are we willing to share space and resources to protect life-forms that far outdate the evolution of 'us'?"

When Reed was an aide to Republican Gov. Claude Kirk, he helped stop plans for a massive jetport in the Big Cypress Swamp. He was assisted by the first-ever environmental impact statement, written by Aldo Leopold's son, Luna, showing how disastrous the thing would be. When Richard Nixon was elected president, Reed went to Washington as deputy secretary of the Interior Department, where he was determined to preserve wetlands and wildlife.

He wanted to beef up the law protecting animals and plants spiraling toward extinction. The federal wildlife law at the time had lots of loopholes. Reed and his allies would meet at a Chinese restaurant and hammer out the language for a new law with no wiggle room.

The result of their handiwork, the Endangered Species Act, passed Congress by an overwhelming margin in 1973, and Nixon signed it into law. Among the species immediately protected were several from Florida, including manatees, panthers, and Muir's old bugaboo, the alligators.

Despite the tough new law protecting these critters, Florida continued letting builders destroy their habitat, usually in service of a "need" for new homes during boom times that, during the subsequent bust, proved to be spurious.

Where homes have replaced panther habitat, panthers now prowl the suburbs, peering through sliding glass doors, occasionally gobbling up somebody's cat or dog or goat. They love goats. Panthers are to goats what I am to Oreo Cookie ice cream.

Manatees have lost habitat to the state's rampant waterfront development, with hardly an objection from state or federal officials. Meanwhile, so many of them have been run over by speeding boats that biologists use their scar patterns to tell one manatee from the other.

Manatees also face threats from Florida's YOLO yahoos. In 2013, a woman visiting St. Pete Beach spotted a manatee swimming past and leaped on it as if it were a bucking bronco. Other beachgoers shouted at her. She paid no heed. She was riding a manatee! Woo-hoo!

People snapped cell phone photos that the sheriff later displayed for reporters in an effort to identify her. He had some advice for anyone else contemplating such a stunt: "Go ride a Jet Ski."

The woman, it turned out, had no prior criminal record. She intended no harm. She had simply confused Real Florida, full of real manatees, with Fake Florida, full of theme-park animals that double as rides. She was charged with a misdemeanor and had to go through a pretrial intervention program. Despite what happened to her—not just the criminal charge but seeing unflattering photos of her thighs flashed around the globe—she turned out to be the first in a wave of clueless manatee riders.

A lot of people in Florida can't just watch a wild animal being wild. They haven't experienced Muir's mosquito epiphany. They view the world as if it were a live-action version of TV shows like *Flipper*. Rather than hang back as passive observers, they feel compelled to make themselves the star. Hey, look, it's a baby manatee! Put the kids on its back and post the photos to Facebook! Yee-haw!

What's true on the water is true on the land. In the Florida Keys is a colony of about seven hundred deer the size of big dogs. The Key deer are endangered, but they're so cute that tourists driving through the National Key Deer Refuge can't resist rolling down their windows and offering them treats. That means the Key deer now associate cars with food, and so their leading cause of death is being run over.

Feeding Florida's wildlife can lead to big problems for people too. Florida's black bear population lost habitat to development. Now, like panthers, the bears show up in the suburbs that used to be their home, lolling in hot tubs, hanging out by swimming pools, scaring the bejeezus out of people who just moved in and had no idea Florida even had bears. Following a series of four bear maulings, state wildlife officials announced in 2015 the return of bear hunting for the first time since 1994—although they acknowledged the hunt could not prevent future attacks. The state sold more hunting licenses than there were bears. The hunters then shot so many bears that what was scheduled as a weeklong hunt was shut down at the end of just two days.

It's instructive to look at what caused one bear attack. In 2014, a woman in a Central Florida suburban enclave called Lake Mary discovered five bears rummaging for food in the unsecured trash cans in her garage. Before she could react, one grabbed her and mauled her. Despite the easy accessibility of her own garbage, she told investigators that this attack was the fault of a neighbor whom she referred to as a "whack-a-doo." A former Audubon Society board member, he regularly fed the local bears, getting them to take treats from his hand as if they were stray cats lapping up milk. He boasted that a TV producer had been talking to him about creating a reality show called *The Bear Whisperer.* He and two others were cited and put on probation.

For decades, Florida's roadside attractions employed bears and other animals to draw in the paying customers. Everglades airboat tour captains would toss food in the water to prompt alligators to leap up, giving customers a thrill. It seemed like a harmless practice—but in Florida, nature bites the hand that feeds it.

"Gator Bites Off Hand of Everglades Airboat Captain," said a *Naples Daily News* headline in 2012. Wildlife officials tracked down the gator, killed it, and retrieved the hand, but doctors couldn't reattach it. The sixty-three-year-old captain wound up permanently maimed *plus* facing charges for illegally feeding gators.

Alligators are still a protected species but no longer classified as endangered. To fans of Nat Reed's law, their comeback proves that the Endangered Species Act works. To Floridians, the resurgent gators are like visiting relatives with big appetites, showing up on our doorsteps without an invitation and occasionally gobbling an unwary yip dog.

Some Floridians are more comfortable with gators than you might expect. In 2013, a man carrying a cardboard box walked into a store and tried to trade what was in the box—a small gator—for beer. He quickly learned that gators are not legal tender, even in Florida.

That same year saw a man arrested for illegally picking mushrooms in the Little Big Econ State Forest. He also happened to have a two-foot gator curled up in his backpack. He swore he'd intended to turn it loose. Because he'd been trespassing on state property, getting turned loose was a bigger problem for him than for the gator.

I am not quite as comfortable with gators as the beer or backpack guys. I have petted small ones and seen some mighty big ones up close—canoeing on the Hillsborough River, for instance, and gulping hard when I passed one that seemed bigger than my canoe.

Some Floridians are quite fond of our reptilian neighbors, though. I have found three instances in the past five years where people held wakes or funerals for a wild crocodile they knew and loved (named Blue No. 9, Wilma, and Pancho). Florida, by the way, is the only place on Earth where crocs and gators coexist.

In general, though, many Florida residents, particularly the new arrivals, do not appreciate gators and crocs lurking in their retention ponds. To them, this seems an intrusion, despite the fact that the big lizards were there first.

In 1908, naturalist A. W. Dimock wrote that a Florida alligator is "as harmless as a Florida cow." That opinion is in the minority these days. So many complaints about "nuisance alligators" pour into the Florida Fish and Wildlife Conservation Commission—about thirteen thousand a year—that the agency hired fifty trappers to go out and kill "problem" gators. This effort is called the Statewide Nuisance Alligator Program, SNAP for short, which is proof that sometimes bureaucrats exhibit a sense of humor.

SNAP trappers get a $30-per-gator stipend, but the trappers are expected to make most of their money selling the hides and meat. At one wildlife commission meeting, a commissioner who had a libertarian bent questioned SNAP. When facing roaches or other nuisances, he said, he hired an exterminator, a private sector solution to a private sector problem. The commission chairman told him that was a flawed comparison.

"Unlike roaches, gators do eat people," the chairman said. "You can't just step on them."

To me, though, our gators are not a nuisance. They're certifiable Florida heroes. They are the only critters defending Florida from voracious invaders.

Just as new residents come flooding into Florida every day, so do other things, and by that I mean invasive species. Scientists say Florida has more invasives than any other state. We're talking walking catfish, Asian swamp eels, Cuban tree frogs, Argentine tegus—it's quite a motley menagerie. Sometimes I wonder if we've got a little Statue of Liberty at the state line that says, "Bring me your slimy, your slippery, your sticky . . ."

A lot of these critters got here because someone thought that a king cobra might make a nice pet. For some reason, Floridians find it hard to believe that any animal might not be an apt accessory to our Florida lifestyle—until they do something to remind us that they're wild animals, like escaping to wreak havoc.

I once spent a day hanging out with some wildlife inspectors at the Miami airport, where they caught a man smuggling marmosets hidden under his hat, Cuban parrot chicks tucked in a woman's bra (one per cup), and forty-five red-footed tortoises stuffed in a man's parachute pants. While I was there, a dude with a red bandanna wrapped around his blond hair sauntered up to the intake window and told the uniformed inspector on duty, "Hey, I just bought a tiger off a guy and it didn't come with any papers. I wondered if that's a problem."

You never know where exotic animals will turn up. I live five minutes from downtown St. Petersburg, and for several years one of my neighbors owned a pair of emus that regularly escaped their pens. One of my kids says he has happy childhood memories of watching the neighbors pursuing their fleeing emus back and forth on our brick streets. All that was missing was someone playing "Yakity Sax."

Some of Florida's invasive species have been here a long time—for instance, the monkeys that live in Silver River State Park, near Silver Springs. In the 1930s, the owner of Silver Springs' Jungle Cruise put the rhesus macaques on an island to spice up the ride for tourists. He thought the monkeys would stay put. He didn't realize they could swim.

State park officials estimate there are about a hundred now. They'd love to get rid of them. They consider them a health hazard—let me just drop the magical phrase "rhesus feces" in here and leave it at that—but the tourists love them and would complain if they disappeared.

One of Silver River's macaques wandered over to the Tampa Bay area a few years ago to become the celebrated and elusive "Mystery Monkey of Tampa Bay." The story of that rambling rhesus was so compelling that the *New York Times* ran a profile of it prior to the 2012 Republican National Convention in Tampa. After three years it was finally captured, much to the chagrin of all the journalists who had had fun writing about its (ahem) monkeyshines.

Farther south, the island of Boca Grande has been so plagued by invasive iguanas that county commissioners finally levied a special "iguana tax" to pay for trapping them. The first time I visited Boca Grande, back in the 1980s, I saw iguanas running around on their hind legs like undersized Godzillas. I interviewed Boca Grande's only law enforcement officer, who told me he'd gotten a frantic call from a woman who'd discovered an iguana in her toilet just as she was about to sit down. The officer borrowed some rubber gloves from her, reached into her commode, grabbed the iguana's tail, and carried the critter outside.

"Did you blow its brains out with your service revolver?" I asked.

"It, uh, escaped from custody," he said with a straight face.

Now iguanas are all over South Florida, and their only enemy appears to be the thermometer. When the temperature dips too low, they stiffen up as if frozen and let go of whatever they're holding on to, leading to headlines such as, "Alien Iguanas Fall from Florida Trees During Cold Snap." Just one more dangerous aspect of living in Florida: the risk of being clobbered by a frozen iguana.

The big name in Florida invasives is, of course, the Burmese python, which has done such a fine job of taking over the Everglades and wiping out all the rabbits, raccoons, and foxes that lived there. Pythons have tried to gobble up the alligators too, but the gators fight back.

In 2005, an Everglades National Park biologist named Skip Snow shot a photo of a thirteen-foot python that had tried to swallow a six-foot alligator. As the gator was being swallowed, it apparently clawed at the python's stomach, making the snake explode. Snow's picture rocketed around the globe, turning pythons into the poster species for Florida invasives.

State and federal officials have tried about everything they can think of to rid South Florida of these snakes in the River of Grass. They even held a freewheeling "Python Challenge" in 2013 that attracted fifteen hundred hunters angling for prizes of $1,500 for the most pythons killed and $1,000 for the longest python. Most of the entrants were amateurs, reality show wannabes who wound up dehydrated and sunburned. At the end of the month-long hunt, sixty-eight snakes had been killed out of a population estimated at five thousand to ten thousand. A female python could replace that with a single clutch of eggs.

The most effective killer of pythons in the Everglades is a state employee named Bobby Hill, a paunchy, bearded great-grandpa toting a shotgun. So far he's killed more than three hundred—blasting their heads off and bringing in the carcasses for biologists to examine. Hill grew up in the Everglades and says he can detect the snakes' presence by their musky odor.

"Once you smell it, you don't forget it," he told me, in what would turn out to be the longest sentence I ever heard him speak.

The scientists studying pythons love Bobby Hill, and they loved the python hunt, because every dead python teaches them something new about where pythons live and what they do. Sometimes, though, what they learn is disturbing.

Scientists trying to save an endangered species of rat—yes, a rat, the Key Largo woodrat, to be precise—spent a lot of time and money on a captive-breeding program that Disney helped with (insert mouse-helps-rat joke here). When they turned the captive-bred rats loose in the wild, they attached tiny transmitters to them. One scientist following the rat radio signal wound up coming face-to-face with a python, the first one ever found in the Keys. This meant two things:

1. The python had swallowed the rat, transmitter and all.
2. Pythons can swim. (Yikes!)

Instead of a rat, I wish the first witness to the swimming python had been a human. Can you imagine a tourist strolling amid the dunes and spotting a fifteen-foot python zigzagging up out of the surf and crossing the wrack line?

Still, that wouldn't be the strangest thing to ever show up on a Florida beach.

Young women mock a sign at Miami Beach requiring full bathing suits, 1934. Photos like this were set up by promoters and sent to Northern newspapers during the winter to show how warm and welcoming Florida was by comparison. Photo courtesy of State Archives of Florida.

5

On the Beach

Perhaps this is the most important thing for me to take back from beach-living: simply the memory that each cycle of the tide is valid; each cycle of the wave is valid; each cycle of a relationship is valid. And my shells? I can sweep them all into my pocket. They are only there to remind me that the sea recedes and returns eternally.

—Anne Morrow Lindbergh, *Gift from the Sea,* a book inspired by her time on Florida's Captiva Island

One of the best things about living in Florida is that you can go to the beach whenever you want. Florida has more coastline than any of the other contiguous forty-seven states, so there's nowhere in Florida that's much more than an hour's drive from the shore. From South Florida's Gold Coast to the Panhandle's Redneck Riviera, these strips of sand and surf are definitely worth a visit, because Florida's beaches are frequently singled out as among the best, if not *the* best, in the country.

I know some Floridians who regard the beach as that place that shoves sand into their clothing in uncomfortable places, period. Even some people who have spent big bucks on waterfront property don't understand the point of a Florida beach. In 2012, the owners of a Fort Lauderdale beachfront condo complex got permission from a judge to bulldoze a sand dune because it was blocking the residents' view of the ocean. Despite expert testimony that the dune was important for hurricane protection and sea turtle nesting, the judge said yes, and the bulldozers flattened the dune.

Me? I have loved going to the beach ever since I was a tiny tyke in a puffy swim diaper laughing at the waves. The smell of cocoa butter is my made-leine, and catching that telltale tang of salt in the air always puts a grin on my face.

I love a Florida beach on a spring day when the sky is Tiffany blue and the waves sparkle like diamonds and the water is still cool enough to make you flinch a bit as you step in. I love a beach when the summer sun beats down like Thor's own hammer and the only relief lies in slipping into and under the bathtub-temperature water. I love going to the beach in the fall when it's like a mirror image of spring. I even like it in winter when it's too cold to swim, and all you can do is stroll along watching the gray clouds scudding across the horizon as towering breakers crash into the shore.

When I lived in Pensacola, Navarre Beach was my favorite. I'd drive out there early in the morning so I'd have the place pretty much to myself—just sugar-white sand and endless waves beneath a vast and welcoming sky. It's still known for the untarnished natural beauty of its emerald waters. But as with any place in Florida, there is a lot more to the place than what's on the surface.

Navarre's founder, Guy Wyman, had been an army surveyor during World War I. He fell for a French nurse named Noel. He wanted to bring her home as his wife, but the immigration laws of the time did not allow that. To get around the law, Wyman adopted her as his daughter, and when they got back to Florida, he married her.

When Wyman laid out his beach town, his daughter-wife suggested they name it for the Navarre province in Spain. Then the Depression hit. Wyman couldn't pay his bills. To make ends meet, Noel went to New York to teach French. Absence, for once, did not make the heart grow fonder. Wyman took up with another woman and divorced his wife. He also warned her not to return to Florida, or he'd put a bullet in her.

One account says she came back to harass her ex-husband/father and his new honey-bunny. Another says she just wanted to tend to a pet cemetery she had started. Either way, Wyman shot her dead.

Although this was long before Florida passed the "Stand Your Ground" law, Wyman never did a day behind bars. The authorities reasoned that he had warned her about what would happen, so her death was virtually a suicide. You can understand, though, why the citizens of Navarre have never scheduled a Founder's Day celebration.

One of the most astounding things I've ever witnessed occurred on a Florida beach. It happened on a moonless night under a sky as dark as spilled ink.

I was tagging along with two volunteers from Sarasota's Mote Marine Laboratory who patrolled the beach every night for months, watching for sea turtles struggling up out of the surf to lay their eggs in the dunes.

We spent hours riding up and down the beach on all-terrain trikes until finally we spotted a huge loggerhead dragging herself from the surf. We hid behind the dunes to watch as she dug a hole for her nest, then backed up to it to deposit her eggs.

At that point my guides said we could get closer because the loggerhead mama was so focused on what she was doing she wouldn't notice us. They measured the turtle's shell and clipped a metal ID tag to one flipper in case she ever showed up again.

As the turtle finished, we scurried back to our hiding place. We watched the turtle cover up the nest and push herself back down to the sea once more. As she swam away, we saw each stroke of her flippers light up the dark water with green streaks of bioluminescence, until the streaks disappeared as well.

Two months later, the eggs would crack open and the little hatchlings would push up through the sand and then make a desperate scramble toward the water. Someday some of them are likely to come back to the very beach where they were hatched and lay more eggs, keeping the eternal cycle alive.

My kids love the beach too. When they were small, they would do more than just splash around or build sand castles. They always wanted to search for cool seashells—angel wings, ponderous arks, prickly cockles, kitten's paws. Years ago, we visited Captiva Island, where Anne Morrow Lindbergh wrote her meditative *Gift from the Sea*. While I was helping one of the kids who was learning to swim, the other one paddled off to search the shallows for shells. Suddenly he began yelling, "*Daaaaaaaaaaaaaaaaaaaaaaaad!!!*"

"What's wrong?" I asked, sloshing over to him.

"This one squirted me!" he said, holding up an enormous lightning whelk.

"That's because somebody's still in there," I said, showing him the mollusk's foot. We took a picture of it, then put the shell back.

Such Florida discoveries can be inspiring. In 1948, a New Jersey electrician named Lewis Earle moved his family to the waterfront town of Dunedin, near Clearwater. There his teenage daughter Sylvia discovered that the Gulf of Mexico was virtually in her backyard. She spent all her spare time exploring it, noting all the marine life. At age sixteen, she took her first scuba dive in the Gulf, and the sea became her passion.

These days, Sylvia Earle, now in her seventies, is an internationally recognized marine scientist. She's known among her colleagues as "Her Deepness," because she holds the record for the deepest dive ever made without any tether to the surface: 1,250 feet.

I asked her what about the Gulf hooked her. "It was the sea grass meadows," she said. "They're like the rain forest, only wetter." She said she had been particularly smitten by "the seahorses, and the little pipefish—oh, and the crabs. I *loved* the crabs."

A lot more than just seashells wash up on Florida's beaches. Cleanup crews all over the state go out every morning to pick up hundreds of pounds of seaweed, and they also have found a part of a rocket, a cow's head, an engine block, and one thousand pairs of shoes.

Florida's beaches are a constant reminder of the joys of serendipity. Early Florida settlers counted on using whatever washed ashore to survive— lumber, food, clothing, dishes, and so forth.

Once, in the 1880s, hundreds of casks of Spanish wine landed on beaches along the Atlantic coast—although there was no sign of any shipwreck to explain their origin. On another occasion, a group of settlers found a shipwreck carrying hundreds of coconuts. They planted them, and the trees grew so well that their crop gave Palm Beach its name.

You never know who or what might turn up on our beaches. During World War II, Nazi saboteurs in swim trunks and forage caps landed on Ponte Vedra Beach, ready to wreak havoc. They were captured within ten days.

American soldiers trained on the beaches of Carrabelle for the D-Day landing and griped about the mosquitoes, horseflies, and sand spurs. Worst of all, they complained in song, was that "the heat in the summer is one hundred and ten / Too hot for the Devil, too hot for the men."

These days, as you stroll on a Florida beach, you might run across anything from wild boar carcasses to a severed leg to a giant Lego man. This is not, of course, what all those retirees with metal detectors are searching for, but Spanish doubloons are few and far between. Still, in 2013 alone, the list of things floating off Florida beaches included a purse containing $13,087.88, a diamond ring in a plastic bag, and a burlap sack containing $700,000 worth of cocaine.

Bales of marijuana, aka "square grouper," still show up from time to time, though not as often as they did in the '80s. If the cops find them, they burn them. If they don't, the bales go up in smoke one toke at a time.

Sometimes what turns up is a mystery. In 1986, a dead elephant washed up in Marathon. Nobody knew where it originated. "We had no missing elephant reports," a marine patrol officer said.

Whales, sharks, and dolphins beach themselves with some regularity, no one knows why. The most famous bit of sea life ever to land in Florida was a blob of flesh found in 1896 and dubbed the "St. Augustine Monster." Although there was speculation it came from a giant squid or even a space alien, more recent tests have—to everyone's disappointment—determined it was just whale blubber.

Like the St. Augustine Monster, some of the stuff that shows up on Florida's beaches catches the world's attention. The most recent Florida beach discovery that caused an uproar was the ginormous eyeball that Gino Covacci spotted while strolling on Pompano Beach in 2013. The eye was as big as a hubcap, with a deep blue iris. Web sites around the world went nuts. Did the eye come from a whale? A giant squid? Cthulhu?

State biologists at last concluded it came from a swordfish. How it got there, though, remains a bit of a mystery, since no swordfish have been seen sporting an eyepatch.

So when you visit Florida and stroll on our beautiful beaches, enjoy the view but keep a lookout. You're liable to stumble across all kinds of strange creatures—although by far the strangest are the Floridians.

In February 2013, cops investigating a reported vehicle fire on Jacksonville Beach discovered a twenty-nine-year-old man and a thirty-one-year-old woman having sex amid the dunes. "Witnesses said a couple had been arguing and throwing things from the vehicle when the woman walked away," the *Florida Times-Union* reported. "That's when the man started to light the vehicle on fire, then left it as he went up the beach to meet the woman." Apparently they rekindled (ahem!) their romance.

Or consider what happened in 1995, when two women—a forty-eight-year-old astrologer from Florida named Dixie Bottari and her twenty-eight-year-old daughter Magica, an actress from Chicago—decided to tote a couple of cups of coffee along as they watched the sun set on Belleair Shore. To call Belleair Shore a small beach town containing a few dozen rich people with no sense of humor would be an understatement. As the Bottaris sipped their java, the mayor walked up and handed them each a $30 ticket for violating a town ordinance banning beverages from the beach.

Newspapers all over the country had fun with the story, dubbing it a "brew-haha." The state attorney's office declined to prosecute, so the mayor told the city attorney to do it. But when the town commission met around the mayor's dining table (there is no city hall), the commissioners decided that because the women had been given no warning before they were ticketed, prosecuting them would be wrong.

My favorite Florida beach frenzy story, though, is the tangled tale of "Old Three-Toes."

In February 1948, when Clearwater was a sleepy village of fifteen thousand and the local beaches were covered by sea oats, not condos and T-shirt shops, a beachgoer wandering along the drift line discovered some strange three-toed footprints in the sand.

Something big had waded ashore, walked two miles through the dunes, and then waded back into the sea. The prints it left were fourteen inches long and eleven inches wide, and showed a stride that measured from four to six feet. Soon the mysterious tracks appeared on other beaches, from Honeymoon Island to St. Pete Beach. Local papers ran photos of patrolmen squatting over a big footprint, looking baffled.

"Are the tracks really those of some weird, gigantic animal, a water-dwelling monstrosity that time forgot?" the *St. Petersburg Times* asked.

The public reaction split between door-barricading panic and a puzzled skepticism. If some monster were leaving these tracks, what sort of mayhem might it cause? But if it was just a hoax, why go to so much trouble?

News about the tracks spread. The *Times* reported that the mystery "is getting Florida more national attention than a beach full of bathing beauties." Clearwater had lost some tourist appeal because of a stinky fish kill, but now people were flocking back to the beach.

The reports caught the eye of a suave New York zoologist named Ivan Sanderson who, unlike most scientists, "was always looking for something that would rocket him into stardom," said his biographer, Richard Grigonis. Sanderson had parlayed several African jungle expeditions into a bestselling book, then became the first person to display live critters on TV. He also coined the word "cryptozoology," meaning the search for legendary or undiscovered creatures.

On behalf of the *New York Herald Tribune* and NBC, Sanderson spent two weeks here investigating what he dubbed "Old Three Toes." He interviewed witnesses. He examined plaster casts of the prints. When more tracks appeared along the Suwannee River one hundred miles north of Clearwater, he dug up one to take home for further study.

Sanderson concluded it could not possibly be a hoax. The impressions in the sand were too deep to have been made by a man or a machine. In fact, he said, he'd seen the creature himself while flying over the Suwannee. Old Three

Toes, he said, was grayish-yellow, at least twelve feet long, with large, flipperlike arms. It made big waves, as if kicking with powerful legs.

So was it a swimming dinosaur? A supersized alligator? No, Sanderson contended, it was a big bird. A *really* big bird. From far beyond Florida.

"The imprint is, in fact, very much like that of a vast penguin," he wrote. However, he readily admitted that his theory sounded "balmy," conceding, "Who ever heard of a 15-foot bird?"

The tracks of the Giant Penguin of Clearwater—or whatever it was—reappeared a few more times, but after 1958, they vanished. Thirty years passed, during which Sanderson wrote books about Bigfoot, the Bermuda Triangle, and UFOs. Old Three Toes, he wrote, was the one creature that left behind the most convincing evidence of all.

Then, in 1988, a *Times* reporter interviewing two local missionaries got a break. They told her she really ought to talk to their friend Tony Signorini, a pillar of the Catholic Church. Ask what he's hiding, they said, smirking. When the writer showed up at Signorini's auto repair shop, he pulled a box from beneath his workbench and showed her a pair of feet.

Iron ones. With three toes.

There never was a Giant Penguin. Signorini was Old Three Toes. The whole thing had been an elaborate hoax dreamed up by his former boss, Al Williams.

To strangers, Williams seemed gruff and antisocial. That rough exterior was just the mask worn by an inveterate prankster, a guy who'd put a mule in a jail cell just to stump the police. According to Signorini, in 1948 his boss had seen a photo of a fossil dinosaur footprint in *National Geographic*. After studying it, Williams announced he and Signorini could have some fun with it.

They designed feet to match the photo, then had them cast in iron. They bolted a pair of high-top canvas sneakers to the iron feet, loaded them into a rowboat, and headed out into the Gulf.

When Williams pulled the boat in close to the beach, Signorini tied on the feet, stepped out into shallow water, waded ashore, and set off down the sand. To create a long stride, Signorini would stand on one leg, swing the other one back and forth to build momentum, then take a leap. When he was done, he waded back to his boss's rowboat.

Each foot of what he called "Dinny the Dinosaur" weighed about thirty pounds, which means Signorini was hopping around with sixty pounds of iron. Years later, thanks to Signorini's son, I tried one on. I could barely lift my leg. But Tony Signorini back then was a vigorous man in his twenties, his son pointed out. He relished pulling a fast one on most of the town, not to mention one snooty out-of-town expert.

By the time Signorini told his story to a reporter, he was the last of the principals left. Williams had died in 1969, and Sanderson departed this dimension in 1973.

Despite Signorini's confession, some of Sanderson's followers refused to believe he'd been bamboozled by small-town pranksters. In the book *Chronicles of the Strange and Uncanny in Florida,* Greg Jenkins points out that there were eyewitnesses who said they saw the creature, including Sanderson himself.

However, three biologists I consulted agreed that what Sanderson saw was most likely a manatee—not a familiar sight back then the way manatees are now. As for the other witnesses, Jeff Signorini said his father and Al Williams put some of their friends up to calling in fake reports, as well as collaborating with some friendly cops who didn't mind seeing Clearwater attract tourists again.

In 2012, Tony Signorini died at age ninety-one. His family made sure to mention in his obituary that, along with being a World War II flight engineer and a faithful member of the church, "Tony was famous for being 'The Clearwater Monster,' a hoax that made national news."

The funny thing about Florida's beaches is that, despite how essential they are to Florida's current image and economy, the early settlers had no use for them. They regarded the beaches about the way they regarded all the swamps and marshes they encountered: If you couldn't plant anything on it, it was worthless. Then, too, they were mindful of Jesus's parable about the foolish man who built his house upon the sand.

"No one thought of building much near the ocean, because it would eventually sweep everything away," a pioneer named Charles Pierce wrote of growing up here in the 1870s. "Beach land was cheap, particularly compared with the good farmland behind it."

Instead of homes and condos, Florida's beaches mostly contained only "a dense ocean hammock with tall banyans, gumbo-limbos, and sea grapes, beach grass and open sand with not a sign of man or his works . . . The entire coast was windswept and throughout most of the year infested with mosquitoes."

The beaches were so deserted back then that when ships were smashed to bits in a hurricane, any survivors who made it to shore had to wait a long time to be saved. One crew nearly starved to death. After that, the federal agency in charge of lighthouses dispatched crews to build along the Atlantic coast ten Houses of Refuge designed to withstand every kind of foul weather. They were stocked with food and dry clothes, and furnished with a cistern of fresh water. Then the government hired keepers (including Pierce's father) to maintain the houses and watch for stranded seamen.

By the start of the twentieth century, though, the tide had turned. "It is already very evident that about everyone who visits this gulf bay desires to go to the gulf beach and take a dip in the surf," a Panama City paper reported in 1909.

Now all the wealthy Yankee tourists wanted to frolic at the shore, inhaling the healthy sea air and roasting clams. Nobody wanted Houses of Refuge. They wanted stately pleasure domes. Builders began offering beachfront houses, and not even Jesus could keep people from building on the sand.

On the land that the settlers once disdained as barren sprouted a rich crop of vacation homes and condos. The beaches became a big business as stores and bars and restaurants sprang up too, all catering to the hedonistic sun worshippers who arrived pale of skin and eager for good times. Between the bars and tattoo parlors you'd find the Florida kitsch—Goofy Golf courses and game arcades and water slides. In some places, the attractions that sprang up along the beach eclipsed the beach itself.

"The gorgeous beach has been mugged and gagged, left nearly invisible from the highway," complained one writer after surveying what had become of Panama City.

Some of the tackiest tourist trappings grew out of the tradition of Spring Break, which began with a Christmastime collegiate swim meet in Fort Lauderdale in 1935. Swimmers from Colgate University went home to freezing New York and spread the word that warm beaches awaited in Florida. Soon the date of this pilgrimage shifted from Christmas to Easter break, someone invented the wet T-shirt contest, and by 1959 some twenty thousand sweaty teenagers were flocking to Fort Lauderdale to scorch their skin in the daytime and dance, drink, and do the horizontal bop at night. Occasionally they would vary the routine of this baccalaureate bacchanal by sneaking a live gator or a dead shark into the hotel pool, fighting with cops, fighting with each other, crashing cars, wandering around naked, and being treated by paramedics who just sighed at another round of projectile vomiting.

By the '90s, Fort Lauderdale had had about enough and began enforcing beach rules, an unheard-of attitude toward Florida tourists. As a result, the Spring Break scene shifted northward to the Panhandle, mostly to Panama City Beach, where the merchants were eager to attract even the poorly behaved students as long as they brought enough cash.

Thus we had the spectacle of the good churchgoing people of the Panhandle sending out flyers and taking out ads that all but guaranteed students that if they showed up in Florida with enough cash, they could expect to—as

Jimmy Buffett put it so succinctly—"get drunk and screw." But in 2015, a Spring Break party at Panama City Beach led to gunfire that wounded seven people, and a video went viral of a gang rape on the beach. At last city officials thought that maybe things had gotten out of hand. They banned drinking on the beach. Indoor imbibing was still all right, though.

The problem with all this wasn't the commercialism, the violence, the greed, the heavy drinking, or the hypocrisy. Nor was it that while Florida was calling all these people to come to our beaches, it was allowing some cities to continue dumping sewage offshore, which led to the occasional closing of the beaches because of the high fecal coliform count (plus rashes).

No, the problem was that beaches don't stay still.

As I mentioned before, the Florida landscape is a treacherous terrain, never as steady as it seems. In this instance it's not sinkholes but sand that's the danger.

Beaches are not fixed in one place like concrete. They move. They absorb the power of the pounding waves and one part of the beach loses a little sand and another part gains. If you build something on a beach, pretty soon your building will be on the brink of falling into the ocean. (See: the parable about the foolish man.)

So did Floridians move their buildings? Did they start building farther away from the water? Don't be silly. No, they sought money from the federal government to pay for "beach renourishment."

Engineers have been dredging sand up from the ocean bottom offshore and pumping it up onto the land since 1922, when Coney Island's beaches needed what plastic surgeons like to call "enhancement." Since then, more than three hundred major renourishment projects have been pursued nationwide, dumping a total of 517 million cubic yards of sand on the country's waning beachfronts.

Guess which state has the biggest number of federally funded renourishment projects?

Florida's beaches have benefited from more than 140 designed and engineered projects over the state's 825 miles of sandy shoreline. Thirty-five of Florida's sixty-seven counties have used taxpayer money to artificially enhance their beaches, plumping them up like a fading star injecting collagen in her lips.

"Sand is to Florida what snow is to Colorado," explained a politician nicknamed "Mr. Sandman" for his ability to round up taxpayer money for rebuilding his district's beaches. Of course, snow in Colorado generally doesn't cost the taxpayers in other states a dime—whereas everyone in the United States is paying for rebuilding Florida's beaches.

The shifting of the sands has become the province of politicians, experts at pushing renourishment projects based on the clamoring of their constituents rather than a determination of actual need.

Sometimes they even exceed what their constituents want. In the 1980s, Captiva Island had so little sand left on its beaches that a tropical storm washed out the only evacuation road. The residents, all fairly well-off, agreed to tax themselves to pay for new sand. Then their congressman stepped in.

Porter Goss was a former CIA agent who had fallen in love with this area while training for the Bay of Pigs invasion, as did quite a few of his cloak-and-dagger colleagues. When this group retired to Sanibel, Goss led the push for incorporation, became the town's first mayor, was appointed a county commissioner, then got elected to Congress—proving the CIA can take over even American governments.

Goss was a staunch probusiness, antitax Republican, a cautious belt-and-suspenders guy (he showed them to me once to prove he wore both). Yet as the region's congressman, Goss pushed his colleagues to approve spending $1.8 million from taxpayers around the country to do the job that his constituents had been willing to pay for themselves. Even before the new sand was dumped onto the shore, waterfront property prices soared, creating private profit from public funding.

Then, in the mid-2000s, six beachfront landowners from the Panhandle city of Destin challenged this whole renourishment system. They contended that it took their property rights.

State officials had maintained that newly deposited sand didn't belong to the beachfront property owners but to the public paying the bill. The Destin group argued their property rights should extend until the beach touched the ocean, no matter what additional sand had been pumped up on the beach. If their property didn't extend that far, they said, then they should be compensated for the government taking their land.

Local and state government officials blanched at the thought of having to pay out millions of dollars to the very homeowners who would benefit most from the renourishment.

When the case got to the Florida Supreme Court, the Destin landowners lost, 5–2. They appealed to the U.S. Supreme Court in 2009. The justices who heard the case had a lot of questions about Florida beach sand: Where it comes from. Where it goes. Where spring breakers like to party. A year later, eight of the justices reached a unanimous decision: The homeowners were wrong and the state was right. The ninth justice recused himself—he owned beachfront property in Florida.

Of course, the ongoing alterations in our world because of climate change further point up the foolishness of building a house upon the sand. Rising sea levels are already taking a toll on low-lying Florida. It's more visible in natural areas than along beaches, where people have built seawalls or the Army has dumped more sand. At Waccasassa State Park in Levy County, palm trees are toppling over dead as rising salt water creeps up the beach. At Rookery Bay Preserve near Naples, saltwater mangroves have invaded what used to be freshwater marshes. Employees of the state Department of Environmental Protection may have been told to steer clear of using the term "climate change," but the signs that it's real are showing up in a big way.

In spring 2014, the Third National Climate Assessment warned that Florida is particularly vulnerable to climate change. It predicted increases in harmful algae blooms, worsening seasonal allergies, and heavier flooding in low-lying areas. Sea levels have already have risen by about eight inches since reliable record keeping began in 1880, the report noted, and they are projected to rise another one to four feet by 2100. That's already making rain-related flooding in the streets of coastal cities such as St. Augustine and Miami a lot worse. Meanwhile, salty water pushing inland under the ground will invade Florida's aquifer, tainting it and forcing local and state officials to find other, more expensive sources, the report said.

Yet right after the report came out, Gov. Rick Scott and the state cabinet voted to approve expanding a Miami-area nuclear power plant at the edge of the Atlantic. Rising seas? What rising seas?

That's always been our way here in Florida. We say we love the beach and the ocean, and then we do what we can to ruin them or ignore their threats. Heck, we've even been known to drive our cars on the beach—and turned it into a multibillion-dollar business.

A motorcade crosses Tampa Bay on the brand new Sunshine Skyway Bridge on Labor Day, 1954. Before the bridge was built, the only way across the bay was by ferry. In 1980, a freighter called the *MV Summit Venture* crashed into the bridge, knocking it into the bay and killing 35 people. Photo courtesy of *Tampa Bay Times*.

Road Warriors

There was nothing to talk about anymore. The only thing to do was go.
—*On the Road* by Jack Kerouac, who finished editing the book in Orlando, and also wrote *The Dharma Bums* and other works while living in Florida

When I was teaching my teenager to drive, one thing I made sure he practiced was how to maneuver through a road that's under construction.

"You need to know this because, at any one time, half of the roads you'll drive on will be under construction," I said, inventing a dramatic statistic just to make sure he paid attention. "And then when they're done with those, the road crew will begin work on the other half."

Despite my made-up percentage, the fact is that a lot of Florida roads are under construction a lot of the time. Sometimes it seems like no matter which party controls the governor's mansion or the legislature, the most powerful man in the state is the owner of Bob's Barricades.

Bob's Barricades, in case you're unaware of it, is the largest privately owned traffic barricade company in the United States, and it is based in Florida. Every driver in Florida knows the name because all the barricades provided by Bob's Barricades have BOB'S BARRICADES printed on them, and so we get to study them at our leisure while trapped in traffic.

Of course, the owner of Bob's Barricades is *not* named Bob. His name is Happy. A Florida newspaper ran a story about the company under the wonderful headline: "Happy Is the Man Behind Bob's Barricades." Happy has been in the barricade business nearly forty years—much longer than Bob the ex-cop, who sold the business decades ago.

People complain about a lack of seasons in Florida, but you can always tell when fall arrives because there's an increase in Bob's Barricades lining the highway. Instead of piles of leaves, we have road crews languidly waving you to a stop. Major road construction begins in the fall because the rainy summer has ended and the contractors know that they can count on dry weather for the next several months.

Of course, fall is also when a lot of snowbirds land back in Florida from the North or Canada. They stay three or four or five months, and they tend to drive a tad slooooooowly. If you've driven in Florida in the fall and winter, you have been behind their cars, which all travel a minimum of three miles with their left blinker on before turning right. They're usually doing 15 in a 35 mph zone. Get behind one of these slowpokes on a two-lane road with more traffic stacked up behind you, and you have experienced what is known as a Florida Parade. All that's missing is the marching band.

Such traffic tie-ups can drive you over the edge, especially if you're trying to get home from a long day at Disney or SeaWorld or Universal. California is notorious for its car-based culture, but Florida is just as addicted to pavement. Sometimes I think our state motto might as well be "Florida: Asphalt Über Alles." (Other times I think it should be "Florida: Where Are My Pants?!")

With the exception of a few walkable downtowns, if you want to go anywhere in Florida, you've got to get behind the wheel. We guarantee you'll need a driver's license and a car because we've sprawled our subdivisions all over the landscape, putting them as far as possible from the mall and the grocery store and any other business you need. Then we complain about the price of the gas we're wasting. A lot of those subdivisions were built without sidewalks as a money-saving measure, which means you can't even walk safely anywhere in your own neighborhood.

Meanwhile, our elected leaders appear allergic to mass transit. In 2011, Gov. Rick Scott rejected $2 billion in federal aid to build a high-speed rail line between Tampa and Orlando, claiming it would cost too much. I should mention that paving and road-building companies are major political donors—but I'm sure that had nothing to do with why the state Department of Transportation buried reports that found bid rigging, sham bids, and collusion among its contractors. When Scott was seeking reelection in 2014, he needed to show the voters he was creating jobs, so he announced the state would build more roads and widen the old ones. See, that's not just asphalt out there—it's an economic stimulus!

Our carcentric culture leads to lots of stories about Florida drivers doing wacky things while behind the wheel to save time. My favorite is the one about the woman in the Keys who, while on her way to see her boyfriend, asked her ex-husband—yes, he was in the passenger seat——to take the wheel. She wanted to look nice for her date, so while her ex was steering, she got out a razor to shave what news accounts later referred to as her "bikini area."

It did not end well.

Florida tends to rank high on the list of states that are unsafe at any speed, and not just because of the six hundred people who got illegal driver's licenses through a scam apparently copied from a *SpongeBob SquarePants* episode. It's because we have such a diverse mix of drivers and their bad habits—for instance, people who will suddenly stop for no apparent reason and people who won't stop for anything. Is it any wonder our drivers go berserk so often? Thriller writer Edna Buchanan says she survives the traffic here by constantly repeating this mantra: "Every other driver on the road is insane and wants to kill me."

Our road rage incidents do tend to be wilder than those of any other state, featuring not just rude gestures but also ramming vehicles, shots fired, and the brandishing of odd weaponry. An AP report on a 2000 battle between a pair of Panhandle pickup drivers noted that it involved "a rake, chainsaw, baseball bat and pregnant woman." In a 2013 confrontation in Fort Myers, one driver pulled a shotgun from his car trunk, only to see the other driver respond by pulling out his own sawed-off. They ended up in a high-speed chase, and before it was over, one had blown out the other's windshield. My favorite one, from the *Gainesville Sun,* had a more karmic outcome: "Man in Road Rage Incident Run Over by Own Truck."

Florida's requirement that we drive everywhere we want to go is also why we have so many elderly drivers. They have no choice. The result is a phenomenon I have heard referred to as Sudden Elderly Acceleration Syndrome, in which a gray-haired driver mistakes the gas pedal for the brake and gives a business a new drive-through. In 2012, incidents of SEAS got so bad that the U.S. Postal Service ran ads asking Floridians to *please* stop ramming their post offices.

When I say "elderly" drivers, I am not talking about someone who recently qualified for AARP. As of 2012, Florida had 455 licensed drivers who were one hundred or older. Of people who are between ninety-one and one hundred, there are 65,000 with licenses. Maybe some of them shouldn't be driving anymore—but if you take away their car keys, they will be stranded as surely as if you'd dropped them on an ice floe.

Trying to get where you're going using a bicycle or walking means taking your life in your hands (or feet). In 2015, Florida ranked first in the nation in bicyclist traffic deaths, and a 2014 study reported that among urban areas,

Orlando topped the list as the most hazardous city for pedestrians, with 583 deaths. In second, third, and fourth places: Tampa, Jacksonville, and Miami.

I thought of this while reading a 2014 story about an impatient driver from DeLand who cut around a pickup only to find a pedestrian crossing in front of her Kia. She ran him down and kept going. When the cops caught her, she explained that she didn't hit the guy on purpose, but he "was in my way."

My friend Lance is, to me, the Ultimate Pedestrian. He walks three miles to work every day. Despite Florida's reputation for running over walkers, he told me he hasn't ever felt in danger of becoming Flat Stanley. However, he said, he invariably encounters some wise guy in a truck who honks the horn next to him just to startle him, and he sees enough roadside litter to make a TV-commercial Indian chief cry.

The variety of our roadside litter can be astonishing. A South Florida radio station reported that drivers on I-95 have had to dodge such diverse debris as blond wigs, sex toys, dental implants, flying mattresses, and entire refrigerators.

Sometimes the hazards come from up above. In May 2015, someone in Jackson County killed an eight-foot alligator and hung it by a chain from an overpass. Someone driving by crashed into the dangling dead gator. A friend of mine said, "Could you imagine being in the car that hit it?" And I said, "Better yet, imagine being the insurance agent: 'You hit a *what* that was doing WHAT now?'"

This bizarre roadside bounty is not to be confused with the amazing offerings provided by Florida's roadside gift shops. John Rothchild, in his book *Up for Grabs,* recounts his childhood fascination with the cornucopia of crappy crafts found in those roadside stands: "coconut heads carved to look like pirates, pelicans made from seashells, tiny crates of bubble-gum oranges, fish skulls advertised as relics of the Crucifixion, seahorses dried and packaged like beef jerky, perfume tapped from tangerines, stuffed alligators, cans of sunshine, and postcards of beauty queens in low-cut bathing suits." My favorite bit of Sunshine State kitsch is something I found in a combined gas station and geegaw emporium near Naples. It was shaped like a manatee, curled up on its back with its flippers upright, its unnatural pose making it ready to hold a bottle of cheap wine, as if something had driven this endangered species to drink.

Sometimes what you find on Florida's roads is a lesson in political action and reaction.

Every spring through the 1980s and '90s, a phalanx of motorcycle riders would roar into Tallahassee to protest a state law that required them to wear helmets. The law had been passed in the name of safety and keeping hospital costs down, just like seat belts, but to these knights of the open road, this was Big Government Infringing on Their Freedom. Their slogan: "Let Those Who Ride Decide."

Among those backing this antihelmet drive was a forty-year-old Fort Myers woman named Dorothy Lynette Rushton, who also owned a motorcycle-themed beauty salon named Helmet Hair.

At last, in 2000, despite the objections of trauma experts, the legislature passed a law allowing motorcyclists to ride without helmets, provided they carry a $10,000 insurance policy. Gov. Jeb Bush (R-Freedom!) proudly signed it into law. It took effect in July.

Before the month was over, the number of motorcyclists who'd died in crashes had begun rising. Among their number: Helmet Hair owner Dorothy Lynette Rushton. "Officials said Rushton probably would have survived the crash of her 1999 Harley-Davidson had she been wearing a helmet," the *Orlando Sentinel* deadpanned.

In the three years prior to the repeal, Florida averaged about 150 motorcycle deaths a year. As of 2012, the number was 457, and safety advocates in other states were pointing to Florida as a good reason not to repeal their helmet laws.

Yep, that's us: "Florida: Setting a bad example since the 1500s."

Driving around Florida does offer certain pleasures, mostly in the form of memorable roadside signs. In Central Florida, I saw what I think of as the Ultimate Florida Combo Business. It had two signs out front. One said POOLS SPAS and the other said GUNS AMMO.

If you delight in irony, as most Floridians do, you can brighten up your drives by looking for subdivision developments celebrating the things they wiped out—Cypress Lakes, Panther Trace, and so forth. My favorite, found on the outskirts of Naples, said simply WILDERNESS. In Naples, the word "wilderness" apparently means "country club with eighteen-hole golf course, four tennis courts, and five heated swimming pools." Ah, Wilderness!

Bear in mind, of course, that lots of these developments would not exist had the obliging local and state agencies not built roads through previously undeveloped areas. If what they've built are toll roads, they were likely based on phony revenue projections.

The best example of this is the Garcon Point Bridge in the Panhandle, aka "Florida's Bridge to Nowhere" and "Bo's Bridge." Critics called it a boondoggle that would harm Pensacola Bay, spur development on flood-prone barrier islands, and never attract enough motorists to justify its expense. Its main backer, Democratic House Speaker Bolley "Bo" Johnson, had an interest in land at the end of the bridge, and he pushed it through. Building it required bogus traffic projections, pie-in-the-sky financing, and shoddy construction practices. Anglers trying to fish beneath the project narrowly missed being clobbered by debris the builders repeatedly tossed into the water.

The day it opened in 1999, the bridge had already incurred hefty fines for environmental destruction. Meanwhile, Johnson was on his way to prison for not reporting on his taxes the secret payments he'd received from a paving contractor and other businesses. The tolls were so high nobody wanted to drive on it. By the end of Jeb Bush's second term, it was bankrupt.

Florida's early settlers didn't bother with roads. Building a road through the swampy, sandy wilderness was just too difficult.

They traveled by boat. They'd sail along through bays or lakes or along the coast to buy supplies at the nearest trading post, then sail home. Mail was delivered by boat or, along the Atlantic coast, by mailmen who shucked their shoes and hiked down the beach. The story of Florida's barefoot mailmen inspired a novel and then a 1951 movie starring Robert "Love That Bob" Cummings.

The movie version of *The Barefoot Mailman* plays up the risks the mailmen faced on their route—at least one was killed by a gator. But it neglects to mention that they would sometimes take off their pants and shirts and tuck them in their mailbags so they could better enjoy the breeze while hiking their route. Perhaps the producers figured a movie called *The Buck-Nekkid Mailman* would have attracted a less desirable audience.

Moving around Florida on foot or in boats was slow, though, too slow to get a farmer's crop to market before it spoiled. The solution (pushed, you may recall, by a senator with a stake in the business): Build railroads across the new state. That spurred the start of new industries—cotton, citrus, and other crops—because now the product could be shipped long distances.

In the 1880s and '90s, railroads remade Florida and set the template for its economic future as a Ponzi state. Two rail lines were built heading southward, their paths running roughly parallel to each other down the state's two coasts. Standard Oil millionaire Henry Flagler's Florida East Coast line pushed along the Atlantic side of the state, while his rival, shipping magnate Henry Plant, laid tracks for his South Florida Railroad on the Gulf side.

The two Henrys were white-haired gentlemen with matching mustaches who lived a couple of blocks from each other on New York's Fifth Avenue. I like to imagine them as the best of frenemies, like the Duke brothers from the movie *Trading Places*.

They built a series of resort hotels along their rail lines, some of which still stand today. To eyes accustomed to the blandness of modern motels, these gloriously ornate structures like the Breakers and the Royal Poinciana and the Hotel Tampa Bay look as gaudy as your great-grandma's diamond brooch. They were innovative for their time. Flagler's Hotel Ponce de León in St. Augustine was the first large cast-in-place concrete building in the United States.

The railroad men added every Gilded Age amenity available, then invented some new ones. Plant's Belleview Hotel offered Florida's first major golf course, for instance.

The Henrys blanketed the country with ads touting Florida as "America's Riviera," neatly combining patriotism and hedonism in a single catchphrase. They convinced Northerners that the state was, as one historian put it, both "exotically attractive" and "healthfully restorative."

Well-off tourists poured into the state looking for a good time in a mild clime. Real estate men working for the magnates were waiting to sell the vacationers some recently drained swampland. It worked. Tampa, where Plant built not only a hotel but also a port for his steamships, underwent an astonishing transformation, growing from a sleepy backwater of about seven hundred inhabitants in 1880 to a bustling town of more than six thousand ten years later.

Flagler was more ambitious, driving his rail line to Miami in 1896 and finally reaching Key West in 1912, an amazing engineering feat considering the long stretches of water that had to be crossed. Even today, people driving to the Keys are driving on the bed of Flagler's old railroad.

As the man who brought all these towns their railroad and tourists and development, Flagler wielded tremendous power. In 1896, when four hundred citizens met in a pool room to incorporate as a city, they initially offered to name the place for Flagler. He declined, so they named it for their river, the Miami. Flagler had so much power that when he wanted to divorce his second wife, whom he had consigned to an asylum, and marry his children's nanny, the legislature passed a special law making insanity grounds for divorce. Four years later, lawmakers repealed it.

The railroads' growth far outpaced Florida's actual roads, which were just trails made by cattlemen driving their herds to market. When the first automobiles began jouncing along what passed for roads at the turn of the century, they bogged down with depressing frequency. The first St. Petersburg resident to own a car got so sick of getting stuck that he started driving on the city's wooden sidewalks. At that point it wasn't against the law.

Florida's first roads were knee-deep sand that became a quagmire whenever it rained. To bolster their stability, road builders turned to an easily exploited supply of paving material: massive shell mounds built by Florida's pre-Columbian tribes, such as the Calusa. The road builders laid waste to the past to pave the way to the future, and how very Florida is that?

As the state's connected coastal settlements became boomtowns, the folks farther inland sought a similar break. Thus they hailed the arrival of a colorful thug named William "Fingy" Conners.

In his native Buffalo, a childhood dare cost him a thumb but gave him his nickname. Fingy grew up to become a pug-nosed, hydrant-shaped stevedore who could whip any man on his crew. Fingy had big goals and no qualms about how to achieve them. He was able to buy a number of Buffalo saloons, one historian wrote, "when all four members of his immediate family died within months of each other, in precisely the order required for the chain of estates to end up in his own bank account." His ruthless approach resulted in him controlling Great Lakes shipping, the bulk of the U.S. and Canadian grain trade, and New York's Democratic Party all at once.

As a man of wealth and political clout, Fingy felt compelled to socialize with other movers and shakers—although whenever reporters quoted Fingy, he still sounded like a Buffalo dock-walloper. He'd say things like, "Say anyt'in' about Conners but nuttin'. When you say Conners, it means somet'in', or you wouldn't say it!" and "Brains is as cheap as tenpenny nails. I can buy tenpenny nails."

Perhaps it was his wife who prodded him to mingle with high society in Florida. Evidence for this theory comes from George McManus, a young cartoonist who fell in love with Conners's daughter and asked for her hand. Fingy was fine with it, but his wife, Mary, made it clear to McManus that he wasn't from the proper social stratum. McManus got his revenge by drawing a comic strip called *Bringing Up Father* that featured a rich roughneck named Jiggs who appeared to be the spitting image of Fingy, and Jiggs's snooty, social-climbing wife, Maggie. *Bringing Up Father* was such a hit that it was syndicated to three hundred newspapers and adapted into radio shows and movies. Fingy didn't mind. History does not record that his wife deigned to speak of the matter.

So in 1917, the Connerses wound up hobnobbing with the hoity-toity set in Palm Beach, where Fingy heard a speech about the bright future of the Everglades. Convinced, he spent $40,000 on four thousand acres near Lake

Okeechobee and declared he would create the state's largest farm. It also proved to be the state's quickest failure.

Despite this setback, Fingy bought an existing land company and modestly renamed its property on the east side of the lake "Connersville." Next he bought the entire town of Okeechobee. Then, in his most audacious move yet, he proposed building a paved road from Palm Beach to his property in order to give potential buyers better access to this agrarian paradise.

Florida legislators took less than three hours to pass a law that gave him the green light. Fingy then went out and bought some tenpenny nails—excuse me, brains—who figured out how to build a road fifty-two miles through Everglades muck. The Conners Highway—the first road built through the River of Grass—was completed in eight months.

When it was done, Fingy threw a party for fifteen thousand people, many of them the cowboys and Seminoles who would be displaced if his plans to turn Okeechobee into "the Chicago of the South" bore fruit. Although Fingy charged $1.50 at his tollbooth, on opening day some three thousand curious drivers paid to cruise his road. The number fell off considerably after that.

The governor hailed Fingy as "The Great Developer," even though he did nothing but spend money. The *Engineering News-Record* declared the Conners Highway one of the outstanding engineering achievements of 1924. The *Palm Beach Post* declared, "The barriers of America's last frontier . . . fell here today."

Except they didn't. Despite Fingy's great achievement, the only thing Okeechobee and Chicago have in common is that they're both on a lake. Connerton has disappeared from the maps. These days, Fingy's engineering feat is plain old State Road 710, a dusty two-lane blacktop that's so straight it's also known as the Beeline. I've driven it plenty of times, and trust me when I say that wherever she is now, Fingy's wife is probably sneering at her hubby's asphalt monument.

The Florida frontier didn't really begin to fade away until 1949, when the state began requiring cattlemen to fence their land. Too many cows were wandering onto the state's paved highways and colliding with tourists' cars. That the convenience of out-of-state drivers should take precedence over the rights of cattle barons showed Florida was on the brink of a major social and economic change.

Bigger, better cross-state highways appeared. First was the Tamiami Trail, which not only connected Tampa with Miami (hence the name) but also dammed the flow of water into the Everglades, starving the River of Grass until the government spent millions recently to raise about six miles of it and let the water flow again. Building the Tamiami Trail in the 1920s took, as one columnist put it, "a dozen years, eight million dollars, almost three million sticks of dynamite, and one stubborn ox named Blue."

Then came Alligator Alley, originally a two-lane highway across the Everglades. When it opened, drivers trying to pass slow-moving vehicles kept being killed in head-on crashes—so many that the American Automobile Association called for a boycott. There were also problems with buzzards dive-bombing windshields, killing themselves and causing glass-shattering havoc.

Now the road is far safer. It's got four lanes, a divided median, Road Rangers who patrol for stranded motorists, and underground tunnels for panthers to cross safely. These days driving Alligator Alley has become boring, except to those of us keeping an eye on the sky in case those crazy buzzards come back.

The guy who should have received all the accolades Fingy got was Carl Fisher, who built the road that Florida really needed. The Miami Beach developer had helped to promote the construction of the nation's first east–west cross-country road, the Lincoln Highway. He then turned to promoting its first north–south road, Indiana to Miami, later known as the Dixie Highway. Of course, that particular route would lead the Tin Lizzie tourists into the clutches of his real estate salesmen. It didn't hurt that Fisher had an interest in a paving company too.

Fisher had learned the lesson of Flagler and Plant: Build a good transportation system, create a lot of hoopla, and curious tourists will come to Florida to spend their money. The Dixie Highway's success led to the building of Interstate 75, which still brings Midwesterners down the state's west coast, and Interstate 95, which brings New Yorkers to the east coast. That's why so many of the people who live on one side of the Florida peninsula tend to sound, think, and vote differently from the ones on the other.

Fisher's other great achievement was building the Indianapolis Speedway, home of the Indy 500. That race, once the nation's most famous, would be eclipsed by something cooked up by a few mechanics and criminals hanging out at a bar just a short drive from Fisher's Florida home.

Florida has been the setting for some of the major events in sports history. I'm not just talking about the Miami Dolphins' perfect season and the invention of Tebowing.

Babe Ruth hit his longest home run during a spring-training game in Tampa—634 feet. It was airborne for 610 feet, then rolled another 24 feet, bouncing off the old West Coast Inn. Years later, asked what had been his greatest accomplishment, Ruth replied, "The day I hit the [expletive] ball against that [expletive] hotel!"

No Florida sports highlight reel would be complete without a shot of Cassius Clay training at the old 5th Street Gym in Miami Beach. He'd jog backward to and from his hotel in Miami five miles away because jogging backward improved his footwork, and because no Miami Beach hotel would rent a black man a room. On February 25, 1964, in a matchup in Miami, he beat reigning heavyweight champ Sonny Liston, a 7-to-1 favorite, with a sixth-round unanimous decision.

"I must be the greatest!" the twenty-two-year-old Clay shouted after the fight, and then converted to Islam and changed his name to Muhammad Ali. The 5th Street Gym, run by Chris and Angelo Dundee, became the epicenter of the boxing world, at least until Ali hung up his gloves.

But the most important sports-related event that ever occurred in Florida involved a meeting at a bar, where the booze was free and the women plentiful.

The leader was a mechanic from Washington, D.C., named William Henry Getty "Bill" France, the son of a bank employee. In 1930, while driving to Miami, France stopped off in Daytona for a swim and knew he didn't want to go any farther.

"When I saw Daytona Beach," he said years later, "I thought it was the prettiest place I'd ever seen."

In Daytona, France opened his own car-repair shop. He was keenly interested in making cars go fast, and in Daytona he had a lot of company. Daytona Beach had hard-packed sand that stretched for twenty-three miles to Ormond Beach. Between the dunes and the surf, the beach was about five hundred feet wide at low tide—perfect for driving a car at top speed.

Earlier in the century, Henry Flagler, who had built a hotel in Ormond Beach, held beachside auto races between the two towns to entertain his wealthy guests. As the drivers roared around an oval marked out with barrels, hundreds of spectators perched in the high dunes as if sitting in a grandstand.

The drivers of those early cars all had one thing in mind: going faster. In 1910, Barney Oldfield drove his Benz Lightning straight down Daytona Beach at 131.724 mph, faster than anyone had ever traveled before in any vehicle.

"Everything before me would be enshrouded in a haze, and I would suddenly feel as though I were in the middle of a nightmare and about to jump off some mountainous precipice," he told a reporter. His record, he added, "is as near the limit of speed as humanity will ever travel."

He was wrong. People kept posting new records at Daytona. In 1933, a Brit, Sir Malcolm Campbell, became the first man to exceed 250 mph, hitting a top speed of 253.97 mph. By 1935, he had topped that with a new mark of

276.82. Campbell wanted to be the first to reach 300 mph, but he did not believe Daytona's beach was stable enough. He shifted to a place about as far from the ocean as possible: the Bonneville Salt Flats in Utah.

Panicked at the thought of the race drivers and their fans leaving for the Beehive State, Daytona Beach merchants decided to sponsor a race themselves, with a track that was partly on the sand and partly on Highway A1A. They lost money on that 1936 race.

The next year the Elks Club tried it, with the same result. But the Elks couldn't complain about the number of drivers who had signed up—for that, they had to thank Bill France, who was in charge of it. Racing on the beach may have started as a rich man's amusement, thanks to Flagler, but thanks to France it was about to become the biggest blue-collar sport in history.

By then the local racers were gathering regularly at France's garage to gab. France was a big man, the guy who in a group photo always stood in the back row, looming a full head above everyone in front. The racers knew the six-foot-six France was a kindred soul, a man devoted to speed. As a teenager he used to swipe his family's Model T and go race it, then sneak it back home when he was done, leaving his father baffled about why his tires went bald so fast.

France still craved the roar of engines and the thrill of competition. He had entered the 1936 city-sponsored race, finishing fifth. That was far behind the winner, Carl "Smokey" Purser, another local mechanic who had honed his driving skills ferrying illegal liquor between Daytona and the Midwest. Purser used to joke that he was a "sea lawyer" because he handled "cases at sea"—cases of illegal booze brought in by boat, that is. Sometimes, to dodge Johnny Law, he drove his route dressed as a priest. Sometimes he drove it in a truck labeled FRESH FISH with a few real fish tossed into the back to give his load an authentic stench. At a racetrack, Purser wanted to win even if he had to cheat. He once pulled a gun on an inspector trying to check his engine after a race.

Now France's fellow racers asked him if he'd take over promoting the 1938 race. He did it, with financial backing from a local restaurateur. France raced too and finished second. The first-place man was Purser again—but instead of stopping just past the finish line, the way he was supposed to, Purser kept going straight into town. France figured out that Purser was headed for a garage to hide how he had illegally modified his car. But if Purser was disqualified, that would make France the winner under what everyone would see as suspicious circumstances. That could hurt his future as a race promoter.

In the end, Purser was disqualified, and somehow the third-place driver was declared the winner and France remained in second. More important, the event covered its expenses and made a small profit. So France promoted another race, and another, and soon he was promoting races up in the Carolina Piedmont region as well.

Although he was a high school dropout, France knew the race game. He knew how to line up drivers and make an exciting spectacle to attract paying fans. France's business style, as one historian noted, "brilliantly mixed the smile, the handshake, and the clenched fist."

France was not too particular about who he'd partner with to get a race going. His 1940 and 1941 Daytona races were sponsored by the Central Labor Union of Daytona Beach. His copromoter was none other than Smokey Purser.

World War II interrupted the fun—it's hard to race when gas is rationed—but once the Axis surrendered, France went back at it. Often his drivers were competing at tracks built by moonshiners, trying to win purses put up by people in the illegal liquor trade. Racing proved to be a good way to launder all that inconvenient cash.

France noticed that the prizes and rules often varied widely from race to race. He wanted the races to be uniform—and he wanted to be the one making the rules.

On December 12, 1947, France invited a bunch of his racing buddies—drivers, mechanics, and promoters, many affiliated with the numbers racket or moonshining or both—to join him at the Ebony Bar in the Streamline Hotel, an Art Deco–style building on A1A in Daytona. About thirty of them showed up, most expecting nothing but a good time with free booze and curvy models that France had hired from the local charm school.

Over the course of three days, France convinced them to adopt his ideas for an organization that would oversee stock car racing, setting standards, rules, and regulations for all races, guaranteeing purses, and creating a point system to name a national champion. They called it the National Association for Stock Car Automobile Racing, NASCAR for short. It formally incorporated in February 1948.

The first official NASCAR race took place in Daytona just before the incorporation papers went through. The race drew fourteen thousand spectators who paid $2.50 a head to watch Red Byron take the checkered flag. In addition to the stock car race, France staged quite a spectacle—midget cars, time trials, and, most important, a big motorcycle race known as the Daytona 200.

Eventually France retired from racing to become NASCAR's chairman and CEO—in effect, the dictator who ran NASCAR his way, period. He designed the Daytona International Speedway, creating a track far larger than any beach oval. At 2.5 miles around, it was the same size as Fisher's Indianapolis speedway, but its turns were banked 35 degrees, compared to 12 degrees for the venerable Indy. Ever since France kicked off the first race at the track in 1959, it has remained NASCAR's season-opening event.

When the Daytona race was broadcast flag-to-flag nationwide for the first time in 1979, a brawl broke out at the end of the race between Cale Yarborough and brothers Donnie and Bobbie Allison. That helped boost racing's popularity tremendously. Who wouldn't love mixing fast cars with boxing?

France ran NASCAR like his personal business, hiring family for key positions. No other sports organization in America operates the same way. Imagine if the National Football League or Major League Baseball had one single owner who ran the whole show with his kids.

France's dictatorial ways, his capricious judgments, and his tendency to continue paying the same size purses even as the gate receipts ballooned created friction. Some NASCAR drivers began talking of a union. Although he had once worked with a union to sponsor races, France told the drivers he would shut down every track rather than let them unionize—shut 'em down, tear 'em up, and plant corn. He vowed to never employ a single union member anywhere in NASCAR, and then added, "If that isn't tough enough, I'll use a pistol to enforce it. I have a pistol and I know how to use it. I've used it before."

The drivers, normally wild and unruly men, obeyed France's edict. There was no more talk of unions.

But unions weren't done with NASCAR. As France was far too busy now to deal with motorcycle races, the Central Labor Union took over running the Daytona 200 on the beach. To attract more competitors, they began adding additional events, and the "Handlebar Derby Week" was born. Today it's known as Bike Week, a ten-day revel for thousands of revving Harleys, burly men in beards and bandannas, and tattooed women in bikinis, all of it fueled by heavy doses of booze and other intoxicants. By 2014, Bike Week was pumping more millions than the Daytona 500 into the Daytona economy.

The Daytona 200, like the 500, ended up moving off the beach and onto the racetrack because too many buildings and people began crowding onto the beach. But you can still drive your car on Daytona Beach, albeit much more slowly than Barney Oldfield did. This, of course, means that from time to time someone runs over a sunbathing tourist or a sea turtle nest. But the occasional mangled body means nothing compared to maintaining a local tradition—at least that's what the locals say.

As for NASCAR, France eventually retired, and as a king hands his scepter to the prince, France handed the keys to his son, Bill France Jr. The younger

France transformed NASCAR into a multibillion-dollar international entertainment conglomerate with tens of millions of fans, a following so passionate it's akin to religious devotion.

Back in the 1960s, when NASCAR was still a small business trying to get bigger, my uncle Philip, a telephone company employee, tried his hand at stock car racing. I remember going to see him at the Pensacola Speedway, watching the pack of clunkers circling the track over and over. I remember wondering if anyone would crash and send a tire flying up into the stands where I was sitting. What I remember the most is how incredibly loud it was, the noise of all those engines echoing off the concrete. Years later, when I covered my first hurricane, I thought it sounded about as loud as one of those stock car races.

Eventually, Uncle Philip got into a crash, flipping end over end over end. Fortunately, he had done a good job welding his roll bar, and he walked away. It was a wake-up call for him, according to my Aunt Janice, and he gave up racing.

Wrecks are always going to happen in racing. Some fans even look forward to a spectacular crash, the wild explosion, the smell of burning fuel. The question, though, is what about the driver?

In 2001, the *Orlando Sentinel* ran a series about NASCAR crashes that suggested the deaths of three drivers could have been avoided if the organization required a particular type of harness. The stories were based in part on information from the drivers' autopsies, which under Florida law were open to public scrutiny.

Other Florida newspapers had looked at autopsy reports for investigative stories—for instance, reporting on what happened to a Clearwater woman who died while in the custody of the Church of Scientology. I worked with a colleague on a story about a police shooting where the autopsy revealed the dead man could not possibly have been doing what the cop said he was doing when the bullets began flying. Other entities had used this access for less public-spirited purposes, including a Web site operator who posted autopsy photos of famous people.

A week after the series ran, there was another horrendous crash at Daytona. This time the dead driver was NASCAR's biggest star, Dale Earnhardt. The *Sentinel* asked for the autopsy report—and ran into a political buzz saw.

The driver's widow sued to block the release of the report. She did not want anyone to see the autopsy because she considered everything about her husband's very public death to be a private family matter. NASCAR agreed, perhaps for different reasons. Although the *Sentinel*'s editors made it clear they did not intend to publish any autopsy photos but only show them to a head trauma specialist, the judge approved a temporary injunction.

While the court case was going on, a state senator from Jacksonville named Jim King—a rotund gasbag generally liked by reporters because he was quick with a quip—filed a bill to keep those pictures away from the *Sentinel.* Under King's bill, the only way anyone could see an autopsy report would be to go to court and get a judge to agree that releasing it would serve a public purpose. Of course some other party could then object and tie up the proceedings. Either way, it turned a simple process into one that was lengthy and expensive and uncertain.

The bill was immensely popular with everyone except journalists. King said he was getting hundreds of e-mails a day from NASCAR fans praising him for what they saw as protecting ol' Dale's privacy. Meanwhile *Sentinel* editor Tim Franklin said he was getting calls and e-mails that "called me names you wouldn't hear in church"—even though the paper's goal was trying to keep more drivers from dying, something you might think the fans would support.

Often bills take months to work their way through the Florida legislature. Some wrongfully convicted death row prisoners have waited years for legislators to pass a bill that would pay them back for the state ruining their lives. But those bills didn't have the backing of NASCAR and its fans. The legislature approved King's bill with a speed that would have made Barney Oldfield dizzy, and then someone from the clerk's office walked it over to the governor's office and Jeb Bush signed it into law with the Widow Earnhardt looking on and smiling.

That's the kind of thing that routinely happens in Florida politics, in the building they call the "Tower of Power." Its true nature is plainly visible as you drive your car on the road that leads to downtown Tallahassee.

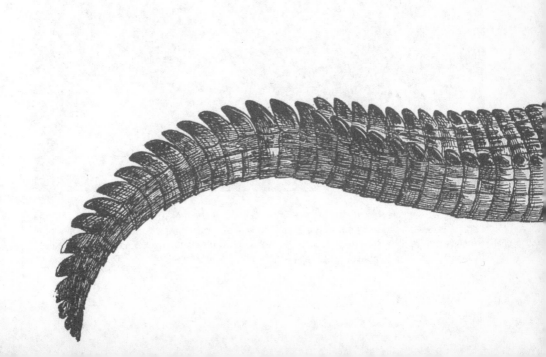

State Sen. Dempsey Barron, D-Panama City—at the time the most powerful man in the Florida Legislature—tries to walk out of the Senate chamber carrying Kim Vande Vusse, a mermaid from Weeki Wachee Springs, who was there to kick off the annual Tourism Day in 1983. Photo by Donn Dughi. Photo courtesy of State Archives of Florida.

7

The Tower of Power

I look forward to the time when these buildings of government
are empty.

—Gov. Jeb Bush, upon being sworn
in for his second term, January 2003

As you drive toward downtown Tallahassee on the Apalachee Parkway,
Florida's state Capitol Building rises boldly from the horizon. First you see
the twenty-two-story executive branch building known as the "Tower of
Power" bluntly thrusting itself toward the sky. Draw closer and you see that
the tower is flanked by the two domes of the legislative branch, one for the
House and one for the Senate.

A few years ago, an online poll selected this as the most phallic public
building in the world.

The architect behind this unintentionally hilarious edifice was neither
Beavis nor Butthead. Instead it was Edward Durell Stone, who designed the
Kennedy Center and the original building of New York's Museum of Modern Art. *Time* put him on its cover in 1958.

Stone may not have planned for Florida's new Capitol, unveiled in 1977,
to be so naughty. On the other hand, Tallahassee politicians rejected his original design, so perhaps this X-rated version was his response, a bird dipped in
concrete for permanent flipping.

"There was never any mention of the shape," a reporter who covered the
cabinet meetings on the building plans told me, "although I have always suspected each member was just waiting for somebody else to speak up." No one
did—and as you may have guessed, there were no women in the cabinet then.

In the Capitol's marble halls, no sign boasts about its phallic victory. However, on the first floor is a bronze plaque that suggests that what the building looks like on the outside accurately reflects the character of the politicians on the inside. It says, "This plaque is dedicated to Senator Lee Weissenborn whose valiant effort to move the Capitol to Orlando was the prime motivation for the construction of this building."

Let me explain. Tallahassee has been Florida's capital city since the 1824, when the few people who lived here mostly lived in Pensacola and St. Augustine. Putting the capital halfway between them in Tallahassee was the only possible compromise. By the 1960s, though, what's now known as the Old Capitol Building, opened in 1845, had become too cramped and archaic. Weissenborn tried persuading his fellow legislators to relocate the capital because Orlando was closer to the state's modern center of population. Of course, it also happened to be his home district, making his constituents the biggest beneficiaries of such a move.

Sentiment, tradition, and cold hard cash kept the state capital where it had always been—far from the voting crowd. After all, what Florida politician really wants to be close to "the people?" Ick.

Hence the decision to build a new, genitalia-shaped capitol, containing this snide little plaque sneering at Weissenborn for trying to accommodate the voters. On the plus side, the plaque guarantees Weissenborn a bit of immortality that eluded the people who posted it.

Tallahassee has been like this from the start. When Ralph Waldo Emerson visited in 1827, he called it "a grotesque place, selected three years since as a suitable spot for the capital of the territory, and since that day rapidly settled by public officers, land speculators and desperados." I think if he came back today, he'd write, "See previous report."

The desperados are still around. A study released in 2012 found that from 2000 to 2010, Florida led all the other states in total convictions of officials and staff who broke federal corruption laws. Our tally of 781 beat what were then the three more populous states: California, Texas, and New York.

"Florida has become the corruption capital of America," Dan Krassner, the executive director of a watchdog group called Integrity Florida, told the *New York Times*. I don't think he was as proud to announce that fact as I was to hear it. My reaction was: We're Number One! Yay, Florida! Our elected representatives are helping maintain full employment in the legal and prison industries!

Every state has sleazy politicians, but Florida's pols really take the cake—

as well as the knife, the plate, and all the candles. "You could hold a film festival of all the undercover sting operations and perp walks involving public officials," *60 Minutes* noted in a 2005 report called "Florida: 'A Paradise of Scandals.'" One example they cited: Miami commissioner Humberto Hernandez, who was indicted for bank fraud and money laundering, yet won reelection and continued to serve until he was convicted of voter fraud too. Then he went to the hoosegow—meanwhile trying in vain to appeal on the grounds that his wife had run off with his attorney.

Some people think Florida's corruption is confined to the southern end of the state. It is true that in a three-week period in August 2013, the FBI arrested the mayors of three towns in Miami-Dade County on charges they took bribes. (Two were sentenced to prison, while one was acquitted but had to fight to get his job back.)

Actually, corruption cases pop up all over. In 2009, the feds busted officials in bucolic Dixie and Levy Counties for taking bribes from an undercover agent using the same name as a porn star. The agent testified he'd been sent there to nail one corrupt local official, but found nearly everybody else was eager to take a payoff too. In my Panhandle hometown in 2002, four of the five Escambia County commissioners were busted, leading to jokes that you can't spell "Escambia" without "scam." That case involved a $90,000 cash bribe hidden in a cooking pot, a star witness who owned a drive-through funeral home, and a couple who used money from a shady land deal to buy their daughter-in-law breast implants.

But Tallahassee is the true center of the slick and the slippery. In the 1970s alone, when the Democrats ruled the roost, we saw the education commissioner convicted of taking kickbacks, conspiracy, perjury, and evading taxes; the state insurance commissioner convicted of extortion and mail fraud; the state comptroller defeated for reelection after pleading the Fifth during a federal grand jury investigation; the lieutenant governor censured for using state employees at his home and farm; and two state supreme court justices who resigned rather than face impeachment on ethics charges. And that was just the executive and judicial branches.

Over in the legislative branch, our lawmakers often end up being lawbreakers. We have had legislators busted for everything from Medicare fraud to paying a prostitute for oral sex to buying Jacksonville Jaguars season tickets with federal funds intended for poor kids' day care.

One thing you seldom see is any sense of shame. One state representative was convicted of not reporting to the IRS the secret payments he was getting from a paving contractor. My paper reported he then "traveled his district while wearing an electronic monitor on his ankle, meeting with voters, and even attending a banquet to accept an award of appreciation from the Police Benevolent Association."

Irony hangs heavy over many of these cases. The state representative caught with the prostitute? He belonged to a prayer group known as the God Squad, earned a perfect rating from the Christian Coalition of Florida, and signed a letter criticizing Disney World for providing insurance to partners of gay and lesbian employees. The letter said Disney was promoting an "unnatural" lifestyle. When the cops approached this lawmaker's pickup, they could see the hooker bent over his lap, so in addition to being arrested for soliciting, the father of six was charged with committing "unnatural acts." He ended up resigning his seat, pleading guilty, and being sentenced to probation—an all too natural act for many Florida pols.

Sometimes the illegality is widespread. During the 2015 legislative session, the House adjourned three days early without a budget, which the supreme court said violated the constitution. The Senate admitted that the maps it created for redistricting were illegal too. Then Gov. Rick Scott admitted illegally hiding public records—and used $700,000 in public funds to pay a settlement to the attorney who'd caught him doing it. The only ones penalized for all this were the taxpayers.

I like to imagine this is Weissenborn's Revenge. Tallahassee is so distant from most of the population that legislators, cabinet officials, and the like feel immune to public scrutiny, which leads them into trouble.

Politicians who are isolated from their constituents instead listen to the people they see the most: lobbyists. The lobbyists are so friendly! And always ready to steer money to a campaign! They're basically ATMs in alligator shoes! Corporations now spend more money on lobbying Florida legislators than on electing them. They can even arrange for such perks as secret hunting trips to a Texas ranch stocked with game. Legislators happily accepted that gift, no questions asked.

It's not just the money that puts the lobbyists in charge. Florida's legislators lack the experience that the lobbyists have. Florida voters set term limits when they passed the "Eight Is Enough" constitutional amendment in 1992, in hopes of ridding the state of entrenched politicians. Since that amendment took effect in 2000, one veteran legislator complained recently, "term limits have produced a large number of leaders who really don't have the experience to sit down and make the deals, who don't have the experience to know that 50 percent of what you want is better than zero percent of what you want." Because of that lack of experience, lobbyists have become essential to the legislative process. They are more knowledgeable about what the laws say than the people in charge of writing them—so guess who writes them instead?

On one golden occasion, a state representative with the marvelous name of Baxter Troutman was at a committee hearing to explain a bill he'd sponsored that environmentalists opposed. Whenever a colleague asked a question, Troutman had no answer. He repeatedly deferred to the lobbyist for the Association of Florida Community Developers. That's who had written the bill.

That same year, sugar lobbyists wrote a bill to delay the cleanup of pollution in the Everglades, and a lobbyist for BellSouth wrote a bill that raised telephone rates for residential customers. Both passed and were signed into law by Gov. Bush. Those were the only major pieces of legislation that passed that year.

To avoid Baxter Troutman Syndrome, smart lobbyists make sure their pet legislators get a list of talking points and stick to the script. When it's time to argue for their bill, they "all stand up with their little . . . piece of paper, and they don't even know what's in their own bills half the time," one veteran lobbyist said.

That lack of expertise (not to mention any sense of accountability) explains why the legislature is constantly coming up with ideas that leave everyone rolling his or her eyes, such as:

- Letting utilities charge customers in advance to pay for building multibillion-dollar nuclear plants, which are then canceled because they cost too much—but nobody gets a refund.
- Outlawing "Internet cafés" where elderly retirees gamble their pension checks away—and making the language so broad as to accidentally outlaw the entire Internet.
- Banning gay marriage but somehow neglecting to ban bestiality. When they did ban bestiality, after a couple of tries, they sort of accidentally outlawed all sex.

In general our politicians do tend to be more entertaining than the duly elected dullards elsewhere. One recent candidate for mayor of North Miami contended she had been the target of voodoo intimidation. (She lost.) A St. Petersburg council candidate climbed on his roof in a tunic and twirled two poles to ward off the Mayan apocalypse (averted apocalypse, lost race). A gubernatorial candidate reported raising $182,000, enough to qualify for matching funds from the state—but most of the names on her donor list didn't exist (arrested, lost race).

My favorite Florida politician is Rep. Richard Kelly, one of seven members of Congress snared in Abscam, an elaborate 1979 sting involving undercover FBI agents and phony Arab sheiks. This is the case that inspired the recent movie *American Hustle*. As usual when dealing with Florida, the truth is far stranger than fiction.

Kelly, a Republican, had been a prosecutor and a Pasco County judge, clashing with his colleagues so frequently that some called him a nut. Kelly had himself examined by doctors, who declared him sane. When he was elected to Congress in 1974, he boasted that he was the only member officially certified as not cuckoo.

Not long after being reelected to his third term, Kelly dumped his third wife and married his secretary. He was riding high until the FBI caught him on videotape stuffing $25,000 and some Honduran cigars into his pockets. Kelly's defense: He took the money because he was running his *own* investigation, and this was evidence. Prosecutors, jurors, and the voting public's reaction: Suuuuuuuuuuure you were. He served thirteen months in federal prison—then divorced the secretary and married wife number five.

Kelly is among the Florida politicians who have, over the years, boosted our state's reputation for odd behavior. I've previously mentioned Sen. Yulee, who claimed to be descended from Moroccan royalty. Gov. John Milton was so ardent a supporter of the Confederacy that when it was clear the South had lost the Civil War, he committed suicide—on April Fool's Day. He claimed the Yankees were "so odious that death would be preferable to union with them." Even odder was U.S. Sen. Charles W. Jones, who in 1885 abandoned his congressional post to stalk a woman in Detroit and deliver speeches to his mirror.

Some went even farther off the deep end. In 1890, the mayor of Cedar Key, William Cottrell, set himself up as an island-nation dictator. He hired a thug to serve as marshal, and they walked around toting shotguns, doing whatever they wanted to whomever they wanted, including ordering random passersby to head-butt each other. Cedar Key was, according to the *New York Times*, "Under a Reign of Terror."

Then Cottrell and his minions attacked the federal customs agent and ran him off. President Benjamin Harrison responded by dispatching a Navy cruiser to invade Cedar Key and capture Cottrell.

Harrison told Congress that invading Cedar Key was "lawful and necessary." He said he'd received a letter appealing for help in deposing the mayor—but not from one of the town's council members or business leaders. They were too cowed by Cottrell.

"It is a very grim commentary upon the condition of social order at Cedar Key that only a woman who had, as she says in her letter, no son or husband who could be made the victim of his malice, had the courage to file charges against this man," Harrison said. (Sadly, he did not mention her name.)

When the sailors invaded, Cottrell fled. He was caught in Alabama, where he made bond, then got into a drunken dispute with a chief of police and was shot dead.

The last time I visited Cedar Key, I searched its history museum in vain for any mention of the only American mayor ever deposed by a military coup. Were I the king of Cedar Key, the town would throw an annual Cottrell Days Reign of Terror Festival with a parade and a street fair, and the celebration would culminate in a reenactment of the invasion. Someone playing the deposed mayor would run screaming through town, pelted with popcorn by the delighted tourists (at $4 a bag, of course). It could be bigger than Gasparilla!

Perhaps Cottrell should have stuck around. A history of violence turns out to be no deterrent to winning public office here. Gov. Milton, for instance, had shot someone else before he shot himself. In 1934, Florida elected as governor Fred P. Cone, a Democrat, who as a young man had shot the White Springs postmaster for the crime of being Republican. The postmaster survived, and Cone's uncle persuaded him not to press charges. Then Democratic officials prosecuted the postmaster for covering up a felony—namely, his own shooting.

The king of crazy Florida politicians is Sidney J. Catts, a backwoods Alabama preacher who moved to the Panhandle looking for fresh opportunities. In 1915, Florida Baptists held their annual convention in Tallahassee. Church members there—including Gov. Park Trammell—agreed to put the delegates up in their homes. The Rev. Catts landed at the governor's mansion, and he found the place intriguing. He inspected it from attic to ground floor and asked lots of questions. On the convention's last night, Catts asked Trammell the question that had been on his mind from the start: "How much do you pay in rent?"

Trammell proudly informed his visitor that the taxpayers provided him with this elegant residence rent-free. Catts was so impressed that a few weeks later he announced he was running for governor.

Catts had never run for office, yet he displayed a flair for the dramatic that veteran politicians would envy. He would show up at campaign appearances with a pair of six-shooters, bragging that he'd been targeted by assassins from the Catholic Church. Then he'd bellow to the cheering crowds, "The Florida crackers have only three friends: God Almighty, Sears, Roebuck, and Sidney J. Catts!"

He won, but he got in trouble for appointing his cronies and family members to state jobs. Later he was indicted on charges of taking payoffs in exchange for pardoning inmates but was acquitted. Just before he died, he also beat a charge of aiding a counterfeiting ring amid testimony that he routinely concealed $5,000 in his shoes.

In the years since then, we have had other quirky governors. Claude Kirk brought a woman known only as "Madame X" to his inaugural ball. "Walkin'" Lawton Chiles showed up for his second inauguration wearing a coonskin cap and toting a potato gun with which he merrily fired spuds into the next block. But no one's ever matched crazy Rev. Catts—although columnists keep suggesting that the jury is still out on the mansion's current occupant.

Fred Cone would be shocked to discover that being a Florida Republican is no longer a crime punishable by shooting. The shift from a single-party state to one where each party has a chance to act foolish began during the Reagan Revolution of 1980 when we elected Paula Hawkins, "the Battling Housewife from Maitland," as a U.S. senator. She was the first woman in U.S. history ever elected to a full term in the Senate who wasn't succeeding a dead husband.

She proved to be just as entertaining as any Democrat. During the height of Florida's cocaine wars, she proposed a solution she was sure would end demand for the Peruvian marching powder: abolish the $100 bills some people used to snort the drug. She once invited reporters to a luncheon of steak, asparagus, and strawberries so she could discuss cracking down on food-stamp cheaters.

Dave Barry described her as having "huge perky eyes and a huge perky smile. She has perky hair. She wears lots of perky makeup and some big perky diamonds, which bring her weight up to maybe eighteen pounds." She wore so much makeup, Barry wrote, she looked "like a person attempting to sneak valuable possessions through customs by hiding them under her mascara."

Hawkins lost her bid for reelection to Gov. Bob Graham, who keeps detailed notes on every mundane thing he does all day and, as Barry pointed out, "speaks with all the spontaneity of highway construction." Graham, now retired, and U.S. Sen. Bill Nelson—who has hunted pythons with a machete and once flew on the space shuttle—remain the last Democrats with any statewide popularity. Both are in their seventies.

Republicans now control the governor's mansion and both houses of the legislature. What's odd about that is that a majority of Florida voters are Democrats. Some states are red. Some are blue. Florida is as purple as a stone bruise.

How can Florida be so politically contradictory? Many Florida voters are new to the state. They have no knowledge of what happened prior to their arrival. They don't know the issues or the candidates. Thus they tend to base their votes on who has the slickest TV ads, or who's favored by their coworkers who have been around for a couple of years and thus seem like experts.

Right now, thousands of Puerto Ricans are flooding into Central Florida, fleeing lousy conditions back home. Everyone's wondering what effect these new Florida voters—many of them registering as independents—might have on the presidential election. I'm curious about what changes they might also cause in local and state government.

Despite their newcomer status, Florida voters can be some of the most persistent supporters of democracy in the world. Some stood in line for seven hours to vote in the 2012 presidential election. Seven hours! People won't stand in line that long to ride Space Mountain!

People who are so passionate about the power of the ballot box are clearly not to be trusted with something as important as deciding elections. No wonder our pragmatic legislature wants nothing to do with those folks. Thus our lawmakers have so gerrymandered their districts that voting on their races tends to qualify more as a hobby than a right.

We voters get our revenge, though. When aspiring pols want to run for a statewide office, we subject them to what can only be called, under the Geneva Conventions, torture. We make them eat rubber chicken and grovel to rich people so they can raise ridiculous sums of money they spend on advertising in ten—count 'em, *ten*—different media markets. We require them to traipse all over the state making ridiculous promises that everyone expects to hear and nobody believes.

We even make them participate in such events as the Wausau Possum Festival. Begun in 1970, the festival honors the humble marsupial that got the Panhandle hamlet through the Depression by providing an acceptable alternative to edible food. The event occurs in August, our hottest month, when anyone with a lick of sense would be indoors with the AC cranked and a cool drink close by. Festival attendees must survive a parade past the Wausau Possum Monument, a beauty pageant, and an auction. During the auction, politicians from around the state bid on live possums, which they then hold high for the crowd to observe and approve. The possums are then released into the wild. The politicians remain captive.

My favorite photo of Jeb Bush was taken at the Possum Festival in 2002. The photo shows Bush perspiring heavily as he grasps his possum's tail. He and the possum have similarly grim expressions, as if to say, "Let's get this over with."

Florida voters aren't just torturers. They also are fickle and forgetful and unpredictable. They can hand all the state's electoral college votes in 2008 to a left-leaning Democratic senator like Barack Obama, then in 2010 choose as their governor a Tea Party–touting GOP candidate like Rick Scott. And then do it again.

For me, Scott has been a bonanza of bizarre, in large part because before he was elected to the state's top job, Scott had zero experience in politics, just like Sidney Catts.

He's a wealthy man, the founder of a hospital chain that eventually pleaded guilty to fourteen corporate felonies and paid more than $1 billion in fines, the largest penalty for Medicaid and Medicare fraud in history. Scott, who contended he didn't know what his underlings were up to, had resigned his post by the time the indictments came out. He was never charged. But during a civil court deposition he pled the Fifth Amendment seventy-five times, a fact brought up repeatedly by opponents in both his campaigns.

He ran a race that could be politely called "unorthodox." He skipped debates, or sent surrogates (including his mother) to speak in his place. He refused to sit for any newspaper editorial board interviews, even with conservative papers likely to endorse him. He was hilariously awkward on the stump. While speaking, he often flailed his arms like a marionette whose puppeteer got soused before the show instead of after. He overcame these handicaps by spending $73 million of his own money on TV ads that repeated the word "jobs" approximately 4,263 times. He won by a 1 percent vote margin.

The Democrat he beat, Alex Sink, was the great-granddaughter of Chang, one of the original "Siamese twins," Chang and Eng. She was married to a Tampa lawyer who lost a bid for governor to Jeb Bush in 2002. She was also former president of the most hated bank in Florida. To top it off, she got caught cheating during a TV debate with Scott, getting an answer texted to her by an aide. Nobody wondered if Sink had taken a dive, but only because this is the kind of exploding-cigar candidate Florida Democrats usually come up with.

As governor, Scott has upheld the finest standards of Florida quirkiness. When he announced a meningitis hotline, it turned out to be a number for sexy talk. He boasted during the campaign about adopting a "rescue dog" which, after he won, disappeared. It turned out to have come from a fancy salon, not a pound, and had been sent back because its barking scared people. At a luncheon at which Scott intended to charm black lawmakers into supporting his initiatives, he offended them by suggesting they had all grown up in the ghetto.

Scott proved to be just as adept at foreign relations. On a trip to Spain, he met King Juan Carlos, who had recently had to apologize to his nation for going on an expensive elephant-hunting trip to Botswana while his country suffered high unemployment. As the king greeted him, Scott blurted out, "I've ridden elephants. I've never tried to shoot one."

Scott's gaffe made him, and Florida, an object of ridicule all across Spain. When he arrived back home, all he could say was, "If I did anything . . . wrong, I apologize."

It turned out that the trip to Spain had been sponsored by a big sugar company, which used the opportunity to lobby Scott. He later approved a no-bid lease for the company to farm state-owned Everglades land for twenty years. Scott has made no apologies for that, even though he likes to boast of being an Everglades champion.

He became the least popular governor in America, yet in 2014 Scott beat former Gov. Charlie Crist to win reelection. Crist is a clever campaigner—after all, the Tan Man had been elected attorney general despite flunking the bar exam twice, and before that was elected education commissioner despite no experience in that field at all. But he carried more baggage than all the carousels at the Miami airport. He had been a Republican governor who ran for the U.S. Senate as an independent, then registered as a Democrat to run against Scott.

Scott made his opposition to Obamacare a centerpiece of his reelection campaign. He even stopped at a senior center to chat with the retirees there about all the awful things Obamacare was doing to their Medicare. He told them he wanted to hear their horror stories. The only problem was he'd picked a senior center in Boca Raton, a Democratic stronghold. The seniors told him they liked Obamacare just fine. After the *Sun-Sentinel* wrote about this, *Gawker* declared him to be "the dumbest politician in the history of all politicians."

Even people in his own party agreed.

"Rick Scott doesn't seem to have any political skills at all," said Tom Slade, former cochairman of Scott's campaign and ex-chairman of the Florida GOP. "I'd give him a B for governing. I'd give him an A for strangeness."

To beat Crist, Scott had to spend the equivalent of $1,200 a minute every day, every hour on TV ads. Toward the end, still trailing, he tossed another $13 million of his own money into the race. He had to spend that much to counteract not only his own lack of charisma but also the hilarity that swept the country when he refused for seven minutes to take the stage for a televised debate with Crist.

As nearly any reporter in the state could tell you, Crist carries a small electric fan everywhere he goes so he can avoid looking sweaty. His staff had quietly installed a fan under his lectern prior to the debate, but after Crist strolled out and took up his position, looking cool and comfortable, Scott refused to join him. Scott's people contended the fan was a forbidden device and until it was removed, no debate would occur. Eventually they worked something out, Scott emerged, and the debate proceeded, although afterward "Fan-gate" was all anyone wanted to talk about.

Since his razor-thin reelection, Scott has continued to govern exactly the way he did in his first term. When the legislature failed to pass a budget in 2015 and the state teetered on the brink of a shutdown, Scott was nowhere near the crisis. He was cutting the ribbon for a new convenience store in Naples.

So far, it appears Scott's political ambitions are limited only by how much money he has left in the bank. Running for president, he said in 2015, would be "more interesting" than running for U.S. Senate.

No Floridian has ever won the presidency, although some have tried, most recently Bob Graham. As of 2015, though, four full-time Floridians and one part-timer were running, most prominently the Florida GOP's Batman and Robin, Bush and Rubio.

Bush has more of a record to talk about, both for good and ill. The grandson of a senator, son of a former president, the brother of another, he's one of those rare politicians who prefer governing to campaigning.

He stepped into the governor's office in 1998 with a set of aims he called Big Hairy Audacious Goals, or BHAGS, and spent eight years pushing them with a single-minded intensity. Mostly they involved privatizing as much of state government as he could, thus allowing him to cut taxes, boot state employees, and create a class of companies that showed their gratitude for their new contracts by donating to the GOP.

Early in his 2016 presidential bid, a lot of GOP megadonors gave money to his political action committee, convinced he would be the 2016 nominee. But like all other Florida politicians, once he was on the national stage, he came across as too strange, too goofy, too gaffe-prone. He stumbled, he slipped, and suddenly he was losing to professional bloviator (and part-time Palm Beach resident) Donald Trump.

Jeb is supposed to be the smarter brother, yet despite his high IQ, he somehow has a hard time remembering to watch his tongue when he's near a microphone. In 2000, to protest Bush's plan to repeal affirmative action in state contracting and higher education, two African American legislators staged a sit-in at the governor's office. Ticked off at this intrusion, Bush told his staff, "Throw their asses out"—apparently unaware a reporter could hear him. His staff tried to spin the story so it was the media's buttocks that Bush wanted booted, but not one black person in Florida believed that story.

Later, during a cabinet meeting where the topic was endangered species habitat, Bush quipped that the people of San Francisco may be endangered and, "that's probably good news for the country." When the room erupted in laughter, Bush added, "Did I just say that out loud?" Yes, and into a live microphone.

His problems extended beyond his loose lips to his appointees. Always a forward-looking tech guy—he was the first Florida governor to respond to citizens via e-mail—Bush named one of his longtime political supporters as Florida's first-ever chief technology officer. The fact that the man had a bankruptcy in his past and a 1985 grand theft charge (later dropped) didn't count as much as his loyalty, at least until he was accused of falsifying a letter to get a Tallahassee bank to lend his computer business $35,000. (A judge later tossed the charge because prosecutors had only a copy of the document, not the original.)

Bush picked another longtime supporter—a former *Playboy* bunny–turned-lawyer named Cynthia Henderson—to head up the Department of Business and Professional Services. When she became the target of ethics complaints, instead of prodding her to resign, Bush moved her over to the agency overseeing the state's management services. Rumors spread that Bush was protecting her because they were having an affair. He denied it, saying, "I love my wife. There is nothing to this rumor. It is an outright lie."

But his wife, Columba, caused him some heartburn too. She went on a five-day shopping spree in Paris, then tried to mislead customs officials about $19,000 in new clothing and jewelry she had brought back. She was briefly detained at the Atlanta airport and had to pay a $4,100 fine. Bush said she lied to customs officers because she didn't want him to know how much she had spent—although why she couldn't tell customs the truth and just lie to her husband was a question no one asked.

Bush has been out of office since 2007, but he hasn't stopped fumbling lines. He's claimed that "immigrants are more fertile," told the middle class to work harder, contended that the "anchor babies" applied more to Asian immigrants than Hispanics, suggested the government spends too much on women's health—the list goes on, each accompanied by a Bush attempt at explaining what he meant wasn't what everyone heard.

Bush even bobbled the one question he should have anticipated. A Fox News anchor asked if he would invade Iraq the way his brother did, but knowing what we all know now, namely, that anyone claiming to have seen weapons of mass destruction in that country was selling swampland. Bush said yes he would, then backtracked, then tried again, and never quite recovered. Still, say this for him: He never stopped trying to answer the question. He never said, "No comment."

Meanwhile, his protégé was hard on his heels, and soon surpassed him.

When state Rep. Marco Rubio first got to Tallahassee, he looked so youthful that Bush's lieutenant governor ordered him to go make copies. She thought he was someone's just-out-of-college aide.

Two years later, after Rubio had locked up enough votes to guarantee he would become Speaker, Bush anointed him his ideological heir by presenting him with a golden sword. (As a Floridian, Rubio no doubt already had his own machete.) He said the sword had belonged to someone named Chang.

"Chang is a mystical warrior," Bush explained. "Chang is somebody who believes in conservative principles, believes in entrepreneurial capitalism, believes in moral values that underpin a free society." Bush did not explain how the sword helped achieve those goals, instead adding, "I rely on Chang with great regularity in my public life. He has been by my side and sometimes I let him down. But Chang, this mystical warrior, has never let me down."

This is not normally the way we swear in House Speakers, but Bush wanted to do something dramatic. After all, Bush had been backing Rubio ever since his protégé had been a twenty six-year-old lawyer running for a West Miami council seat. Now they were both in positions of great authority in state government. Imagine all they could do!

Rubio certainly had a dramatic tenure in the legislature. While speaker he:

- Tried to get rid of property taxes and replace them with a higher sales tax.
- Spent hundreds of thousands of tax dollars on renovations to the House, including a members-only dining room.
- Gave staff members six-figure salaries, which meant some of them earned more than their counterparts working in the governor's office.
- Charged thousands of dollars in grocery bills, repairs to his family minivan, and wine purchases to a GOP credit card that was supposed to be used only for political purposes. Rubio said he'd paid back all personal expenses, but the fact that he had used what was in effect a business credit card to cover his own piddly day-to-day expenses raised questions about his judgment.

- Made a $200,000 profit selling a house to the mother of a chiropractor who was lobbying for a state insurance law change. Rubio had opposed the change, but after the house sold, he changed his position.
- Owned a Tallahassee home with another Miami-area pol, Rep. David Rivera, who investigators say essentially lived off campaign donations for a decade without listing it as income. Rivera has been under investigation for months over other campaign shenanigans.

Rubio comes from a far humbler background than Bush. While Bush's grandfather was a senator, Rubio's grandfather cobbled shoes in Havana. Rubio's family fled Cuba before Castro seized power. Rubio's dad, rather than serving as president, tended bar at one of Miami Beach's Art Deco hotels. Unlike his mentor, Rubio's adult life has meant a frequent, frantic scramble for money.

Thus, when Rubio left the House, he needed a job. He approached Florida International University about teaching classes on government. The catch: He had to raise the money to pay for his own salary and expenses. A billionaire auto dealer named Norman Branam put up $100,000 to create the position for Rubio. Branam also hired Rubio's wife, a former Miami Dolphins cheerleader, to work at his foundation.

Rubio has cultivated a lot of wealthy friends. The most influential is sugar baron Jose "Pepe" Fanjul, who has repeatedly donated to Rubio campaigns. When Rubio declared his intention to run for president, he stepped off the dais and into a big hug from Fanjul. Is it any wonder he supports government subsidies for the sugar industry?

Both Branam and Fanjul were crucial to Rubio's long-shot run for the U.S. Senate, when he beat ex-Gov. Charlie Crist so badly Crist was driven out of the GOP. Since then, though, Rubio's most notable achievement occurred when he delivered the Republican response to President Obama's 2013 State of the Union address, suddenly developing a dry mouth that could be cured only by fumbling for a bottle of water on live TV. He tried to turn it around by selling souvenir water bottles with his logo on them. But that hardly substitutes for filing bills, sitting in committee meetings, or just showing up for work, something No-Show Rubio has had problems with once he began running for president.

Of course, achieving national attention for something you do in Florida is no guarantee of a bright political future. Just ask the state official I like to think of as the quintessential Florida Woman.

In November 2000, Bush was still in his first term as governor, and his brother, Texas Gov. George W. Bush, was doing his best to beat Vice President Al Gore for the right to succeed Bill Clinton as president. But Florida's ballot counting was so bollixed up, nobody could tell who had won.

For thirty-six days between Election Day and the end of the counting, Tallahassee became, as one columnist put it, "the hub of the universe, the adrenaline capital of the world, the omphalos of the Biggest Political Story Ever." The Showdown in the Sunshine State proved a great economic boon to the capital, particularly its "dry cleaners . . . the restaurateurs, the newsstand operators, the hoteliers, the purveyors of overcoats and umbrellas . . . the deliverers of shrimp po'Boys and onion bagels, and, most important, the barkeeps."

The 2000 recount also marks the beginning of the modern attitude toward Florida, swinging from "what a nice place to visit" to "what a bunch of *weirdos*!" Everyone outside Florida stared unbelieving at the spectacle playing out on their TVs. As a former Florida resident named David Barstow wrote in the *New York Times,* "The nation seems uneasy about entrusting this election's grand finale to Florida . . . a sleepy, seasonless place where reality routinely exceeds the imagination of its sharpest satirists."

I will spare you a recap of every twist and turn that occurred during the five weeks when Florida's election results were in dispute in what seemed like every court in every county. The whole wacky spectacle ended at last with Bush defeating Gore by 537 votes (or a 5–4 U.S. Supreme Court ruling, depending on your point of view).

I just want to point out that the person who did the most for shaping the modern attitude toward Florida was the inadvertent star of this sixty-seven-ring circus, a citrus heiress and java junkie named Katherine Harris. How she got to that point tells you a lot about how Florida politics works—or doesn't.

Harris grew up in the bucolic town of Bartow, the daughter of a wealthy banker and the granddaughter of Florida's most famous citrus baron, Ben Hill Griffin Jr., whose name adorns the stadium at the University of Florida. At sixteen, she was named Miss Polk Agriculture. Schooled in Spain and Switzerland, she earned a master's in public administration from Harvard and settled into the upscale gulf-front enclave of Longboat Key near Sarasota.

Harris arrived in Tallahassee in 1994 as a state senator representing the Sarasota area. Some in the GOP were touting her as a sure bet to be the first woman ever elected governor of Florida. She was attractive, vivacious, and very, very rich.

One of her major campaign benefactors was an insurance company named

Riscorp, which donated to lots of other politicians too. After Harris's election, Riscorp got her to sponsor a bill to block its competitors from getting a greater share of the workers' compensation market.

In 1998, gubernatorial candidate Bush picked the incumbent secretary of state, Sandra Mortham, as his running mate. GOP leaders recruited Harris to run for Mortham's old job, which would put her in charge of Florida's elections, its museums, its historical archives. But that's not what she wanted. What she really wanted was to oversee international trade. However, that's the job of the secretary of commerce, a post that wasn't open.

Because she'd been tapped as Bush's running mate, Mortham attracted attention as never before, producing lots of stories about several of her prior political missteps. To avoid hurting Bush, Mortham dropped out of the race for lieutenant governor and said that instead she'd run for reelection. But Harris refused to drop out of the secretary of state race, so now Mortham and Harris went head-to-head in the GOP primary.

Then federal prosecutors revealed that Riscorp had been handing out gobs of illegal campaign contributions to Florida politicians. Five company executives pleaded guilty and the company's founder was sent to prison. Prosecutors did not charge any of the politicians. They said they had no proof the elected officials who took the money knew what was going on—not even then-Insurance Commissioner, Bill Nelson, a Democrat and future U.S. senator.

The biggest recipient of Riscorp's cash? Harris, who got more than $20,000. The Riscorp files contained a memo that said, "Katherine's office called and asked if we could give them different addresses to list for each of the checks. All of the checks show the P.O. Box 1598 address and if they submit these the newspaper will probably make the connection and track them all back to Riscorp." Riscorp even paid for an ex-employee to work on Harris's state Senate campaign.

Harris told a *St. Petersburg Times* reporter that she hadn't known about any of this before investigators questioned her.

Mortham had also gotten some Riscorp cash—about $5,000. So Harris ran TV ads blasting her opponent for taking "illegal contributions from insurance executives," the very thing Harris had done. She beat Mortham.

Instead of boning up on election law prior to the 2000 race, the new secretary of state became quite the globetrotter, spending millions of the taxpayers' dollars visiting Australia, Brazil, Venezuela, and other countries for "international relations." Harris saw nothing wrong with becoming honorary Florida cochair of the Bush campaign, even helping him campaign in New Hampshire. After all, Florida attorney general Bob Butterworth—a Democrat who would end up issuing opinions on election law—served as honorary cochair of the Gore campaign. The theory is that in Florida everyone's conflicted, so no one is.

Then the election turned out to be too close to call and suddenly everyone in America was looking to Harris for answers. Her televised news conferences were not reassuring. The late-night comics mocked her as Cruella de Vil come to life.

She didn't help her reputation when she showed up at the annual football game between longtime rivals Florida State and the University of Florida, which took place in Tallahassee right in the middle of the counting controversy. Jeb Bush and two of the Democratic-appointed Florida supreme court justices sat together in the FSU president's box. When Harris arrived, she began gabbing with reporters, apparently without listening to herself. She told Dan Abrams of NBC: "You know, there are times when my lawyer will discuss some legal issue with me and I won't really understand what he's talking about until I hear you explain it on television."

A little after 7:00 P.M. on November 26, 2000, Harris effectively killed the Gore candidacy. The Florida Supreme Court had set a 5:00 P.M. deadline for recount results. Palm Beach County, home of the confusing butterfly ballot, had missed the deadline, but county officials kept counting, hoping an effort at a manual recount of all ballots would still be considered valid, in keeping with the law's intent.

But Harris certified the results without Palm Beach.

"It was as if the air had been sucked out of the Emergency Operations Center, where the recount unfolded over the better part of two weeks," the *St. Petersburg Times* reported. Her decision to not count the Palm Beach ballots "was a turning point for Gore, giving Bush's lead an air of credibility that the vice president never managed to overcome."

Harris's post-2000 career was one long downward spiral. Gov. Bush and GOP legislative leaders quietly slashed her international travel budget. She decided to run for Congress but first held an awkward press conference at which she confessed she had to resign as secretary of state because she misunderstood what was required under the election laws she was supposed to administer. Her mostly Republican district elected her to Congress anyway—but while there she ran into a scandal nearly identical to the one involving Riscorp but again avoided any charges.

When she ran for Bill Nelson's U.S. Senate seat, she behaved so erratically that headline writers used words like "unhinged."

She said things on the stump that were either lies or hallucinations. She professed herself to be a staunch Christian, comparing herself to the Old Testament hero Queen Esther, but behind the scenes she berated her staff in ways that were hardly Christ-like. They abandoned her in droves and told reporters how crazy she seemed. They said she required them to plot the location of the nearest Starbucks to every campaign stop, because that's about all she was living on. As her campaign staggered to its conclusion, she promised to put $10 million of her own money into the race, but didn't. In the end, to no one's surprise but hers, she lost. She has never tried for office again.

Her name resonates even today, a living symbol of Florida's cuckoo elections. In the 2008 HBO movie *Recount,* she was portrayed by Laura Dern as someone who's too self-centered and clueless to understand the stakes of the game, much less its rules.

I only wish J. Emory "Red" Cross got as much attention.

"Red" Cross had his quirks too. He made up his own nickname so the voters would remember him when they saw it on a ballot. As a member of the state Senate in the 1960s, he had a habit of strolling the halls of the Capitol in a white suit.

In his time in office, first as a prosecutor, then in the House, and later in the Senate, he saw things he didn't like.

"The people were getting ripped off by secret meetings not knowing what public officials were doing behind closed doors," he said.

What the politicians were doing was enriching themselves and their cronies at the public's expense—and some of those doing it were Cross's own pals. It made him sick.

"I had a very good friend who was on the road board helping his buddies," Cross said. Cross's friend would tip them off about where Interstate 75 was going to be built so they could buy land needed for the highway and sell it to the state for a profit. "It just wasn't right."

In the mid-1950s, Cross, who represented the Gainesville area, got to talking with a University of Florida journalism professor named Buddy Davis, who as a reporter for the *Florida Times-Union* in Jacksonville had covered the legislature. They agreed that the state needed a law that would shine a light into the darkest corners of government.

"I always believed the people had a right to know about this," he said.

Cross drew up a bill to require open meetings and open records. Any public official who tried to sneak around the public would face a fine of not more than $500, or jail for up to six months, or both. He introduced his bill and . . . nothing happened. A year later, he tried again. Same result. A decade passed. Every year he introduced the bill and every year he couldn't get it out of committee.

Back then a group of Democrats from the rural Panhandle, called the Pork Chop Gang, controlled the legislature. Their districts included more pines than people, and they cared about only one constituent: Ed Ball, the rich, profane, and combative owner of the state's biggest bank, biggest railroad, and biggest paper mill, not to mention politicians and judges.

But the U.S. Supreme Court's one-man, one-vote decision in 1964 broke the Pork Chop Gang's stranglehold on state government, giving urban progressives more power in the legislature. Cross was at last able to get his bill passed and signed by Gov. Kirk. They called it "the Sunshine Law."

Florida's Sunshine Law became a model that other states copied. Every reporter and every voter should send up a hallelujah for Red Cross, the man who opened the doors of government and let the light in.

Although Florida legislators have repeatedly slipped in exemptions and exclusions, the law remains mostly intact. It does more than just force Florida government to hold itself open to scrutiny. It's the reason why every police report on a guy high on flakka having sex with a tree is available to the public. It's the reason why reporters get to sit in on the public meetings where someone freaks out and does a Nazi salute. So if you enjoy reading all those weird Florida stories, you too owe a debt of gratitude to Red Cross.

But there's no plaque in the Tower of Power for Red Cross.

That's not surprising, really. In Florida, we seldom recall the heroes of the past, just as we spend little time considering the future. Instead we're most concerned with the present and with hanging on to what's ours—or taking what's someone else's, using whatever weapon is handy.

Two women and a girl show off their rifle skills, St. George Island, 1924. In Florida a gun is sometimes used as a magic wand, something you wave around to make problems go away. Photo courtesy of State Archives of Florida.

8

The Gunshine State

Say hello to my little friend!
—TONY MONTANA (AL PACINO), FIRING AN M16A1
MACHINE GUN AT ENEMIES INVADING
HIS MIAMI MANSION IN *SCARFACE*, 1983

In 1969, *Monty Python's Flying Circus* ran a sketch about a self-defense instructor, played by John Cleese, who showed his students how to fend off an assailant wielding a banana. A banana! Can you imagine?

In January 2014, one of the first Florida crimes of the year involved a Port Richey man accused of attacking his girlfriend with a banana. A banana! Can you imagine?

We Floridians can be a disputatious lot, with scorching weather and long lines making us hot under the collar. As our argument escalates, we reach for whatever equalizer might be handy.

Take food. In 2013 we had these headlines: "Sister Jailed for Flinging Peanut Butter in Argument over Dog," "Spring Hill Man Charged with Striking Wife with Turkey Neck," "Myakka City Man Threw Bowl of Chicken Wings at Wife," and "Florida Man, 36, Assaulted Teen Relative with Taco Bell Burrito."

Even the cops seem amazed at what passes for weapons. One day while filling in for another reporter, I drove to the jail to pick up the overnight arrest reports. On top of the stack of paper, placed there by the jail staff so I wouldn't miss it, was one about a Gulfport woman arrested for clonking her boyfriend over the head with a lawn gnome. Not just any lawn gnome, either—a New Orleans Saints lawn gnome.

Florida fights often involve neighbors. So many of us are new arrivals that we haven't yet built up any trust with the folks next door, or even learned their names. We avoid speaking, at least until we start squabbling about whose dog pooped on whose property. That's when we learn that anything can be a weapon. *Anything.*

In 2007, two Destin men were fighting. Destin bills itself as "The World's Luckiest Fishing Village," and thus the handiest weapon was a catfish. One man hurled it, and the sharp fins stuck in the other man's back. Lifeguards had to cut away the fish and call an ambulance as cops took the fish flinger off to jail.

A 2002 fish fight between two Madeira Beach men ended when one stabbed the other with the swordfish's bill. A similar stabbing occurred in Carl Hiaasen's 1989 novel *Skin Tight*—the one time Hiaasen managed to beat reality.

The all-time best odd-weapon story occurred in 2004, when a Port Orange man was charged with battery on his girlfriend. The weapon he swung at her midsection: a three-foot alligator that he'd been keeping in his bathtub. Sadly, no one reported on what injuries—mental or physical—might have been suffered by the gator.

I admit laughing at the gator keeper and the gnome knocker, but I wonder about our inclination to giggle about these domestic disputes. If you polled people on whether domestic violence could be funny, most would tell you no.

Remember the famous scene in the 1932 movie *The Public Enemy* where Jimmy Cagney smashes a grapefruit into Mae Clarke's face? It was brutal, not amusing. Cagney's character was angry, and the grapefruit was close by. If this happened now in, say, Boca Raton, it would become "Florida Man Attacks Girlfriend with Grapefruit." Cagney would be mocked on Twitter, blogged about on *Huffington Post*, hooted at by late-night comics. Nobody would think about poor Mae Clarke.

Not every attempt at using alternate weaponry works. In 2008, a man walked into a DeLand liquor store and demanded $50, menacing the clerk with a pair of flip-flops and a palm frond. A customer grabbed a barstool and chased him off.

Or consider the 2013 incident in which a forty-one-year-old man held up an Ocala convenience store with a gun-shaped piece of cardboard covered in tin foil. The clerk told the robber to take whatever he wanted. The robber couldn't open the register, so he grabbed a charity's donation bucket and ran.

His loot: $14 in change. A customer recognized the Tin Foil Bandit, and the cops (ahem) foiled his crime.

Then there was the guy who in 2012 robbed a Manatee County 7-Eleven by holding his fingers in the shape of a gun. He made off with a cheeseburger, beer, and some condoms.

Samurai swords are surprisingly popular. It's as if Quentin Tarantino ruled the state. In August 2013, the *Orlando Sentinel* announced: "Samurai Sword–Wielding, Knife-Throwing Man Lost It over Missing Can of Shrimp, Report Says." A month later, the University of Florida student paper *The Alligator* had this: "Gainesville Man Threatens Workers with Samurai Sword." I am partial to a 2013 samurai sword story from my own paper: "Clearwater Police Arrest Man Wielding Samurai Swords." What I like is that he had two swords, one pointed at his *own* chest. He held the police at bay for two hours.

One thing you rarely see in these stories, though, is where the sword came from. Was it a cheap souvenir? Or an authentic Hattori Hanzo sword?

One exception that I've seen enriched the story, although technically what was involved was not a samurai sword: In December 1992, a lawyer stopped at a Pensacola mall's Christmas gift wrap desk and asked if they had Hanukkah paper. They did not. This upset him so much he marched over to Cutlery World and picked out a $417 item, the "Robin Hood sword." He told the cashier, "I want that sword *now.*"

The cashier was busy with other customers and told him he'd have to wait. The lawyer put his credit card on the counter and said, "Ring it up. I'll be back." He walked out. He came back three times to check before the cashier handed it over—in a box.

The lawyer marched back to the wrapping desk, took the sword from the box and raised it as if about to chop a security guard in half. Two customers tackled him, and he was arrested. But at least he had a nice souvenir (once it was released from the evidence room).

The oddball weapon you hear about the most in Florida stories is the machete. Sometimes it's used in combination with other weapons: "Fight Involving Machete, Frying Pan Land Flagler Mom and Son in Jail."

I once wondered if we have so many machetes here because they're issued to new residents as they cross the state line, but a representative for Machete-Specialists.com told me that "a pretty significant chunk" of their sales are to Florida customers. The reason is our thick, fast-growing vegetation. The University of Florida says machetes are a perfect solution for gardening problems: "If you have an overgrown corner of your landscape, a machete can help you easily remove vines and semi-woody perennials."

Land surveyors often have to hack through underbrush to clear a sight line. They usually use a machete or a bush axe, which has a long handle attached to a teardrop-shaped blade. During the summer I spent on a survey crew, I collected lots of blisters swinging both, but I preferred the machete—and not just because I could pretend to be Indiana Jones. It just felt right in my hand, and I suspect that's a big part of its appeal for my fellow Floridians.

How popular are machete crimes in Florida? In December 2013, my colleague Michael Kruse pulled together a list of things that Floridians had used machetes for that year:

1. Rob a pizza place.
2. Kill a gator.
3. Chase a burglar.
4. Critically injure a home invader.
5. Attack Grandma.
6. Attack a man in the woods.
7. Attack police officers . . . at the police station.
8. Slice a neighbor on account of sickly trees.
9. Charge a neighbor on account of a stolen chicken.
10. Slash the arm of a ranting drunk on Cudjoe Key.
11. Decapitate pythons in a state-sanctioned snake-catching contest.
12. Search for Civil War ruins.
13. Threaten fellow college football fans.
14. Run through Jacksonville yelling, "Kill me, I want to die," before breaking into a home and ripping the toilet out of an upstairs bathroom while foaming at the mouth, then shattering a window and falling two stories to the ground.

If those folks had used a gun instead, they might not have made the news at all (well, except for that last one).

Florida's shape is open to interpretation. People have compared it to a penis, a uvula, and a skillet. The most popular comparison, though, is a handgun. The grip is the peninsula. The hammer is Jacksonville. The Panhandle is the barrel. That means my hometown of Pensacola is the muzzle. Maybe its name should be "POW!"

The gun is an apt symbol. A common way to celebrate New Year's in Florida is to fire a gun into the air, which inevitably leads to someone getting hit by a bullet falling back to earth, gravity being the law even here.

One reason so many bullets fly at New Year's is that we've got so many guns. In December 2012, state officials announced that Florida had hit a milestone of one million concealed weapons permits, more than any other state. The agency that announced this was *not* the Florida Department of Law Enforcement. It was the Florida Department of Agriculture and Consumer Services, which you might think would be too busy with farm implements and rip-off artists to pay attention to who's got a Glock in his pocket.

If you're a hard-core, National-Rifle-Association-sticker-in-the-car-window person, you are probably convinced that a million concealed weapons is a good thing. The more guns that are out there, the less chance bad guys will shoot anyone, right? That might be true in other states, but I'm not sure it applies here in Florida. Some of my fellow citizens act as if guns are not mechanical devices that propel projectiles through the air using gunpowder, but magic wands that can be waved around to make problems disappear.

Case in point: In July 2015, two volunteers in Lauderdale-by-the-Sea went out searching for sea turtle nests. They were confronted by a drunk who said he didn't like turtles. One volunteer pulled out his concealed weapon, explaining later he thought it would "defuse" the situation. Instead, in the ensuing scuffle, he was shot with his own gun, right in the left buttock.

That's not even counting the accidental shootings that have occurred. In Florida the number of accidental shootings is double the national average—often occurring when someone packing a concealed weapon goes bowling, checks into a hotel, or reaches for a cigarette, and the gun goes off. That hotel misfire wounded five people.

Antigun folks talk about Florida having a frontier mentality, but when Florida was a frontier in the 1820s and '30s, concealed weapons were frowned upon. A man who carried a concealed weapon and killed someone was not eligible for a manslaughter charge. Toting a hidden weapon showed premeditation—"a settled, rancorous malice," one judge said. A legislative council tried to forbid the carrying of concealed weapons, but failed.

Why do so many Floridians carry concealed weapons now? Some gun dealers credit their increase to the election of a black president, even though a majority of Floridians voted for him. Some Floridians feared—with zero justification—that Barack Obama would seize guns and ammunition, so they bought a lot of both. One Palm Beach County gun dealer said, "Barack Obama is the best gun salesman since Samuel Colt."

Some of the increase is fueled by tourism. Florida does not require you to be a resident to get a concealed weapons permit. You just need to show that you're over twenty-one and of sound mind, have no disqualifying convictions, and display a rudimentary proficiency with a firearm. Then you're free to stroll around Disney with your Beretta—or you would be, except Disney bans firearms.

But guns get in anyway. In 2013, a grandmother visiting Animal Kingdom found a Cobra .380 caliber semiautomatic on the seat of the Dinosaur Ride. A man with a concealed weapons permit said the gun fell out of his pocket during the ride. He was promptly escorted off the property by security. I would have let him stay but required him to wear a dunce cap with mouse ears.

I suspect so many Floridians carry concealed weapons because of the news that so many Floridians carry concealed weapons. It's a combination of peer pressure and fear—call it fear pressure. Let's say you get into a spat with your neighbor over hedge trimming. Do you want to be the one who brings clippers to a gunfight?

Because of the demand, Florida has more places to buy a gun than there are post offices for people to crash their cars into. Not everybody who's buying a gun in Florida is planning to use it in Florida, though. Guns bought here wind up being used to commit crimes in other states. Florida ranks in the top ten of states sending guns to do dirty work elsewhere.

Florida's guns fire shots heard 'round the world too, aiding coups and assassinations. In 1989 and 1990, weapons from Miami gun shops were used to kill three candidates in Colombia's presidential election, the *New York Times* reported, adding that Florida arms traffickers have "tried to ship weapons out in refrigerators, washing machines, scuba tanks, fire extinguishers and even stuffed animals and toys."

My favorite Florida gun-smuggling story happened in 1994. A Miami woman and a Delray Beach man bought lots of pistols from a Pompano Beach dealer, then went to Publix and bought ten frozen turkeys. They unfroze the turkeys, stuffed a few guns inside each one, and refroze the birds. They then flew to Haiti with the cold turkeys in their checked luggage. I am now writing a script for a holiday TV special titled *The Thanksgiving When the Turkeys Were Full of Guns and Salmonella*.

The most famous concealed weapons permit in Florida history was issued in 2009 to George Zimmerman of Sanford. It didn't get to be famous for three years, but then it was impossible to ignore.

At 7:11 P.M. on February 28, 2012, Zimmerman, twenty-eight, a volunteer neighborhood watch captain, spotted someone strolling through the drizzle in his gated subdivision. Zimmerman called police on his cell phone and described the subject: "Black male, late teens, dark gray hoodie, jeans or sweatpants walking around area." Why was Zimmerman suspicious? "He's got his hand in his waistband. Something is wrong with him."

The dispatcher told Zimmerman to wait and let the cops handle the situation. Instead, Zimmerman got out of his car and followed the man. A holster tucked in Zimmerman's waistband held a Kel-Tec 9mm PF-9, one of the lightest, thinnest handguns around. It's made in Florida and not intended for hunting or target practice. It's made for shooting people at close range.

The two men confronted each other. A struggle ensued. Zimmerman, losing the fight, pulled his gun and shot the stranger dead.

The person he'd gunned down was not an intruder. The teenager's name was Trayvon Martin. He was armed with nothing but some Arizona Iced Tea and a bag of Skittles. He also wasn't scoping out the two-story town homes for a burglary. He lived with his mother in Miami but was visiting his father in Sanford. He'd been staying in a rented town home in the development—just like Zimmerman. Moments before he died, he had been on the phone, telling a friend that some "creepy-ass cracker" was following him. To Martin, Zimmerman—who was half Hispanic, not an actual Florida Cracker—was the menacing stranger, not the other way around. For one final irony, the name of the development is the Retreat at Twin Lakes, although retreating is the exact opposite of what they did.

The Sanford police detective who investigated the shooting initially wanted to charge Zimmerman with manslaughter. Neighborhood watch volunteers aren't supposed to follow anyone, much less get in someone's face. And carrying a gun? Also against the rules. But weeks passed, during which everyone from the president on down offered an opinion, and no charges were filed. Police said Florida's "Stand Your Ground" law on self-defense had them unsure what to do. At last, in April, a special prosecutor appointed by Gov. Scott charged Zimmerman with second-degree murder.

The July 2013 trial took four weeks, with dozens of witnesses. The jury of six women deliberated for twelve hours, then sent out a note asking for a clarification of their instructions on the lesser charge of manslaughter.

In the end, though, they acquitted him. Afterward, a juror told CNN they voted that way "because of the heat of the moment and the 'Stand Your Ground.' He had a right to defend himself. If he felt threatened that his life was going to be taken away from him or he was going to have bodily harm, he had a right."

After the trial, Zimmerman got his gun back; visited the Cocoa factory where it was made; got arrested again after a fight with his estranged wife and father-in-law (no charges were filed); was accused of domestic violence by his new girlfriend (charges later dropped when she recanted); rescued a couple from an overturned SUV; was pulled over three times for traffic infractions; insulted people on Twitter; and got into a road rage incident where he told the other driver, "Do you know who I am? I will [expletive] kill you." A year later, he encountered that same driver again and was injured by flying glass when the driver shot out his car window. Now Zimmerman knows what it feels like to be on the other end of a gun. Oh, and he painted some pictures of Confederate flags to sell as a fund-raiser for a gun shop that wouldn't admit Muslims.

The one thing Zimmerman did not do—but should have—was write Marion Hammer a thank-you note.

Who's Marion Hammer? A 4-foot-11 grandmother with a bowl haircut and a fondness for lipstick the color of arterial blood, for one thing. She's also the most powerful woman in Florida. She even has power over the birds of the air.

Florida legislators spend a lot of time thinking about our state symbols. Florida has a *lot* of them, including a state flower (orange blossom), state butterfly (zebra longwing), state shell (horse conch), state reptile (alligator), and state soil (Myakka fine sand). Not long ago our lawmakers got into a snit over whether the state pie should be pecan or Key lime. (Key lime won.)

Of course Florida has an official bird. No, it's not the construction crane. It's the mockingbird. But the mockingbird is also the state bird of four other states. Twice Florida's schoolchildren have tried to change the state bird to something exclusive to the Sunshine State, and twice that effort has been blocked by one woman: Marion Hammer.

In 1999, more than ten thousand schoolchildren signed a petition to change the state bird to the Florida scrub jay. Supporters of the scrub jay boasted about how gentle it is, that it will eat peanuts right out of a person's hand.

"Begging for food isn't sweet," Hammer told legislators. "It's lazy and it's a welfare mentality." They voted to stick with the mockingbird.

Ten years later it was the osprey, a graceful raptor. The change was now supported by twenty thousand kids. Again, Hammer stuck up for the mockingbird. Again, lawmakers listened to her instead of the kids.

How could Hammer wield more power than thirty thousand children? Because since 1978 she has been the National Rifle Association's top lobbyist in Florida. On the wall in her Tallahassee office is her concealed weapons permit, License No. 0000001.

She fired her first weapon when she was six years old. She met her husband while shooting. In the 1990s, she became the first female president of the national NRA. Now in her seventies, she's as powerful as ever, rattling off testimony in her deep, penetrating voice, handing out endorsements and campaign contributions, and occasionally advising legislators on what guns they ought to buy. She may be the most influential lobbyist not only in Florida but nationwide.

She does more than shoot down gun control bills. She's constantly trying to loosen up the existing laws.

In 1987, Hammer got the legislature to pass Florida's concealed weapons law. That law, the first of its kind in the nation, was then copied by forty other states.

In 2008, despite opposition from Disney and the Chamber of Commerce, she pushed through a bill that allows employees to bring their guns to work.

In 2011, she persuaded legislators to pass the Firearm Owners' Privacy Act, better known as "Docs vs. Glocks." It forbids physicians, including pediatricians, from discussing the risks of firearm ownership with their patients. Since Gov. Scott signed it into law, ten other states have introduced similar bills.

Most important for Zimmerman, in 2005 Hammer pushed the legislature to pass the Stand Your Ground law, the first one of its kind in the nation. Previously Florida law said you had a right to protect your home from intruders—the so-called castle doctrine, as in "a man's home is his castle." But if you were involved in a confrontation elsewhere, such as a Sanford roadside, you had a "duty to retreat" and wait for the cops.

Hammer's bill made your castle portable. It said anyone "who is not engaged in an unlawful activity and who is attacked in any other place where he or she has a right to be has no duty to retreat and has the right to stand his or her ground and meet force with force, including deadly force if he or she reasonably believes it is necessary to do so to prevent death or great bodily harm to himself or herself or another or to prevent the commission of a forcible felony."

Law enforcement officers throughout the state objected. John Timoney, then Miami's police chief, called it the "License to Murder" law: "Trying to control shooting by members of a well-trained and disciplined police department is a daunting enough task. Laws like Stand Your Ground give citizens unfettered power and discretion with no accountability. It is a recipe for disaster."

But thanks to Hammer, the bill passed the House 92–20 (among those voting for it: future presidential candidate Marco Rubio) and zoomed through the Senate 39–0. Gov. Jeb Bush signed Stand Your Ground into law, calling it "a good, common-sense, anticrime issue."

In the first five years after the law passed, reported "justifiable homicides" tripled. Hammer's law repeatedly allowed drug dealers to avoid murder charges when they shot rivals or their own customers. In 2008, two Tallahassee gangs got into a gunfight that killed a fifteen-year-old. Prosecutors charged the shooters, but a judge dismissed the charges. They were standing their ground.

"The law has proven especially effective in providing legal cover if the victim is black," my paper reported.

The best example of what Stand Your Ground can do comes from Pasco County, where a man shot a romantic rival five times—four as the man tried to run away. Charged with attempted murder, the shooter claimed a Stand Your Ground defense, and it worked—the jury acquitted him. Left unanswered: How can you be standing your ground if the other guy is busy *fleeing* your ground?

To persuade legislators to pass the law, Hammer told a story she has told many times. In the 1980s, a carload of drunks followed her into a Tallahassee parking garage, shouting obscenities and making plain what they intended to do with her. She reached in her purse for her Colt. "I pulled the gun out, brought it slowly up into the headlights of the car so they could see it, and heard one of them scream."

The ruffians fled, she said. The moral: Having a gun saved her life. Of course, Hammer didn't actually fire it—unlike Zimmerman.

Another anecdote got the Stand Your Ground bill rolling, a story from 2004 when Hurricane Ivan pummeled the Panhandle. That story, told over and over to and by legislators, was this: One night after the hurricane passed, amid rampant looting, an elderly man and his wife were sleeping in their ruined home near Pensacola, trying to protect what they had left. Suddenly, a thief broke in and attacked them. Fortunately, the homeowner had a gun and wounded the intruder. Then he waited an agonizing six months as prosecutors debated whether to charge him. He even had to pay an attorney, at a time when he couldn't spare a dime. He avoided prosecution, but the process, legislators said, was not fair. The law needed to be changed.

Nearly everything in that story was distorted or wrong, except for the part about the hurricane.

James and Kathryn Workman were asleep not in their storm-damaged home but in an RV parked outside it. The intruder who burst in was not a looter. He was a Federal Emergency Management Agency contractor. Rodney Cox had come down from North Carolina to help with rebuilding. He had a wife and two kids back home. That night, he'd gotten drunk and lost, then burst into the trailer. Cox wrapped his arms around the seventy-seven-year-old Workman, who struggled to get free and then fired two shots. Cox died before he reached the hospital.

The prosecutor took less than three months, not six, to decide not to charge

Workman. The couple never had to hire a lawyer. When the *Pensacola News Journal* asked the prosecutor whether the law should be changed in light of the case, he said, "I think the law's fine as it is."

But that's not what Marion Hammer thought, and so that's not what legislators—including Marco Rubio—or Gov. Bush thought.

Zimmerman's acquittal produced a deluge of stories about how messed up the Stand Your Ground law is. Gov. Scott set up a nineteen-member panel to review it and suggest changes. They spent six months traveling the state and taking public testimony. But because the panel included two lawmakers who helped draft the law, two others who voted for it, and a fifth who sponsored "Docs vs. Glocks," no one was surprised it proposed no major changes. They did, however, suggest a tweak to discourage neighborhood watch volunteers from acting like cowboys. So far, no legislator has filed a bill to make that happen.

That means it's up to Florida's law enforcement officers to figure out how to deal with a million or so people armed to the teeth, ready to shoot anyone who seems threatening or even insulting. Of course, because they're working in Florida, the cops are also dealing with the dumbest, drunkest, craziest criminals in the nation, and any one of them could go—dare I say it?—viral.

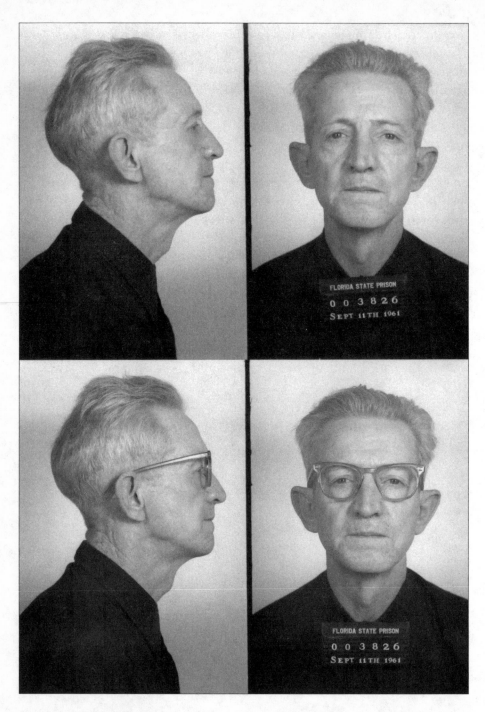

Prison mug shots of Clarence Earl Gideon, Florida State Prison, Raiford, 1961. He forever changed the American justice system—with a little help from his cellmate. Photo courtesy of State Archives of Florida.

9

Bad Boys

"Why do you love Florida so much?"
"Because I need nonstop stimulus. Living here is like being in a permanent studio audience for *Cops*."

—TIM DORSEY, *CADILLAC BEACH*

Over the years, a lot of TV shows have been set in Florida. They have featured everything from a red-haired ukulele player (*Arthur Godfrey and His Friends*) to four daffy female retirees (*Golden Girls*) to a clever dolphin (*Flipper*) to a ditzy magical spellbinder (*I Dream of Jeannie*). Crime shows set in Florida have been particularly popular—the silly sleaze of *Silk Stalkings,* the jaunty thrills of *Burn Notice,* and the sunglass-snatching drama of *CSI: Miami,* to name a few.

But nothing compares to *Miami Vice.*

The show debuted in 1984 while Miami was still reeling from the Mariel boatlift, a race riot, an influx of Haitian refugees, and the rise of the trigger-happy cocaine cowboys spraying bullets all over I-95. The murder rate soared so high that the medical examiner had a bumper crop of corpses. He had to borrow a refrigerated truck from Burger King to hold the overflow. Magic City seemed more desperate than enchanted, while Miami Beach consisted of nothing but decrepit hotels full of elderly people eking out an existence while dodging muggers and junkies.

Yet *Miami Vice* made it appear to be a gleaming cityscape full of neon and glitz. The producers concocted this image based on a single factoid: One-third of all unreported income in the country moved through South Florida.

"That means one-half of one percent of the nation's population is responsible for twenty percent of the under-the-table money," explained Anthony Yerkovich, who wrote the pilot episode. "Statistically, that's a forty-to-one disparity. Any area that generates forty times more unreported cash than the rest of the country is worth writing about."

Miami Vice starred Don Johnson and Philip Michael Thomas as Crockett and Tubbs, a pair of designer-clothed undercover cops out to nail drug kingpins and arms dealers. Its focus on style and music rewrote the script for how a TV show should look and sound, influencing all the shows after it.

It didn't just change the TV landscape. It changed the actual landscape too.

The show was filmed on location, which was easy because the streets tended to be empty and any building the producers wanted was open. As the show grew in popularity, though, the swank nightclubs and hotels that the show's designers created in the run-down buildings began popping up in real life, a Potemkin village turned 3-D. *Vice* had convinced investors (many of them looking to launder that unreported income) that its vision of Miami Beach could work.

The TV people had pulled off the Florida dream: They told a lie about Florida that came true.

Florida's cops also owe a huge debt of gratitude to Crockett and Tubbs. *Vice* made them all seem like supercool crime solvers, ready to take on any case no matter where it might lead.

The truth, of course, is more complicated.

Florida's law enforcement officers are definitely a special breed. Every day they're confronted with Florida crime, which is not like crime anywhere else—attackers swinging samurai swords, car wrecks involving a driver shaving her "bikini area," etc.

You might argue that Florida cops have it easy because while Florida's crooks may aspire to be the Joker, mostly they're just a joke. There was the fugitive who was caught because he responded to people who were making fun of his wanted poster on the Pasco County sheriff's Facebook page. Or the fleeing motorcyclist who was doing 150 mph until he ran out of gas. Or the hiker who called 911 to report that he was lost and being pursued by wild hogs. When the cops arrived, they discovered he had an outstanding warrant and a backpack full of stolen goods—including a GPS unit he'd never tried.

Sometimes it seems like Florida itself helps thwart the bad guys. I can name at least two instances where fleeing perpetrators were apprehended with a major assist from an alligator and one in which a burglary suspect hiding from the cops was fatally chomped by an eleven-footer. Talk about taking a bite out of crime!

Florida's crooks can be creative, stealing everything from motorized scooters to school buses to fire trucks to a front-end loader (the ultimate slow-speed chase). They've stolen twenty-six chameleons, a truck carrying thirty-six thousand pounds of Crisco, a giant chicken statue—you name it.

Florida cops are often called on to handle situations not covered by their training. On a single weekend in June 2013, Tallahassee police officers had to capture an escaped llama and, meanwhile, Pasco deputies went after a runaway kangaroo.

The three-hundred-pound llama was easier—a lasso, a Taser, and six officers took it down. As for the kangaroo, the deputies tried tranquilizer darts and a Taser, to no avail. Finally a spectator—a onetime high school wrestler—just tackled it. Once he'd brought the marsupial down, deputies used duct tape to bind its legs. The wrestler briefly became a celebrity, until the kangaroo died. The cause, said wildlife officials, was "excited delirium," which also serves as a pretty fair description of most weekends in Florida.

Tasers have become the go-to weapon for Florida cops. I've lost count of how many stories end with the cops whipping out a stun gun. The most outrageous was a 2013 story from Maitland that was headlined, "Naked Man Walking Dog Shocked with Taser, Arrested." Remember, he was naked—it's not like he had a concealed weapon.

The rise of the Taser toters began in 2007, when Sen. John Kerry gave a speech on the University of Florida campus and was confronted by Andrew Meyer, a columnist for the student paper, the *Independent Florida Alligator*. During the Q&A session at the end, Meyer stood at a microphone to pepper Kerry with questions. He uttered what the *Washington Post* later described as a "non-family friendly word" and his mike was cut off.

Even though Kerry said he wanted to answer, the campus police moved in. Meyer began shouting, demanding to know why he was being arrested. It was then, as he noticed the cops reaching for their belts, that he let out a plaintive wail that echoed throughout the nation: "Don't Tase me, bro!"

Let the record reflect that no bro Tased Meyer. Instead, it was Officer Nicole Lynn Mallo who zapped him, triggering screams of agony, as well as what one bystander called "a stench that was not overpowering, but it was unsettling."

When a video clip of the incident went up on YouTube, it quickly went viral—not as a serious confrontation between overly zealous cops and an overly dramatic college kid, but as a comical cri de coeur.

Meyer spent a night in jail but the charges were dropped as his star rose. Stories appeared in papers all over the country, leading to an interview on

NBC's *Today* show. Devo and other bands included his catchphrase in songs, the *New Oxford American Dictionary* listed "tase/taze" as one of the top words of the year, and the *Yale Book of Quotations* called it the most memorable quote of 2007. As for Meyer, he copyrighted his four-word outcry, then used his Web site to sell T-shirts carrying the slogan. He went to law school but—exhibiting what may be symptoms of lingering mental damage from the incident—he became a writer.

He never did get Kerry's answer.

I suspect the primary qualification for being a cop in Florida is the ability to keep a straight face while writing up reports.

Imagine the lip biting that's required when an officer writes in a report, "The female stole a lab coat, commandeered a golf cart and was spraying people with fire extinguishers as she drove around." Or when a cop describes a DUI suspect as "wearing zombie contacts" while "dressed as a pig in a nude color bathing suit." Or when an officer notes that, "When I asked her if she understood her rights, she began screaming that she was fighting with her sister . . . over a vibrator and her boyfriend." Or noting that a man who danced on top of a patrol car said he did it to ward off vampires because he wanted to "stop the slaughter of small children."

I can't tell you what a delight it is to read Florida police reports because of how often you run across sentences like, "I had the defendant secure the squirrel and then exit the vehicle" and "As I was handcuffing him, he told me that he had jurisdiction over me since he was the director of the CIA."

I spent four years covering criminal courts and saw plenty of comedy. I saw the trial of a bigamist whose defense was, "I forgot I was married," and the jury believed him. I covered another where a pair of bumbling hit men got lost trying to find their victim in St. Petersburg and wound up in Tampa.

I saw some sick and twisted things too, involving murder and rape and a mother who secretly dosed her child with potions that made him sick so she could get a doctor's attention.

I also witnessed some outstanding police work. One case I covered involved a guy named Jimmy Randall, suspected of killing at least five women. He'd get high on crack, pick up a prostitute, choke her, then dump the body in a secluded location. One day a corpse turned up near a single muddy tire print. Detectives traced that tire print back to the Firestone place that sold the tire, which led them to Randall.

Forensics experts discovered that the bodies had a sprinkling of dog hair on them. They also spotted a tiny piece of paper stuck to the breast of one woman. Randall's live-in girlfriend—a former prostitute—had a dog, and so a couple of female deputies knocked on the door and pretended to be part of a new dog-washing service. They convinced Randall's girlfriend to let them in to give the dog a free introductory bath. The hair they collected was similar to that on the bodies.

The dog, a little pug, proved to be the source of the tiny piece of paper too. Randall's girlfriend smoked. When she finished a cigarette, she dropped the butt on the floor. The dog picked up the butts and chewed them. This canine craving for nicotine left tiny flecks of paper scattered on the floor. The forensics lab was able to pull some human saliva out of that paper from the one victim and match its DNA to Randall's girlfriend. A jury agreed that proved the victim had been killed in Randall's apartment.

The reason this case stays with me is because of the dog with a fondness for cigarettes. A serial killer might have gotten away with his crimes if not for the pug named Princess Penny Pickles.

One of the things I learned in covering courts is that you can never predict what a jury will do. Perhaps because so many of us are transient and feel no strong connection to our community, our juries can produce some awfully lenient verdicts.

A Florida jury acquitted World Series hero Jim Leyritz of DUI-manslaughter in a wreck in which a thirty-year-old mother died. But they did convict him of drunk driving in connection with that wreck. Another jury acquitted a Clearwater police officer of a manslaughter charge for shooting an unarmed man. Then a civil court jury said the cop was to blame, after all—but not the city that employed him, so the dead man's family was not entitled to damages.

The most forgiving jury in Florida history was the one that heard the case of four white Miami police officers charged with murder in the 1979 death of a black insurance executive named Arthur McDuffie, a Marine Corps veteran. McDuffie died four days after he went out riding on his motorcycle and wound up in a coma, courtesy of the pursuing officers.

The officers said he'd been driving recklessly and suffered his injuries when he tried to flee them and crashed. The truth was that the cops had caught up to McDuffie and beat and kicked him mercilessly, cracking his skull like an egg because they were angry that he'd run from them. A medical examiner testified that the fatal blow was "equivalent to falling four stories and landing between your eyes." The cops doctored the crime scene to hide what they'd done. It came out anyway.

"My child is dead, they beat him to death like a dog," McDuffie's mother said.

Because of pretrial publicity, the case was moved to Tampa, where an all-white jury voted to acquit the cops. Miami's predominantly black Liberty City erupted in three days of riots that left eighteen people—eight white, ten black—just as dead as Arthur McDuffie.

The antics and achievements of Florida's real-life cops and criminals have become staples of American TV, thanks to onetime Broward County sheriff Nick Navarro. As a lawman, Navarro was part bloodhound and part publicity hound. He approved letting TV cameras ride along with his officers for three months to produce the first season of a groundbreaking show called *Cops*.

Cops premiered on March 11, 1989, and became an instant smash. Even its theme song, "Bad Boys," by the reggae group Inner Circle, became a hit. Filmed in a documentary style, *Cops* focused only on what the cops said and did, and what the perps they busted said and did—no voice-over, no commentary, and no laugh track, no matter how bizarre the situation. It set the template for the battalion of reality TV shows that eventually took over the tube—not just the other cop shows, such as *Unleashed: K9 Broward County*, but also shows about celebrities and their families.

One of Navarro's deputies, Linda Canada, became the show's first breakout star. The five-foot-five blonde "looked like Farrah Fawcett with a badge," the local paper reported. Viewers saw her dressing in provocative clothing to go undercover as a hooker. They saw her in a tight uniform telling a sketchy hitchhiker, "Get off my street!" They even saw her exchanging kisses—and, eventually, accepting a marriage proposal—from her boyfriend, another deputy. Fan mail poured in along with calls from radio stations, followed by an interview on *Entertainment Tonight*. A profile in *People* called her looks "arresting."

Despite the show's fly-on-the-wall style, *Cops* producers sometimes tinkered with "reality." In 2002, they persuaded a Tampa police officer to dress up as a clown, complete with a bulbous red nose and a white van advertising his services for children's parties. They sent him out in costume to solicit hookers. When a woman climbed into his van, "Coco" would spray her with Silly String, take a hit of helium from a balloon, and then, in a high-pitched voice, inform her she was under arrest.

Cops shied away from showing anything not flattering to its title subject. It didn't show viewers Navarro leading raids on gay bars, then later having to write a check to make up for an improper search. It didn't delve into Navarro's repeated arrests of rappers 2 Live Crew for obscenity, an obsession that led to his defeat at the polls in 1992. Nor did it mention Deputy Canada's lawsuit against her own department for sexual discrimination.

A true TV portrait of Florida crime would have to go beyond what's on *Cops* to include the darker side of law enforcement. Plenty of Florida cops are decent, hardworking people, but some of those sworn to uphold the law veer to the wrong side of it. Florida cops have gotten in trouble for everything from hanging out in a strip club while they were supposed to be on patrol to stealing thousands of dollars from their own union to raping female drivers after pulling them over. One even posted nude photos of herself online— photos that she'd taken in her cruiser while she was supposedly on duty.

We've even had cops get in trouble for trying to avoid getting in trouble. A Hollywood cop crashed into a civilian's car and then he and some of his colleagues created a fake crime scene. Under their scenario, the other driver lost control when her cat jumped out her car window. One of the cops described their fakery as "do a little Walt Disney." Uncle Walt would've warned them to keep an eye out for the cruiser's dashboard camera.

It's easy to say that these are just a few bad apples, but the problems can go deeper. In 2013, the U.S. Justice Department blasted the Miami police for a pattern of using excessive force and repeatedly dropping the ball on investigating officer-involved shootings.

That same year, the chief of the Miami Gardens Police Department had to step down after the *Miami Herald* revealed that his officers had been systematically harassing and abusing black residents. They did their worst to an African-American employee of a Quick Stop. He'd been stopped by police 288 times, or once a week for four years, and arrested 62 times for trespassing—in the store where he worked. A subsequent investigation by Fusion TV found that they also stopped for questioning a five-year-old on a playground and a 99-year-old man they described as "suspicious."

Meanwhile, most of the Lakeland Police Department became tangled in a bizarre sex scandal that prompted the New York *Daily News* to dub them "Florida's Horniest." In the end, twenty-seven employees were disciplined, including about a dozen officers who resigned in lieu of termination and three who were fired. Also fired: the woman at the center of the scandal, whom the city then had to pay $28,500 to drop a complaint about workplace harassment.

The poster boy for bad cops in Florida is German Bosque, who over the course of twenty years was fired five times by different departments, and arrested three times—charged with stealing a car, trying to board an airplane with a loaded gun, and driving with a suspended license. He was also the subject of forty internal affairs cases, sixteen of them for battery or using excessive force. Inspections of his patrol car turned up a counterfeit $20 bill, cocaine, and a crack pipe.

Yet somehow Bosque managed to hang on to his badge until he was dubbed "Florida's Dirtiest Cop" by a *Sarasota Herald-Tribune* investigation that asked why departments kept hiring him. He was fired by the Opa-Locka Police Department and arrested again, this time for kidnapping someone trying to file another complaint about him. He was convicted and sentenced to nearly a year behind bars. After he gets out, it wouldn't surprise me a bit to see a Florida department rehire him. I mean, look at all his experience! He's looked at crime from both sides now!

You could complain about the bad cops to the police chief or sheriff . . . except they get in trouble too. In 2014, the former chief of the Longwood Police Department was indicted on charges he accepted $30,000 in bribes to hire an ex-felon as a cop, providing him with badges and guns. The ex-con cop was promoted all the way to commander before the scheme unraveled.

A month later, the chief of the Atlantic Beach Police Department resigned amid an investigation that uncovered a variety of drugs in his home. Hidden in a bag of dog food, the investigators found a duffel full of steroids. The investigation started because the chief, instead of buying his drugs on the street or stealing from the evidence locker, had cleverly ordered his drugs online, which attracted the attention of Homeland Security.

Corruption can spread beyond just a cop or two and infect the entire department. For decades, the town of Waldo, near Gainesville, was known as Florida's worst speed trap. Then a trio of patrolmen came forward to say they were under orders to meet a quota for tickets every month, causing an uproar. The city soon disbanded the department, leaving city officials scrambling to find some other source of revenue to replace all those speeding fines. However, the chief faced no criminal charges because requiring a quota for tickets wasn't illegal (the legislature corrected that in 2015).

A similar speeding-ticket imbroglio in the nearby town of Hawthorne led to the revelation of such a tangle of scandalous behavior by city officials that legislators threatened to dissolve the town. You *know* how much our legislators hate corruption.

Fortunately, we've got some fine, upstanding prosecutors and judges to uphold the law and . . . oh, wait, they've got problems too. In 2014, for instance, a Gainesville prosecutor resigned after being accused of using his cell phone to shoot video of a woman stripping down in a tanning booth, while three judges from Broward County were busted for DUI. The third one hit a police car in the courthouse parking lot. We've had judges who got in trouble for being drunk on the bench, for retaliating against a party in a case for refusing the judge's Facebook friend request, and for getting into a fistfight with a public defender outside the courtroom.

My favorite story of a legal eagle getting his wings clipped happened in 1996, when the U.S. attorney in Miami got in trouble for biting a stripper named Tiffany. That night South Florida's top federal prosecutor ran up a $900 bill at the strip joint. The next day he sent his father back to try to buy the original of his charge slip back for $1,200—thus tipping off Tiffany and her husband that the guy who'd sunk his teeth into her arm might be important. Prosecutor Kendall Coffey ended up resigning, but he maintained a high profile in private practice—first as the lead attorney for Al Gore during the 2000 election debacle and later as an expert commentator on CNN on the sex scandal that cost New York governor Eliot Spitzer *his* job.

Florida's law enforcement folk have long treated the law as something malleable, to be molded into whatever shape meets their needs.

In 1836, the Florida Keys' richest and most unscrupulous wrecker, Jacob Housman, got fed up with the restrictions of the salvage court in Key West, the seat of Monroe County. He used his influence with the legislature to create a new county called Dade. He made the county seat the town that was the base of his wrecking operation, Indian Key.

The new county had three county officials: a sheriff, a clerk of court, and a justice of the peace. Part of their pay was based on fines collected for arrests and trials. There was only one problem: They couldn't find any illegal behavior other than Housman's. So the sheriff and the justice concocted charges against "the best and most respected citizens," reported one early settler. "The craziest accusations were made against some of the best people."

Nobody ever went to trial, mind you. It was easier to just pay the fine. The whole thing was handled discreetly, and the sheriff and justice made a bundle—until they were caught.

Sometimes the law was twisted so far out of shape that it seemed like it might snap back. In 1860, Tampa's newspaper reported that the city had been "infested with gamblers, burglars, thieves, robbers and cutthroats" to the point that lawmen could not cope. Fortunately, the paper said, vigilantes had taken the law into their own hands, stringing up anyone deemed a threat. Thus, the paper noted without a trace of irony, "There is not a town or county in the whole South that can boast a more law-abiding people than the city of Tampa." The leader of the lynch mob was a lawyer named John Wall. His peers were so horrified by his embrace of mob rule that they elected him the first president of the Florida Bar Association.

For years cops looked the other way when hookers picked up well-heeled tourists or gambling halls operated in the open. Whatever made the out-of-towners happy made the city's business leaders happy, and so the cops learned to bend the rules to keep the Florida Tourism Machine running on all cylinders. Sometimes they even catered to the tourists' desires personally. In the 1960s, witnesses reported seeing Key West's finest dealing dope—from the police station.

Key West, sometimes known as "Key Weird," has produced some particularly colorful stories of bent lawmen, many of which I heard from Allison DeFoor, a former Monroe County sheriff and judge, famed both for his ability to spin a yarn and for his lack of height. In the 1970s, when DeFoor was a fresh-out-of-law-school prosecutor, he was called to the scene of a stabbing at a rowdy shrimpers' bar. The diminutive DeFoor was, at the time, attending one of Key West's first Fantasy Fests dressed as a plain green M&M (his wife, who was dressed as the peanut variety of M&M, was pregnant at the time—hence the costumes). And so he had to show up at the scene of the crime still wearing his bulky candy outfit. It was preferable, he said, to wearing just the leotard.

When I asked DeFoor about Keys corruption, he told me so many stories so rapidly that after about an hour of taking notes, my pen exploded. My favorite was the Key West police lieutenant who got caught dragging a stolen safe down the middle of Duval Street with help from a city councilman. The cop later became a Mafia button man.

In the 1980s, drug smugglers were dropping off Burger King bags full of cocaine at Key West's city hall, and the FBI labeled the entire police department a "continuing criminal enterprise." The long list of government officials busted for taking drug money included the fire chief, Joseph "Bum" Farto, renowned for wearing all-red suits and rose-colored glasses while tooling around in a green Cadillac with a license plate that said EL JEFE. Before he could be sentenced, Farto disappeared, leading everyone from Jimmy Buffett to tourists at Mallory Square to wear T-shirts asking WHERE IS BUM FARTO?

Trying to tell the good guys from the bad guys has always been tough in Florida. In 1961, a TV show called *Everglades!* aired, created by the same folks who made *Flipper* and *Sea Hunt*. It starred Ron Hayes as a cop patrolling the River of Grass in an airboat. The show—which also featured future stars Dawn Wells and Burt Reynolds—had for its technical adviser and occasional Hayes stand-in a former game warden named Sigsbee Walker. What the show's producers didn't realize was that Walker was also Florida's biggest moonshiner and alligator poacher. It was like casting Al Capone as Eliot Ness.

The good-guy/bad-guy confusion only got worse in the cocaine cowboy era. At one point, some undercover cops in Miami who were masquerading as drug dealers busted a group of drug dealers who were masquerading as cops.

But one pair of bent Florida cops did more to change the TV landscape than *Cops* and *Miami Vice* combined.

John Sion couldn't sleep. He tossed and turned until, at 2:50 A.M. on this spring night in 1977, the college student got up and switched on the ham radio he loved so much.

Voices floated out of the speaker. At first Sion, reading a book, didn't pay attention. Then he heard one say, "The numbers didn't work . . . I got it open anyway . . . The registers are empty." Sion realized he had stumbled onto a burglary. He grabbed a cassette and taped more than seven minutes of chatter.

Sion gave a copy to a police buff neighbor, who passed it along to a Miami Beach detective. The cops who listened to Sion's tape were shocked. They recognized the voices. The burglars were two colleagues, Noel Chandler and Robert Granger.

The Miami Beach PD has had a long and occasionally spectacular run of crooked cops, starting with the chief who in 1925 was convicted of running a dope ring. But this was something beyond even that.

The case landed in the hands of a state attorney's investigator named Martin Dardis. Just five years before, Dardis had broken open the Watergate scandal, although he rarely gets credit for it. Dardis—not Woodward and Bernstein—traced money found on the Watergate burglars through a Miami bank to Richard Nixon's Committee for the Re-Election of the President, which led to uncovering the rest of Nixon's misdeeds.

By walking the streets mentioned on Sion's tape and chatting with business owners, Dardis figured out that the cops were breaking into businesses that Chandler visited while on duty. Chandler would return after dark to break in while Granger stood lookout, the two communicating via walkie-talkies. They drove to the scene of one break-in in a squad car they'd checked out from the police motor pool.

Nailed by Dardis, the pair hired an attorney named Joel Hirschhorn, whom the *Herald* described as "the finest pornography lawyer in Miami." A jury convicted them in 1977, but Hirschhorn appealed over a fairly new legal issue. He objected to TV stations filming the trial.

Because of the development of smaller, quieter cameras, Florida's supreme court had approved a year-long experiment with allowing TV cameras in trials. Stations needed the approval of only the judge to film a trial. Throughout 1977, TV stations covered everything from traffic court hearings to supreme court arguments.

One of the first trials to be broadcast produced a classic Florida irony. Facing a murder charge, Ronny Zamora, fifteen, offered a novel explanation for gunning down his eighty-five-year-old neighbor, then driving her Buick to Disney World: he had become so intoxicated by TV violence, he couldn't tell the difference between reality and fantasy. A public TV station broadcast the TV-intoxication trial gavel-to-gavel, and excerpts went out across the country. Everybody—the judge, the prosecutor, the jurors, even the defense attorney—said the TV experiment worked just fine, except for Zamora, who was convicted. He complained that his attorney had turned the trial into a media circus.

During the crooked cop trial, a TV station put a camera in the courtroom and provided pool coverage for another one. Neither broadcast more than about three minutes of the trial. To Hirschhorn, that was enough. He appealed all the way to the U.S. Supreme Court, contending that if a defendant in a televised trial were acquitted, "his unwanted television notoriety will follow him to the grave." News organizations filled the court's in-box with arguments that broader public scrutiny of the courts would help keep a trial fair.

Despite Hirschhorn's argument, in 1981 the Supreme Court approved allowing cameras in state courts. Federal courts still won't allow TV or even still cameras, but state courts let cameras cover nearly everything. Imagine how different American TV would be without coverage of sensational trials like the O. J. Simpson murder case. For a while, an entire cable channel, Court TV, devoted itself to broadcasting trials. And it's all thanks to a couple of crooked Florida cops, a porn lawyer, an insomniac college student, and the guy who cracked the Watergate case.

Like bell-bottoms, Florida crimes go in and out of fashion. In Tampa in the 1920s and '30s, the hot crime (so to speak) was arson. The end of the Florida boom and the start of the Depression left a lot of people unable to afford their houses. Criminals could pick them up cheap and torch them for the insurance. In 1931, one official estimate said 85 percent of all fires in the city were deliberately set.

In the 1960s, the fad became hijacking jets to Cuba. The first one happened in 1961 aboard a National Airlines jet bound for Key West. The plane had just taken off when a Miami electrician named Antulio Ramirez Ortiz walked into the cockpit, put a knife to the pilot's throat, and said, "If I don't see Havana in thirty minutes, we all die."

When the plane landed, Cuban soldiers hauled Ramirez off to prison and sent the jet on to Key West, where it arrived a mere three hours late. In the months that followed, so many Cuba-bound copycats sprang up that by the end of the summer Congress passed its first law against skyjacking.

In recent years, we've seen fads for crack, mortgage fraud, identity theft, meth making, insurance fraud, flakka possession, and pill mills. A *Wall Street Journal* analysis found that three times more stockbrokers in South Florida had red flags on their disciplinary records than in the rest of the United States. They clustered here because there are so many rich old people just waiting to be fleeced.

Amid these crime waves, Florida has played host to a few star-quality criminals. In the 1920s, the Ashley Gang—led by Bonnie and Clyde forerunners John Ashley and his wife, Laura Upthegrove—robbed banks and hid in the Everglades. The one-eyed Ashley (aka the Swamp Bandit) would taunt Palm Beach County's sheriff, sending him bullets with his name written on them. The sheriff vowed to kill Ashley and wear his glass eye as a watch fob.

In 1924, Ashley's teenage nephew put on a long black dress, a white blouse, and a hat with a veil and pulled off Florida's first cross-dressing bank robbery. Not long afterward, deputies nabbed Ashley and three other gang members driving across a bridge over the St. Sebastian River and shot them dead.

The cops swore Ashley and the others had been trying to escape. Thirty years later, the last surviving deputy admitted they had gunned Ashley down in cold blood. In 1926, a despondent Laura Upthegrove drank poison so she could join Ashley in death. They were buried together in a secluded woodland area. It's now in the middle of an upscale subdivision.

Kate "Ma" Barker became the FBI's Public Enemy No. 1 when her gang went on a spree across the Midwest and the South. In 1935, she and one of her sons holed up in Ocklawaha. A dozen agents surrounded the place. A four-hour gun battle ensued. Just as the agents were running out of ammo, the firing from inside ceased. The agents said they found Ma Barker and her son lying lifeless in pools of blood. In 2012, the longtime owners of the Barker house put it on the market for $1 million. The sales brochures played up the fact that the walls still had bullet holes in them.

"It could be a bed-and-breakfast," the broker said. "You could have weddings there." So far, none of that's happened.

Realtors have had better luck with Al Capone's Miami Beach mansion, which has been sold and resold repeatedly. He bought the place for $30,000 in

1928 from one of the Busch family heirs whose fortunes had declined during Prohibition just as Capone's were on the rise. The original Scarface, Capone plotted Chicago's notorious St. Valentine's Day Massacre from his sumptuous Florida home. He threw wild parties around his saltwater pool, annoying nearby neighbors. One story says a neighbor who was friends with President Herbert Hoover told him about the partying gangster. Hoover issued a two-word order to federal authorities: "Get Capone." They did—on income tax charges, not murder.

But the most influential criminal to ever be busted in Florida was a gaunt, jug-eared thief named Clarence Earl Gideon.

Gideon was a drifter with stooped shoulders, glasses, and four felony convictions. His own biographer described him as "a perfectly harmless human being, rather likeable, but one tossed aside by life. Anyone meeting him for the first time would be likely to regard him as the most wretched of men."

Gideon was born in Missouri. After his father, a shoemaker, died, his mother married a man Gideon did not like. He ran away at age fourteen, came back a year later, and wound up in jail because his mother was angry. He spent the next two decades in and out of prison, learning one important lesson along the way: A man facing criminal charges needs a lawyer.

In 1961—ten years after his last arrest—he was charged with breaking into a Panama City pool hall and rifling the jukebox and register. Hauled before a Bay County judge, Gideon had only one thing to ask: "Your Honor, I request this court to appoint counsel to represent me in this trial."

"Mr. Gideon, I am sorry," the judge replied, "but I cannot appoint counsel to represent you in this case. Under the laws of the state of Florida, the only time the court can appoint counsel to represent a defendant is when that person is charged with a capital offense." Because Gideon had not killed anyone, he could not get free legal help.

Gideon did his best to represent himself but was convicted and shipped off to the state prison at Raiford. He did not give up. He filed poorly spelled handwritten petitions to get his conviction overturned. He argued that he deserved to have an attorney arguing for him. Eventually, his crude petitions found a sympathetic audience in Washington.

In 1963, the U.S. Supreme Court ruled for Gideon, guaranteeing that felony defendants throughout the United States had the right to an attorney. Everyone with a TV knows this right, because on every cop show the detectives tell the suspects: "You have the right to remain silent . . . You have the right to an attorney."

Florida quickly enacted a law creating the office of the public defender in every judicial circuit, and other states across the country followed suit.

Gideon won a new trial. With an attorney representing him, he was acquitted. He never got in trouble again. Meanwhile, his story became an award-winning book and then a movie starring Henry Fonda.

Gideon's successful pursuit of justice stands as a testament to what a single person can achieve in the American justice system, wrote Anthony Lewis in the bestseller *Gideon's Trumpet.* His triumph "shows that the poorest and least powerful of men—a convict with not even a friend to visit him in prison—can take his cause to the highest court in the land and bring about a fundamental change in the law."

But Gideon's pursuit wasn't as lonely as everyone believed. He already had help from a lawyer—or rather, an ex-lawyer—named Joseph A. Peel Jr.

Peel had been a West Palm Beach municipal court judge in the 1950s. He was a flashy dresser, always flush with cash, and so crooked he must have needed a corkscrew to get out of bed in the morning. Peel would sign warrants for the cops to raid illicit casinos and then tip off the gamblers. He took payoffs from guys hauling illegal liquor. A local hood had an ambitious plan for Peel to be elected state attorney, then Florida attorney general, then governor.

But another judge found out and threatened to expose him. Peel faced disgrace and disbarment at the hands of Judge Curtis E. Chillingworth.

One June afternoon in 1955, Chillingworth and his wife, Marjorie, vanished from their waterfront cottage in Manalapan. When Chillingworth didn't show up for work, police went to the cottage. They found blood on the staircase to the beach and footprints leading to and from the water.

Five years passed with no arrests, until two hoodlums were busted for a murder in Miami Beach. They confessed to the 1955 Chillingworth killings too. They had kidnapped Chillingworth and his wife, beat the couple, tossed them aboard a boat, roared out several miles into the Atlantic Ocean, wrapped the couple in chains, and tossed them overboard.

"Remember I love you," Chillingworth said to his wife.

"I love you too," she replied, just before the killers threw them into the water.

And why had the killers done this horrible thing? They said they "did it for Joe"—to help Peel keep climbing the ladder to the governor's mansion.

In 1961, Peel was convicted of being an accomplice in the murders and sent to Raiford, where he and Gideon became cellmates. They discussed Gideon's case and the ex-judge agreed to help. As Gideon drafted his appellate motions, Peel looked over his shoulder, telling him what to say.

Defense attorneys still honor the memory of Clarence Gideon, yet no one has suggested a salute to the real brains behind his Supreme Court success—the crooked, murderous Judge Joe Peel Jr., who somehow managed to do at least one noble thing in his wicked life.

A final note: Gideon did not argue his own case in front of the Supreme Court. Instead, the court appointed a brilliant Florida attorney named Abe Fortas to do it. Fortas, a dapper man with a charming manner, was subsequently appointed to the high court.

But Fortas was secretly taking payoffs from another Floridian, corporate raider Louis Wolfson. Nicknamed "the Junkman" because he got his start in his father's Jacksonville junkyard, Wolfson's companies built the Glen Canyon Dam and produced the earliest Mel Brooks and Woody Allen movies. His Harbor View Farm produced Affirmed, the 1978 Triple Crown winner.

In the mid-1960s, the Junkman ran afoul of the Securities and Exchange Commission, and he was sentenced to a year behind bars. Wolfson tried everything to get out of it, including recruiting a Miami radio disc jockey named Larry King to hand a bribe to incoming attorney general John Mitchell (King kept the money to pay his own debts, leading to Wolfson charging him with grand larceny and nearly ruining his long broadcasting career before it really got started).

Wolfson also consulted with Fortas about his case. A foundation Wolfson controlled paid the new justice a $200,000 retainer. When *Life* magazine blew the whistle on this shady setup, Fortas became the only Supreme Court justice to ever resign amid scandal.

Like I said, in Florida it can be hard to tell the good guys from the bad guys. Sometimes they switch sides.

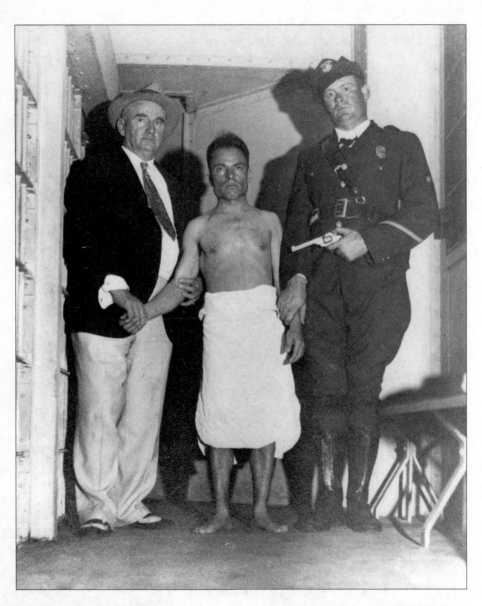

Giuseppe "Joe" Zangara (center), in police custody after his failed attempt at assassinating President-elect Franklin D. Roosevelt in Miami Beach, 1933. His grave marker is made from a license plate blank. Photo courtesy of State Archives of Florida.

Florida, viewed from Space Shuttle Mission STS-95 on October 31, 1998. The far northwestern part of the state is known as the Panhandle. The string of islands at the southern tip are called the Keys. The big blue hole is Lake Okeechobee, and much of the land south of the lake is what's left of the Everglades. Some people think the state is shaped like a gun, others like an uvula or some other body part. (Photo courtesy of the National Aeronautics and Space Administration)

In 1994, at a phosphate mine near Mulberry, a sinkhole that measured 110 feet in diameter and 200 feet deep opened under one of the mine's toxic waste ponds. The water in the pond drained into the the Floridian aquifer, the source of drinking water for Central Florida. (Photo by Mike Pease. Photo courtesy of the *Tampa Bay Times*)

Florida's State Capitol building, built in 1977, viewed from the Historic Capitol next door. The 22-story structure and the twin domes of the House and Senate on either side—designed by noted architect Edward Durrell Stone—won an online contest as the most phallic building in the world. (Photo by Scott Keeler. Photo courtesy of *Tampa Bay Times*)

Gov. Jeb Bush holds a possum he bought for $500 at the annual Wausau Possum Festival in 2002. The festival traditionally attracts politicians on the campaign trail who are looking for a chance to shake hands, pose with babies, get some local press, and bid on one of the animals that according to legend saved the town from starving. (Photo courtesy of Associated Press)

A tour boat rumbles past a manatee swimming just beneath the surface of Three Sisters Spring in Citrus County, 2014. Manatees are so popular with both tourists and residents that more than one person has gotten in trouble for jumping on a manatee's back and trying to ride it like a pony. (Photo by Douglas R. Clifford. Photo courtesy of *Tampa Bay Times*)

Migratory workers gather at a juke joint in Belle Glade in 1944. Note the armed man keeping order. Florida's gift to the world of words is "jook," aka "juke," thanks to the writings of Zora Neale Hurston. Photograph by Marion Post Wolcott for the U.S. Farm Security Agency. (Photo courtesy of the Library of Congress)

Seminole Tribe of Florida president James C. "Jim" Billie at the opening of a museum devoted to Seminole life and culture, in 1997. Billie is a classic Florida character— profane, charismatic, and as wild and unpredictable as a rattler full of Red Bull. A onetime gator wrestler, he has overseen the tribe's rise to power, fueled by money from its pioneering Indian gambling operation. (Photo by Mike Pease. Photo courtesy of *Tampa Bay Times*)

Three University of Florida researchers—from left, Therese Walters, Alex Wolf, and Michael Rochford—hold up a 15-foot-long Burmese python captured alive in the Everglades in 2009. The python weighed 162 pounds. That visible bulge in the middle is a 6-foot alligator that the snake had swallowed before capture. (Photo courtesy of U.S. Geological Survey)

A family's fun day at Pass-A-Grille Beach in July 2015 is interrupted by an approaching thunderstorm. Florida calls itself "the Sunshine State," but many of its cities get more annual rainfall than notoriously soggy Seattle. (Photo by Scott Keeler, courtesy of *Tampa Bay Times*)

A rhesus macaque roaming the backyards of the St. Petersburg area became known as the "Mystery Monkey of Tampa Bay." It evaded capture for nearly four years, but appeared lonely. In this 2010 photo it stares at its own reflection in a backyard art installation. (Photo courtesy of Don McBride)

Leon County Sheriff's Department deputies capture a runaway llama by using their Tasers. On the same 2013 weekend when this occurred, Pasco County deputies used their Tasers on a runaway kangaroo. (Photo courtesy of Leon County Sheriff's Department)

A flotilla of small boats follow a ship full of rich people dressed as pirates about to "invade" downtown Tampa and kick off the Gasparilla Festival's annual drunken bacchanal. The event honors the rapacious pirate Jose Gaspar, who never existed. (Photo by Fraser Hale, courtesy of *Tampa Bay Times*)

Katherine Harris during her doomed U.S. Senate race. Her performance as Secretary of State during the 2000 election debacle imprinted on the public consciousness the idea that Florida is a place full of wacky people—Florida women and Florida men. (Photo by Ken Helle, courtesy of *Tampa Bay Times*)

Sanibel Island's beaches are famous for the variety of their seashells—so much so that the common tourist act of bending over to scoop them up is known as "the Sanibel Stoop." (Photo courtesy of State Archives of Florida)

Thousands of college students on Spring Break throng Daytona Beach, collecting sunburns, hangovers, and the occasional STD. The Spring Break action has more recently shifted to Panama City Beach in the Panhandle. (Photo courtesy of State Archives of Florida)

God's Waiting Room

When I sentence a man to death by electrocution, it's because I think he deserves the shock of his life.
—*Maximum Bob* by Elmore Leonard, who bought his mother a Pompano Beach motel in 1969 and began writing crime novels set in Florida in 1980

Florida's cops have to be ready for anything. Even a relatively simple matter, like finding a stolen car, can lead to discovering the thief is still in it. Also, she's unconscious. And naked.

Or it might lead to the capture of the nation's most notorious serial killer.

Ted Bundy, connected to at least thirty-six murders across the country, was nabbed in Pensacola by a patrolman. The cop spotted a stolen Volkswagen and chased the driver down on foot. Once captured, Bundy told Officer David Lee, "You should have shot me." Later, when detectives asked who he was, he replied, "I'm the most cold-blooded son of a bitch you'll ever meet."

His trials turned out to be quite a circus, with the law school dropout representing himself. While he was on the witness stand, he proposed marriage to another witness, and she accepted. Didn't save him from the electric chair, though.

People joke about Florida being a place where people go to die. It's not just because we have so many inmates on death row (about 400, second only to California). The city where I live, St. Petersburg, used to be nicknamed "God's Waiting Room" because there were so many retirees here, sitting on green benches downtown, apparently biding their time until the Grim Reaper showed up. Some wags use the term for the entire state, because three million of Florida's nineteen million residents are seniors, the densest concentration of elderly folk in the country.

But some of those elderly folks are not waiting around to die. They're living it up more than they ever did up north.

The Native American tribes that inhabited Florida gave us some wonderfully mellifluous place-names, such as Okahumpka, Wewahitchka, Wacahoota, Umatilla, and Sopchoppy. The settlers threw in some colorful ones too, including Yeehaw Junction and my favorite, Two Egg.

But the oddest community in Florida has the blandest name imaginable: the Villages. The place doesn't generate a lot of strange news, which is part of what makes it so weird—even weirder, I would argue, than Gibsonton, the town full of circus retirees that once inspired an *X-Files* episode.

The Villages is the fastest-growing metro area in America and the largest gated over-fifty-five community in the world. It holds more than one hundred thousand residents, in an area bigger than Manhattan. And everyone gets around via golf cart.

The first time I visited, I couldn't believe it. All the businesses had designated cart-parking areas. I saw golf cart paths going everywhere, with golf cart tunnels and a golf cart bridge over major highways.

Why golf carts? Because nobody there needs a car. Everything they could ever want is inside the gates.

Some of the golf carts "cost upwards of $25,000 and were souped up to look like Hummers, Mercedes sedans, and hot rods," Andrew D. Blechman noted in his book *Leisureville: Adventures in a World Without Children*. The most outrageous one I saw had been remodeled to look like an old-fashioned fire truck, complete with a stuffed Dalmatian.

The carts aren't just for traveling around the three dozen golf courses. In 2005, the Villages made it into the *Guinness Book of World Records* for the world's longest golf cart parade by lining up 3,321 of them.

The Villages holds other records. "We have the highest consumption of draft beer in the state of Florida," one Villages official boasted in 2002. It helps that the community has its own microbrewery that pipes beer beneath the streets to its town square restaurants.

Some distinctions they are not so thrilled about. In 2009, the *New York Post* labeled the Villages "ground zero for geriatrics who are seriously getting it on." The story reported that couples had been caught having quickies in the golf carts, which explained a thriving black market for Viagra. A police officer told the paper, "You see two seventy-year-olds with canes fighting over a woman and you think, 'Oh, jeez.'"

One thing alone is forbidden: children. They can visit briefly, but that's it.

"It's amazing that there's a place in America where children get visitors' passes like international visas," Blechman told me. The Villages is "an endless playground for adults, but I only found one playground for children."

Don't get me wrong. Whenever I have visited the Villages, I met retired college professors, retired engineers, retired scientists, all as nice as could be. They taught me a lesson about relativity. I was having lunch with some Villagers in their late sixties and early seventies who told me that in their minds they picture themselves as being in their forties. They pointed out a woman at another table who was in her nineties.

"Now she's *old*," one of them said. Then my lunch companions told me she'd been married three times—so far.

My buddy Jerry has parents who bought a home in the Villages ten years ago. When Jerry visited after they first moved in, the place creeped him out with its Stepford-like uniformity.

"It was like Disney World for old people," he said.

Five years ago, though, he started thinking of it as being "like an expensive party school." (His dad drove one of the Guinness parade golf carts.) Now he thinks of it as being "a landlocked cruise ship. It's got everything you want to do, sixteen hours a day. But then everything shuts down at ten P.M."

If you stroll around and read the historical plaques, as Jerry did, you learn that the area has a fascinating history, full of Indian attacks, epidemics, shipping accidents, and odd characters like the guy who built a lighthouse on a lake and insisted he be called "the Commodore."

Because this is Florida, you are wise to be skeptical about these markers. They are, in fact, a load of hooey, concocted by the developers over a bottle of scotch and a case of beer.

The real history starts with a trailer park and a dream. In the 1970s, a Michigan businessman named Harold Schwartz bought land that became the Orange Blossom Gardens mobile home park. A decade in, Schwartz got his son, H. Gary Morse, to leave a Chicago advertising firm and join him. They put in a golf course and didn't charge residents to use it. The lure of free golf became the first step in drawing tens of thousands of new buyers.

By 1986, they were selling five hundred homes a year and adding more golf courses, pools, clubhouses, recreation centers, theaters, even a hospital. They put up a statue of Schwartz in a Disney-esque pose. After he died, his ashes were deposited inside the statue.

Schwartz used to circulate and glad-hand the residents. Not his son, though—he was as approachable as the Wizard of Oz. For Morse, the Villages became a private mint. He not only sold the residents their houses, he also owned the mortgage company that financed them. He owned all or part of everything worth owning in the Villages, including the bank, the hospital, the utilities, the garbage collection company, the TV and radio stations, and the newspaper, where never is heard a discouraging word about the Villages.

A friend of mine who worked at the paper said they were told never to mention two things:

1. Anything complimentary about President Barack Obama
2. The numerous sinkholes that open up because of all the water being pumped from the aquifer to keep lawns and golf courses green

Thanks to the Villages, Morse became a billionaire. He used his control over the community to build a powerful political base too. Part of it's the money—Morse and his family donated more than $1 million to Mitt Romney during the 2012 presidential campaign. Part of it's the other assets Morse could offer, such as giving candidates free use of his four private jets. The biggest source of his clout, though, was his role as gatekeeper. All the politicians he supported could visit the Villages for a flag-waving campaign stop. Their opponents couldn't get in, and any protesters were kicked to the curb like last season's golf cart models.

According to the Internal Revenue Service, though, the way Morse built this grand empire is about as rock-solid as the sinkhole-prone ground beneath it. Morse financed a lot of construction using something called a community development district, CDD for short. The district levies fees on the homeowners to pay for roads and other improvements. Under state law, it can borrow money using tax-free bonds. The Villages' CDD paid Morse millions of dollars to buy golf courses, guardhouses, and other amenities from him. But the IRS ruled that the Villages' bonds should not be tax-exempt, because everyone on the CDD board—like everything else in the Villages—was controlled by Morse. Those seats are supposed to be filled by residents, the IRS said.

When he died in 2014, Morse had politicians from both parties going to bat for him with the IRS. But his most potent argument came from the residents themselves. According to Blechman, most show little interest in seizing control of their community from a leader they never see. Like most Americans, they're not interested in local politics. Maybe they'd feel differently if, instead of overseeing construction, the board was in charge of dispensing beer and Viagra.

I suspect there are more strange ways to die in Florida than anywhere else. I'm not talking about being cooked to death in a condo sauna or smacked in the face by a leaping sturgeon or getting trapped in a pet door or blowing up in a hyperbaric chamber for horses (yes, those all happened).

I mean a death that's *really* strange, like the incident in 2012 when a man died while winning a Deerfield Beach pet store's roach-eating contest. The first prize was a python. The medical examiner said the man choked on insect parts. Where, I wonder, is *that* box on the official "Cause of Death" form?

One of the most famous cases of "spontaneous human combustion" occurred in St. Petersburg in 1951. A widow, Mary Harder Reeser, went up in flames. The FBI said she fell asleep while smoking, setting fire to her chair, yet no one could explain why a pile of newspapers next to her never ignited.

Sometimes what's unusual is what happens after death. In 1991, after a sixty-five-year-old man died of a heart attack on the sixteenth green of a Winter Park golf course, the police (after some debate) covered the body with a sheet and let other golfers play through.

It could be worse. In 2015, a guy in St. Petersburg buried what he thought was a dead cat in his yard, only to see it five days later wandering around like a zombie.

That cat was lucky. In Florida, acting like the undead can get you killed. Look what happened with Rudy Eugene, who during the Memorial Day weekend of 2012 stripped naked and attacked a homeless man on Miami's MacArthur Causeway, chewing off his face and growling at anyone telling him to stop. Finally a cop shot Eugene and rescued the victim. Initially Eugene's behavior was blamed on a new drug called bath salts, but eventually toxicology tests revealed that the only thing he'd taken prior to getting zombified was plain old Mary Jane.

For Floridians, one frequent cause of death seems to be falling prey to a serial killer. We've had plenty, because our constantly transient population means plenty of potential victims.

Thus we had Aileen Wuornos, dubbed "America's first known female serial killer," a prostitute who let lonely men pick her up, and then murdered at least seven of them. She said she "flat robbed, killed them, and there was a lot of hatred behind everything."

Her case inspired the movie *Monster,* which won star Charlize Theron an Oscar. She continues to attract visitors to the Last Resort, the Port Orange biker bar where Wuornos drank her last beer. In addition to admiring her framed photo, you can buy T-shirts and bottles of hot sauce with her likeness.

We also had the Gainesville Ripper, Danny Rolling, a cop's son who confessed to killing eight people, decapitating one and posing several others to create a more dramatic scene. Rolling's bloody spree inspired Kevin Williamson's script for the movie *Scream,* which rejuvenated the horror genre.

We had Ottis Toole, a Jacksonville native who was convicted of six murders but likely committed more. Among his Florida victims was young Adam Walsh, whose 1981 killing spurred his father, John Walsh, to start the long-running TV show *America's Most Wanted,* which helped round up hundreds of violent criminals nationwide.

But the king was Bundy, whose crimes were so extensive that he's still cited as an argument for capital punishment. He was executed in the grim prison confines in Raiford in 1989. A thousand people ringed the prison, many waving signs that said BUNDY BBQ and COOK HIM! Someone shot off fireworks as if this were the Fourth of July.

So many TV trucks showed up to cover the execution that a prison official said satellite dishes "were popping up like mushrooms in the field." A TV network offered the Florida Department of Corrections $1 million to be allowed to film Bundy dying. The corrections secretary joked, "Cash or check?" before saying no.

Bundy remains the most famous inmate to be executed in Florida's electric chair, a three-legged oak contraption built at a Jacksonville cabinet shop in 1923. The electrode to be attached to the condemned man's leg was made from an old Army boot and some roofing copper. Despite its origin, the chair was regarded as a major technological advance on hanging.

Some wiseguy nicknamed it "Old Sparky," which sounds more like something from a claymation holiday cartoon ("The Night Old Sparky Saved New Year's"). Yet it stuck.

The question of whose job it was to flip the On switch led to some debate. In 1927, a squeamish sheriff refused to do the deed, as did his deputies, as did the prison superintendent. They spent ten minutes bickering over who was supposed to execute the condemned man, Jim Williams. Already strapped in the chair, Williams listened to them argue, meanwhile perspiring hard enough to fill an Olympic-size pool.

Finally, Williams was sent back to his cell until everyone could figure things out. The execution was never rescheduled. Several years later, Williams jumped off a prison truck to save a woman and her child from being gored by a bull, and the governor pardoned him. But forever after, Williams refused to sit in barber chairs because they reminded him too much of Old Sparky.

For a while, the gruesome duty belonged to the prison warden, particularly during a marathon session in 1936 when four men were executed in one day. In 1941, the legislature authorized hiring an executioner. He (or she) always wore a black hood to hide his (or her) identity. That's been the way it has worked ever since.

Among Floridians, Old Sparky became a popular cultural touchstone, something people joked about as if it were a crotchety but colorful old uncle who lived in a town no one ever wanted to visit. I grew up hearing people joke about sending killers to "take the hot squat."

Old Sparky also became a popular prop for politicians wanting to show that they were Tough On Crime. When Tampa mayor Bob Martinez ran for governor as a Republican in 1986, he promised that if he won, "Florida's electric bill will go up." He's the governor who signed Bundy's death warrant, but that didn't help his reelection in 1990.

His successor, the Democrat Lawton Chiles, signed the warrants for seventeen executions during his two terms, including that of Judi Buenoano, "the Black Widow," the first woman ever electrocuted in Florida. She got away with poisoning two husbands and drowning her paraplegic son during a canoe trip, collecting big insurance payouts each time. But when she tried to blow up her fiancé outside Pensacola's fanciest restaurant, her schemes unraveled.

Chiles's record was topped by Jeb Bush, who in eight years signed twenty-one death warrants that were carried out. Bush's successor, Charlie Crist, signed only five—a clear indication he had no plans to stick around for a second term. Gov. Scott tied Bush's twenty-one in November 2014, the most ever in a single term in office, then surged ahead in his second term. It's ironic because when Scott became governor, he had no idea the job description included putting people to death.

In my time covering courts, I visited death row a couple of times to interview inmates. One, an aluminum siding salesman named Oba Chandler, had killed three female tourists and was suspected of killing more. After our interview, he sent me several follow-up letters in which he had dotted his *i*'s with smiley faces.

I also watched a funeral in the prison cemetery, where the inmates unclaimed by their families are buried. All the grave markers are repurposed license plates made by the inmates.

While there, I tracked down the grave of Giuseppe "Joe" Zangara, a bricklayer who in 1933 tried to assassinate President-elect Franklin Roosevelt after a speech at Miami's Bayfront Park. Zangara was unstable, in more ways than one. He perched on a metal folding chair twenty-five feet from the car where

FDR sat. As he took aim, he yelled, "Too many people are starving!" and emptied his pistol.

But a woman next to Zangara, Lillian Cross, grabbed his arm and beat him with her purse, spoiling his aim. Every shot missed FDR. One bullet killed the mayor of Chicago, Anton Cermak, who'd created the Windy City's Democratic political machine.

"I don't hate Mr. Roosevelt personally!" Zangara told the cops. "I hate all officials and anyone who is rich."

Within a month of Cermak's death, Zangara was tried, convicted, and executed, a record that still stands. His last words to the executioner were, "Push the button."

When I located his marker, it showed how far Zangara has fallen into obscurity: His last name was misspelled.

In 1972, the U.S. Supreme Court banned capital punishment, ruling there was no rhyme or reason to how states were putting inmates to death. The states would have to figure out a way to ensure that death sentences were handed out under a consistent policy.

Florida became the first state with a new system, one that requires juries to weigh various aggravating and mitigating circumstances to pinpoint just which defendant merits execution. However, Florida's new rules didn't require a unanimous jury vote to recommend death. A simple 7–5 majority will do. Florida was the only state to allow a split vote to send a person to die—Until the U.S. Supreme Court declared that Unconstitutional in January 2016. That guaranteed a lot more Florida death causes clogging up the appeals courts. Legislators could have changed the system but refused, confusing the promise of fewer death cases with the image of being soft on crime.

As a result, Florida condemns more prisoners to death than nearly every other state. In 2012, Florida judges sent twenty prisoners to death row, nearly as many as the combined total from Texas and California.

Old Sparky fell into disuse after it set not one but two inmates' heads on fire. It is one thing to electrocute killers, and quite another to turn them into human torches.

The next man scheduled to die was Allen "Tiny" Davis, whose nickname saluted the fact that he weighed 350 pounds. Prison officials feared he might crack their historic hot seat, so they built a sturdier version, just for Davis.

The new chair worked as well as the old one. Photos shot during his electrocution were so horrifying that after that nobody wanted to use either of the electric chairs anymore—except the legislature, which could not give up its electrical addiction. In 2000, lawmakers agreed to let inmates choose between two execution methods: electrocution or lethal injection. So far, every condemned man has opted for lethal injection, which has yet to set anyone's head ablaze.

However, one Florida lethal injection did take more than a half hour to carry out and required a second dose to finish it. That led to a 2007 legislative hearing in which the official executioner—testifying via telephone—admitted, "I have no medical training and no qualifications." (Perhaps that's why his patients always died.)

For the next few executions, prison officials added something new that is, to my mind, classic Florida: a man in a purple moon suit who, after the injection, leans over the dying inmate to check for a pulse.

"The man is a doctor," noted AP reporter Ron Word, who in his career witnessed some sixty Florida executions, "and the gear shields his identity—not just from the prisoner's family and friends, but from the American Medical Association, whose code of ethics bars members from participating in executions."

Another reason for hiding your face while helping with an execution: Florida leads the nation in the number of death row inmates who were exonerated, suggesting that in our rush to execute lots of bad guys we sometimes skip over evidence they might be innocent.

How does that happen? One clue lies in the strange career of John Preston and his superstar K-9 helper. In the 1980s, Preston, a former Pennsylvania state trooper, would show up at various Central Florida prosecutor offices and ask if anyone needed help. If the answer was yes, he'd get some details about the crime and then bring out his dog, Harrass II. That dog was a miracle worker, tracking defendants across busy highways months after a crime, or even sniffing out a trail underwater. The evidence was as phony as the Villages' historic plaques, but the jurors bought it and sent innocent men to prison. Since then several have been cleared—one of them based on DNA evidence from a bloody shirt that Preston's dog "proved" the defendant had worn.

No one has ever been punished for using Preston's evidence—not even the dog.

When Florida became a state, it had hardly anyplace to lock up criminals. The jails then were as secure as a wet cardboard box. People were constantly escaping. (The King of Florida Escapees, by the way, has to be James Shearer, who in 1973 broke out of a prison medical unit in Central Florida, made his way to Tallahassee, and stole a car belonging to the secretary of the Department of Corrections.)

After the Civil War, Florida was strapped for cash. Instead of corralling prisoners behind bars, they were rented out. They dug phosphate for fertilizer and, in camps in the piney woods, they cut timber and harvested turpentine.

The turpentine camp operators relied on prison labor for their hard and dangerous work. They would meet with the local sheriff and concoct "a list of some 80 Negroes known to both as good husky fellows, capable of a fair day's work," according to a 1907 account. The sheriff, who had been promised $5 a head, went after the men on the list with a series of Saturday night dragnets, nailing them on charges of gambling, disorderly conduct, assault, anything that sounded good. The judge, who was in on it, sentenced them to the camps.

As in other Southern states that leased convicts, the prisoners were virtual slaves. They worked in miserable conditions and were supervised by men who believed that their punishment should include the infliction of physical pain and poor medical treatment. A book by a former prison guard dubbed Florida the "American Siberia."

Then, in 1921, a white man from North Dakota named Martin Talbert was arrested in Leon County for vagrancy and sentenced to pay $25 or spend three months at hard labor. Talbert's family wired the money, but the county clerk never recorded it. Talbert was hauled off to a Dixie County camp and put to work cutting timber in the swamp. He contracted malaria and God knows what else, suffering headaches, fever, oozing sores, you name it. Because he couldn't do any work, the camp's whipping boss propped him up—on swollen feet—and gave him fifty lashes. He died that night.

His death set off a national uproar, complete with calls to boycott Florida products. The legislature halted the convict-leasing system, although no one was punished for Talbert's death (in fact, the whipping boss killed another worker in 1926). This set the pattern for Florida's uncorrected corrections department.

Take chain gangs, which were introduced in 1919 because there were so many new roads to be built and maintained to accommodate all the tourists pouring into the state. In 1932, a dead prisoner (white, originally from New Jersey) was found in a two-foot-nine-inch-square sweatbox, naked, dangling from his chain, with heavy wooden stocks clamped on his feet. He'd suffered starvation and torture. Camp officials tried to claim his death was a suicide. A national uproar ensued, prompting Gov. Doyle Carlton to complain about "one-sided publicity" that did not paint "a fair picture" of Florida.

Two camp bosses were indicted for murder. One was acquitted; the other was convicted of manslaughter but never served a day. The sweatboxes and leg irons were still in use in the 1940s, when a counterfeiter and safecracker named Donn Pearce served time at the Tavares Road Prison. Pearce later wrote a novel about what it was like, calling it *Cool Hand Luke*. Part of the movie version was filmed in Florida with the prison system's own bloodhounds.

Then, in the 1980s, we tried juvenile boot camps, a military-type basic training program for juveniles. Screaming drill instructors were supposed to teach unruly boys about "discipline" as they ran obstacle courses and chanted, "I used to live a life of crime, now I'm doing boot camp time!"

The first one opened in Manatee County in 1993 and was soon followed by five more—despite the fact that three out of four kids from the Manatee camp were rearrested within a year after they "graduated." Then—as with convict leasing and chain gangs—something happened that exposed the system for what it really was. In 2006, a judge sent a fourteen-year-old African-American juvenile named Martin Lee Anderson to a boot camp in Panama City. During his first night there, Anderson was running laps and collapsed. Seven guards beat and kicked him for thirty minutes, then tried to revive him by shoving ammonia capsules up his nose while holding his mouth shut. He suffocated.

A security camera taped what happened. A national uproar ensued. Efforts to stonewall the investigation and to claim the teenager had died of sickle-cell anemia fueled the anger. Black college students held a two-day sit-in in the office of Gov. Bush, demanding action. Ultimately, the legislature dismantled the boot camp program, and the seven guards were charged with aggravated manslaughter. But an all-white jury acquitted them, as well as a nurse who'd failed to stop the killing. Their defense: They were just following normal boot camp procedures. Afterward, the family's attorney said, "You kill a dog, you go to jail—you kill a little black boy and nothing happens."

Ah, but if it's an *unborn* child? Then you get some action!

In 1974, a year after the U.S. Supreme Court's *Roe v. Wade* decision, a clinic called the Ladies Center opened in Pensacola. By the early '80s, antiabortion activists were picketing the clinic while other people picketed the picketers. Tensions ran high. At one point someone had a heart attack and died during a pro-life march.

I think the eruption occurred in Pensacola because my hometown straddles two worlds: on one hand, the Bible Belt, and on the other, the live-and-let-live freak show that's part of being a Florida beach town, port city, and Navy town. Thus you had a strong economic demand for abortion but a strong religious opposition to it.

The guy leading the antiabortion protests at the Ladies Center was an ex-Klansman named John Burt who had decided Christianity would be his new cause. He opened a home for unwed mothers called Our Father's House. He once showed up for a TV interview toting a fetus in a jar, which he called "Baby Charlie," to the shock of the on-air talent.

On June 25, 1984, someone blew up the Ladies Center. No one was injured, but the clinic had to move. Six months later, on Christmas Day, two devout twenty-one-year-old Pentecostal church members—with no prior criminal records—planted bombs at the Ladies Center as well as the offices of two doctors who also performed abortions. One of the bombers had a girlfriend, the other a wife, both age eighteen. One of the women later said they'd intended the bombings as "a gift to Jesus on His birthday."

They were rounded up quickly once federal investigators traced who had bought the black powder used in the explosives. They confessed they'd been behind the June bombing too.

The manager of the Ladies Center—who had spent Christmas Eve singing in the Presbyterian church choir—called it "terrorism." John Burt, on the other hand, told the *New York Times* that the bombers were just like John Brown battling slavery.

"When the history of this period is written, it won't be the pickets or the letter-writers who will be the heroes," Burt said. "It's going to be the bombers."

The two bombers got ten years in prison, but that did little to discourage further protests. In 1986, an activist named Randall Terry gathered reporters at a Pensacola Western Sizzlin to announce the formation of Operation Rescue, which became one of the nation's largest antiabortion groups.

Operation Rescue's Pensacola leader was Burt, already back picketing the rebuilt and reopened Ladies Center. He and his protesters would show up regularly to scream and yell at the patients entering the clinic from a sliver of land that Burt had bought next door.

Meanwhile, the doctors who had been bombed dropped out. An Alabama doctor named David Gunn started driving over to Pensacola to meet the demand. One of the frequent protesters joining Burt in yelling at Gunn was Michael Griffin, a former chemical plant worker. In March 1993, while Burt led chanting protesters in front of a clinic, Griffin chased Dr. Gunn down in the back and shot the unfortunately named doctor.

Gunn's murder marked the first time in the nation anyone had killed an abortion doctor. At Griffin's trial, his attorney argued that his client had been brainwashed by Burt, but the jury didn't buy it. The pro-life killer was sentenced to life in prison.

Another doctor stepped in to provide Pensacola abortions. Some people who did not like terrorism volunteered to take turns escorting him for his safety. In July 1994, a tall, sandy-haired former minister named Paul Hill waited outside the Ladies Center for Dr. John Bayard Britton and his escorts, a retired Air Force officer named James H. Barrett, seventy-four, and Barrett's wife, June, sixty-eight, a retired nurse. As the trio pulled into the parking lot in a pickup truck, Hill raised a twelve-gauge shotgun. He blasted away four times, killing Barrett but only wounding the doctor. He stepped closer and fired four more times, killing the doctor and wounding Mrs. Barrett. Police nabbed him moments later.

"One thing is for sure!" he yelled as the handcuffs went on his wrists. "No innocent babies will die in that clinic today!"

I was there for Hill's first court appearance, which occurred in a tiny hearing room in the jail. Rather than spouting slogans or quaking at his fate, the former minister struck me as behaving like a man who has wandered into an appliance store to buy a new toaster but can't make up his mind which brand he prefers. When the judge asked if he needed an attorney, Hill smiled and said, "I don't know how the system works here, sir. What do you think would be the wisest thing?"

It was a moot point, because Hill all but pleaded guilty. At trial he contended he had to kill those two people to stop the killing of the unborn. After he was sentenced to die—news that Hill accepted with that same air of detachment—he regarded himself as a martyr. He never expressed any remorse, and in a death row interview said he could easily advocate the assassination of the U.S. Supreme Court justices who had ruled in *Roe v. Wade*. He was executed in 2003, on a death warrant signed by pro-life Gov. Bush.

By then, John Burt was headed for prison too. He didn't shoot any doctors or bomb any clinics. He had molested a fifteen-year-old girl who'd been staying at Our Father's House. He died behind bars in 2013, an apt fate for a man whose ranting about the sanctity of life led to the death and ruination of so many others.

But Florida's biggest right-to-life battle didn't involve babies.

In January 2000, a five-day trial took place in Pinellas County's probate court. At issue: over about the future of a young woman who had been in a persistent vegetative state after suffering a heart attack a decade before at age twenty-six. She had left no written instructions about what to do if that ever happened to her.

On one side of the trial was her husband, Michael, who testified that she'd once told him that she never wanted to live like this and would prefer death with dignity. On the other side were her parents and brother, the Schindlers, who insisted she would never have said such a thing and that she still had a chance of being revived.

Only one reporter sat in the courtroom. The husband invited her to visit the patient. That's how a *St. Petersburg Times* reporter named Anita Kumar went to the Palm Gardens nursing home to visit the comatose Theresa Marie "Terri" Schiavo.

"She lay in bed, her head slightly elevated. Her brown eyes darted about the room," my friend Anita wrote. "She blinked. And blinked again. She constantly opened and closed her mouth, often leaving it slightly ajar. She turned her head. She moaned softly. I called Terri's name while sitting to her right. No response. I called her name while sitting to her left. No response. I detected no reaction, no turn toward the voice. Minutes went by, and she remained still and quiet."

Within three years, Terri Schiavo (pronounced SHY-vo) would become the center of a lurid political soap opera the likes of which the nation has seldom seen. The cast included Gov. Bush, President Bush, the legislature, Congress, and the pope, not to mention what seemed to be the entire Internet.

Driving a lot of the uproar was a video posted by her parents. The video appeared to show Terri Schiavo nodding and laughing in response to their commands, even following a balloon around her room with her eyes.

"In the video footage, . . . she certainly seems to respond to visual stimuli," Senate Majority Leader Bill Frist, a heart surgeon, said during a rare Easter weekend congressional session called for the sole purpose of ordering federal courts to save Terri Schiavo. Frist said he was commenting "more as a physician than as a United States senator."

The probate judge who heard the case was George Greer, a quiet and studious jurist (who, as it happened, had been one of rocker Jim Morrison's roommates at Florida State). Unlike Frist, Greer had seen more than the online excerpt of the Schindlers' video. He'd watched all four hours of it and come to a different conclusion. A *St. Petersburg Times* reporter named Steve Nohlgren watched it all too and wrote that the times when the patient appeared to react were "rare compared to the times when Schiavo lies in bed, slack-jawed and seemingly unresponsive, her limbs stiff, her eyes vacant, her hands curled in tight contractions." The editing had made all the difference.

When Greer ruled for the husband, ordering the feeding tube removed, the decision touched off a furor that reached all the way to the Vatican. The Schindlers appealed to every court they could think of, including the U.S. Supreme Court, and hired Randall Terry of Operation Rescue for $10,000 to act as their spokesman.

The Schindlers were aided immeasurably by Michael Schiavo's own public persona. While he was still married, he had fallen for someone else and fathered a child. People who couldn't pronounce Terri Schiavo's name—or even spell it—gleefully speculated about whether her husband had cheated on her and tried to murder her.

The judge became the target of threats. "I wore a bulletproof vest for months," he said later. Undercover officers guarded him when he went out for a haircut or to grab some lunch, and twice hustled him out of town just in case.

Gov. Bush, who was exchanging e-mails with the Schindlers, pushed for the legislature to give him the power to intervene so he could order the tube reinserted. Lawmakers passed a bill called "Terri's Law," in effect giving Bush the power of life and death over Mrs. Schiavo, regardless of Greer's ruling. The bill, which Bush called "an act of compassion," was voted on and signed into law in less than twenty-four hours.

The governor promptly ordered the tube reinserted. To defend the move in court, he brought in Ken Connor, a past president of Florida Right-to-Life who had run against Bush for governor in 1994, then became an adviser Bush consulted on judicial appointments.

"He authorized us to advocate with vigor and aggressiveness," Connor said later. "He staked out a position rooted in principle and he never wavered—even though he came under intense criticism from the media and several other quarters."

Florida's supreme court ruled that "Terri's Law" was unconstitutional. Bush wouldn't give up. He ordered the state's Department of Children and Families to petition the court to put the feeding tube back in while they investigated whether Mrs. Schiavo had been abused (she hadn't, and the court said no).

Then Congress stepped in, trying to force the federal courts to take charge of a case that clearly belonged in state courts. After Congress passed a Schiavo bill, President George W. Bush could easily have signed it while vacationing at his Texas ranch. Instead he flew back to Washington, D.C., to do it in the media spotlight.

But while Congress was debating the bill, a Florida senator, Mel Martinez, did a very Florida thing. Martinez, a Republican, accidentally passed along to a Democratic senator a memo from one of his staffers talking about how this Schiavo case was "a great political issue." The Democratic senator, of course, immediately leaked it to reporters.

The Martinez memo—which misspelled Schiavo's first name and also gave the wrong number for the pending bill—contended the case would be great for the GOP: "This is an important moral issue and the pro-life base will be excited that the Senate is debating this important issue."

Except it wasn't such a great issue after all. Polls showed a majority of Americans thought the government should butt out of such an important family decision. On the plus side, *Time* magazine reported, "Suddenly, couples gathered around the dinner table or getting ready for bed were discussing how they would want to be treated near the end of their life and making plans to draft a living will and appoint a health-care proxy."

Despite the urging of Congress and the president, a Tampa federal judge and an Atlanta appeals court both refused to take the case, and the U.S. Supreme Court passed on it five times. All the GOP politicians who, for once, wanted activist judges to jump in and force a federal decision on a state official were left disappointed.

Outside the Hospice House Woodside in Pinellas Park where the patient lay wasting away, a circus had sprung up—people singing, people praying, people chanting. There was "a man playing 'Amazing Grace' on a trumpet as a pickup truck pulled a trailer bearing 10-foot-high replicas of the stone Ten Commandments tablets and a huge working version of the Liberty Bell," the AP noted. To cap off the spectacle, a Georgia juggler drove down with his wife and children to toss his silver clubs in front of the hospice.

"God told me to come and juggle," he explained.

By the end, the Schindlers became desperate. They filed an affidavit that claimed one of their attorneys had grabbed Mrs. Schiavo by the arms and demanded she speak if she wanted to live. Her affidavit said the patient said, "Ahhhh waaaa," which they contended was her trying to say, "I want to live!" It might as well have been "To blave," from *The Princess Bride*. Judge Greer rejected that.

At last, on March 31, 2005, Terri Schiavo quietly starved to death, her husband and his brother by her side, her parents waiting nearby to see her. The medical examiner conducted an autopsy. His findings said she had been in a persistent vegetative state, with no hope of recovery. But there was more—a coda that exposed how very Florida this had been.

"Her vision centers of her brain were dead," the medical examiner wrote. "Therefore, Mrs. Schiavo had what's called cortical blindness. She was blind, could not see."

So there's no way she could have been looking over at her parents at their command or, for that matter, following a balloon with her eyes. In fact, when a writer for *Slate* watched the video all over again, he noticed something that had escaped the attention of Dr. Frist and everyone else: "What's striking in retrospect is what you can't see: the balloon. Without it, you can't tell whether she's following it. In fact, her eyes dart back and forth too quickly to reflect the movements of a balloon, even if it were jerked by a human hand."

You could call it a classic Florida con job, but even the people behind it were fooled.

For most of the combatants, the war was over. Michael Schiavo was at last free to remarry. The Schindlers started a foundation in their daughter's name to watch out for other disabled people. Randall Terry moved to Jacksonville to run for the legislature (he lost). The juggler packed his clubs and went home.

But one person could not let it go. Gov. Bush contacted the Pinellas-Pasco State Attorney's Office to ask for a new investigation regarding Terri Schiavo. Specifically, he wanted a look at how much time elapsed between when Mrs. Schiavo collapsed from her heart attack and when Michael Schiavo dialed 911. The implication was clear: Michael Schiavo had dawdled, hoping she'd die.

Two top prosecutors—men who had handled every kind of high-profile case, including Oba Chandler's triple homicide—looked at the evidence and said, "It is obvious to us that there is no possibility of proving that anyone's criminal act was responsible for Mrs. Schiavo's collapse." They noted they had done a similar review in 2003 at the request of the Schindlers.

Only then did Bush give up. In 2015, while he was gearing up to run for president, someone asked him if he regretted inserting himself in the Schiavo case and causing a constitutional crisis. He said no.

"It was one of the most difficult things I had to go through," he added. "It broke my heart that we weren't successful at sustaining this person's life, so she could be loved by her mom and dad. But the courts decided otherwise, and I was respectful of that."

In 2007, *USA Today* published a list of twenty-five lives that had had an indelible impact on the modern world. Terri Schiavo ranked at no. 12, just below Mother Teresa and talk show maven Oprah Winfrey. A year later, during a televised debate among presidential contenders, one of the senators who'd voted for getting a federal court to second-guess Judge Greer was asked if there was any vote he'd like to take back. He named that one.

"I think that was a mistake and I think the American people understood that that was a mistake," Barack Obama said. "And as a constitutional law professor, I knew better."

That's the thing about Florida: You live and you learn. And, if you go to a particular Florida educational institution, you take off all your clothes.

Children walking to school in rural Dade County, 1937. Note their footwear, or lack thereof. Photo courtesy of State Archives of Florida.

Schoolhouse Rock

I leave you love. I leave you hope. I leave you the challenge of developing confidence in one another. I leave you a thirst for education. I leave you a respect for the use of power. I leave you faith. I leave you racial dignity. I leave you a desire to live harmoniously with your fellow men. I leave you, finally, a responsibility to our young people.
—Inscription on Washington, D.C., statue of Mary McLeod Bethune, Florida educator

When Floridians talk about education, everyone's in favor of it, but hardly anyone wants to pay for it. That's especially true of the millions of retirees who have moved south for the sunshine. They figure they paid their share of school taxes up north. Now their children are grown and they are uninterested in spending a dime on anyone else's brats.

Nevertheless, Florida has managed to be a bold national leader in education. Take our public universities. We have a dozen now, scattered around the state, some apparently set up just to provide jobs for ex-legislators so they can keep drawing a state salary from a place to which they steered a lot of state dollars.

One beneficiary of this was Mike Haridopolos, who while climbing to the post of Senate president was paid $152,000 by Brevard Community College to write a book called *Florida History & Legislative Processes*. Although billed as a "scholarly work," the *Orlando Sentinel* described his 2006 masterpiece as "a 175-page double-space manuscript padded with inane observations" such as the need for candidates to carry cell phones and make sure their names are legible on campaign signs. Haridopolos claimed to be interested in cutting wasteful spending, yet he never returned the money he got for his boondoggle book.

One university-employed politician who's still in office is Sen. Marco Rubio, who teaches political science at Florida International University. He was hired at a time when the university was cutting programs and had laid off two hundred employees. The students seem to like him, though.

Some of our universities have experimented with programs that don't involve hiring politicians. For instance, the Florida Institute of Technology encourages its ocean engineering students to surf for credit. I think the class is called Hang Ten 101.

The universities grabbing the most headlines are the University of Florida, Florida State University, and the University of Miami. A lot of those headlines concern their sports teams, because sports are a Big Deal here. FSU's head football coach, a grown man named "Jimbo," makes way more than the governor—$5 million a year, not counting any attorney referral fees for his players. Meanwhile the college has yanked the phones out of some professors' offices and unscrewed the bulbs in campus buildings to save money.

There is always a lot of excitement over the annual matchup between the FSU Native American Stereotypes and the UF Giant Reptiles with Brains the Size of Olives. The UM Natural Disasters can only dream of generating such merchandise sales—er, I mean, passion.

But if you think these universities are producing nothing but halfbacks and point guards, think again. The University of Florida has crackerjack scientists working in different disciplines—although their most famous discovery is a drink that seems to be more frequently poured out than consumed.

In the summer of '65, a UF assistant coach met with four of the university's physicians. Football players kept wilting in the Florida heat, then getting sick. Could science help? Kidney specialist Dr. Robert Cade and his research team picked ten players for testing. The players were cooperative—for the most part.

"They would not consent to having practice stopped so we could measure their body temperatures rectally," Cade said.

Cade's team determined that the fluids and electrolytes that players lost through sweating were not replaced by merely drinking water. The carbohydrates that the players expended were not being replaced either. Cade's crew came up with a new carbohydrate-electrolyte beverage to be used during games. Because the UF team is the Gators, they called their concoction "Gatorade."

Guzzling Gatorade, the Gators finished that season with a 7–4 record. The next season they racked up a record of 9–2 and won the Orange Bowl for the first time. Soon other teams began buying Gatorade and at some point began dumping coolers of it on the coach's head after a win. Gatorade inaugurated the global sports drink industry, and by 2006 it held more than 80 percent of the $7.5-billion-a-year American market.

But inventing Gatorade is nothing compared to what Florida State created in the early 1970s.

The fiery upheaval of the '60s had brought both turmoil and a newfound sexual freedom to campuses. By the spring of 1973, with the Vietnam War and the Nixon administration both in trouble, college students were ready for a kind of protest that would command attention in the most basic way. At FSU—founded as the West Florida Seminary in 1857—two students cooked up a protest that harked back to Lady Godiva.

Here's how my friend Bill Cotterell, then with United Press International in Tallahassee, tells the story: "The student newspaper, the *Florida Flambeau*, called to tell us it had pictures of two men who jumped from a car and streaked across Landis Green, where another car picked them up. The newspaper was in on the stunt. UPI moved two pictures, carefully cropped so no faces showed but you could tell they were naked. The pictures were used in papers all over the country and shown on a couple network news shows as the closing 'bright' story. By the end of the week, hundreds were dashing around campuses everywhere."

What were those nude students protesting? Hard to say. When you're running naked, it can be difficult to hold a picket sign.

Nevertheless, the fad, known as "streaking," spread rapidly. "Although the exact number of streaks during this time is unknown, one group of researchers gathered data on over 1,000 incidents on U.S. college campuses alone," a historian wrote. "Streaking generated significant press coverage and spawned a plethora of streaker-related consumer items." These included T-shirts, mugs, patches, a "Nixon Streaking" wristwatch, pink underwear embroidered with TOO SHY TO STREAK, and several songs, most notably Ray Stevens's "The Streak."

"I've always taken credit for publicizing streaking," Bill said. "I once told Bob Woodward that he broke Watergate and ran Nixon out of office, but I got thousands of college kids to run around naked, so I felt our career achievement was about equal."

Only one of Florida's presidential hopefuls, Rubio, attended Florida colleges—Santa Fe Community College and the University of Florida, then the University of Miami for law school. Like Jeb Bush and the rest, I did not attend any Florida college, so I have no deep feeling for UF, FSU, et cetera. Instead, my favorite Florida college is—or was—a private, for-profit one in Miami named FastTrain College. It is the most Florida of all the Florida colleges.

According to a federal lawsuit filed in 2014, FastTrain "purposely hired attractive women and sometimes exotic dancers and encouraged them to dress provocatively" to recruit male students. The suit says the college invented this revolutionary recruiting technique to bilk the U.S. Department of Education out of millions of dollars.

Sadly, an FBI raid and a criminal indictment derailed FastTrain.

Education was important to Florida's Spanish colonists. Franciscan friars launched the first religious school in America in St. Augustine in 1606. What's believed to be America's first public school opened there in 1787, serving both white and black students.

When the Spanish departed, interest in education waned until after the Civil War. In the 1870s, Florida at last designated school districts in each county, allowing them to levy taxes to pay for schools, teachers, and textbooks. The man who laid out Florida's school system was state education superintendent Charles Beecher, brother of Harriet Beecher Stowe. When anyone I know complains about Yankee carpetbaggers ruining Florida, I think of Charles Beecher, who made his adopted state a better place to live.

These days when people talk about Florida's schools, they're often talking about Florida's teachers. Florida has some great teachers—selfless people who devote their personal time and hard-earned pennies to improving the lives of young people. Often that involves spending their own money on classroom supplies and working serious unpaid overtime during the school year.

But the most famous teacher Florida has produced is not one of those folks. It's Debra Lafave, who when she hit the limelight was a twenty-four-year-old reading teacher at Greco Middle School in Temple Terrace, near Tampa. Her blond hair and blue eyes made her into a media darling in 2004 even as she faced charges of lewd and lascivious battery on a fourteen-year-old. Her pouty-lipped picture became a fixture on front pages and TV screens around the country. Her attorney said she was too pretty for prison, but her look was just right for a chat with Matt Lauer on the "Today" show. There was talk of an insanity defense, but she ended up pleading guilty to two felonies and serving probation, to the copious disgust of commentator Nancy Grace.

When it comes to learning, I am a fan of the carrot-and-stick approach. Florida already has a carrot for educators by honoring a Teacher of the Year. Clearly what we need is a stick, so I propose we hand out an annual Debra Lafave Bad Teacher Award.

Competition for the Lafave Award is likely to be fierce. Bad teachers are notoriously hard to fire in Florida. Still, we have had teachers fired for having a side job as a bikini model and for having a past career in gay porn. We have had teachers who got in trouble for tapping a student on the head with a banana and for making some kids wear a "cone of shame" dog collar as seen in the Pixar movie *Up*. We have had at least one, a first-grade teacher from Polk County, who faked a fatal illness so she could skip class for an entire year.

We have had some teachers who made headlines because they didn't get along with their students, mocking them as stupid and ugly ("Honey, you look bad every day. Pages will be turning in the yearbook and mirrors will be smashing."). We had others who made headlines by getting along with their students a little *too* well (buying them alcohol, teaching them about twerking, etc.). We have also had teachers who got in trouble for not getting along with other teachers—a Plant City teacher pleaded guilty to trying to hire a hit man to take out a fellow teacher he didn't like. Apparently he was unaware of the rule in Florida that nine-tenths of the people who tell you that they're hit men are actually undercover cops.

Not even a straight-A student can avoid getting sucked into some Florida educational absurdity. In May 2013, a bright sixteen-year-old named Kiera Wilmot was taking her science experiment—it combined toilet bowl cleaner and aluminum foil in a water bottle, creating a small chemical volcano—to be approved by her teacher. Curious friends convinced her to try it first out on a hilltop behind Polk County's Bartow High.

"It did not react the way I expected it to," she said later. "The lid popped off and smoke came out."

Even though she had a sterling record and excellent grades, Wilmot was arrested and expelled for setting off an explosion on school grounds, a charge that somehow ignored the fact that there had been no actual explosion.

The *real* explosion occurred on social media as she became the subject of a worldwide Internet uproar. Scientists rushed to her defense. Ultimately the charges were dropped, she was reinstated, and she and her twin sister were invited to attend the U.S. Space Academy. They graduated together in 2014, with plans to attend Florida Polytechnic Institute—where, presumably, the spirit of scientific inquiry is encouraged, not greeted with handcuffs.

There was a time, decades back, when Florida's best-known educator was Mary McLeod Bethune, a child of slaves who went on to become a teacher, school founder, and one of FDR's advisers. During World War II, she organized the first officers' schools for women. She founded the institution that became

Bethune-Cookman College and served as its president for four years. She also founded the National Council of Negro Women to work on civil rights issues. A statue of her stands in Washington, D.C.

These days, Florida's best-known education expert (other than Ms. Lafave, that is) is Jeb Bush. Yet unlike Mary McLeod Bethune (or Marco Rubio), he never taught a class or presided over a college. His interest in education was purely political.

When Bush first ran for governor in 1994, he was not a skilled politician, so he said what he meant with no attempt at subtlety or subterfuge. When asked what he'd do for black voters, he replied, "Probably nothing." As for the state's educational system, he announced that he planned to dismantle it. Bush had limited personal experience with the public school system—he briefly attended a public elementary in Houston before his mother enrolled him in a private one, and for high school he attended the prestigious Phillips Academy in Massachusetts, where, as he once put it, he "was a cynical little turd at a cynical school." Thus Bush had no feel for how important the public schools might be to parents and kids.

His candor was rewarded by a narrow loss to the Democratic incumbent, Lawton Chiles. His defeat had many causes, but one was that voters disliked Bush's unvarnished hard-right politics.

Bush retreated to his Coral Gables home to figure out his next move. He converted to Catholicism, his wife's faith. He founded a think tank. He traveled the state meeting with minority groups. He visited 250 schools.

Most significantly, he teamed up with the head of the Urban League of Miami to persuade the Republican-dominated legislature to pass a bill authorizing charter schools. In 1996, the two men opened Florida's first charter school. It wasn't in the rich part of Miami-Dade County that Bush called home, either. It was in poor and predominantly black Liberty City.

A charter school is a public school formed by a contract—a charter—between the people running the school and the local school board. In the case of the Liberty City school, it was created through a partnership between the Urban League and Bush's Foundation for Florida's Future. The contract sets out the mission of the school, its performance measurements, its management, financial plan, and overall responsibilities. That leaves the school free to set its own curriculum, discipline methods, parental involvement, and hiring practices. That last became important because the Liberty City school avoided hiring anyone in the teachers' union. Bush had no love for the union, seeing it as a major Democratic Party supporter. To him anything that undercut the union was good.

The teachers' union objected to Bush's school, "mostly because they put [the proposal] together in two weeks," a union official with the delightful name Merri Mann recalled in 2000. "We were like, why are we putting this through so fast?"

The school board staff wanted to rush Bush's approval because they knew he was going to run for governor again. Sure enough, when he did, he touted his Liberty City school experience. When he gave reporters tours, the kids would mob him. Bush gave every appearance of being concerned about poor children.

He was particularly proud of the fact that the school focused as much on character—manners, hygiene, ethics, and respect for elders—as on academics.

"I think it's something that parents want," he said, "but the attitude at many public schools seems to be that we're too busy teaching other things to work on character education. I think that's wrong."

In his 1998 campaign, instead of calling for dismantling the educational system, Bush was now touting a far-reaching reform called the A+Plan. He based everything on the results from the new Florida Comprehensive Assessment Test—the FCAT, or "eff-cat," as everyone immediately dubbed it, much to the chagrin of felines everywhere. Test results would be tied to a grading system for the schools themselves.

Schools where students scored well on the test would get state incentive money to do more, and the teachers might even get bonuses. Students at schools that received F's for two out of four years would not have to stay there. Instead they would become eligible for vouchers that their parents could use to pay the tuition at private schools, or they could transfer to other public schools within their district. Meanwhile, though, third graders might not get promoted and high school seniors might not graduate.

Bush won this election, and also won more power over the educational system than any previous governor. Voters endorsed not only Bush but also a constitutional amendment shrinking the state's seven-member cabinet to four. One of the positions that disappeared was the elected education commissioner. Now the person who filled that post would be appointed by the governor.

Bush resigned from his charter school, and, with the eager help of the legislature, soon had implemented his changes, including launching the largest statewide voucher system in the United States.

Bush's A+Plan was based on the ideal of accountability through testing. But a funny thing happened at the school he'd cofounded. In 1999, the first year of Bush's program, the Liberty City Charter School scored a D.

Its students scored 24 on the state's FCAT comprehensive reading test and 45 on the Florida Writes test. By contrast, the state average for schools was 70 for the reading test and 73 for the writing test. State statistics showed

Liberty City did worse than most of the traditional public elementary schools its students might have otherwise attended.

You could hear the chortling of teachers' union officials from Pensacola to Key West.

"It's very ironic that in this world, where everyone is more closely scrutinized and we're all struggling to meet higher standards, that this school that was set up as a model of how it should be done is a failure," a union official said.

"When people are trying to serve low-income students that historically don't perform as well academically, obviously when the school first starts their grades may not be at the top," Bush's spokesman said. Not mentioned was another possibility: The school had spent too much time on manners and not enough on academics. Also not mentioned: cutting the same amount of slack to other schools full of poor students.

Nevertheless, Bush forged ahead with remaking the Florida schools into a place ruled not by reading levels or graduation rates but test scores. Everything began to revolve around the FCAT. Teachers taught nothing but what would be on the FCAT. Other tests proliferated, to measure pieces of what the children were supposed to know. Testing became so important that some districts devoted a third or more of their school year to it.

Some teachers, fearing for their jobs, succumbed to the temptation to cheat, helping their students score well—until they got caught. Meanwhile the state Education Department wasn't grading the tests. Instead, it had followed the Bush plan and privatized the work, hiring a contractor. In turn, the contractor had hired as test graders "janitors, homemakers, and store clerks," one paper reported. Many of the graders had zero experience in education and no degree in the subject they were grading. It was not a situation that inspired parent confidence.

To top it all off, a science teacher named Robert Krampf discovered some of the official answers were wrong. Worse, on some of the multiple-choice questions, he said, there was more than one right answer.

"I wonder how many students got 'wrong' answers on the FCAT because their teachers taught them too much. How many F schools would have higher grades if those scientifically correct 'wrong' answers were counted as correct answers? How many B schools would get the extra funding that A schools get, if those scientifically correct 'wrong' answers were counted as correct answers?" Krampf wrote on his blog.

Krampf tried in vain to warn state officials about the errors. He spent nearly a year feuding with them via increasingly snarky e-mails before they at last acknowledged the problem and fixed it.

Bush's A+ Plan suffered other setbacks. The Florida Supreme Court said his voucher program was unconstitutional, and he was caught on tape bragging about his "devious plans" to undo a constitutional amendment capping the size of classes.

But he stuck to his goals, achieving results that were, at best, mixed. By the time he left office in early 2007, "fourth-grade reading scores in the state had improved sharply, though eighth- and tenth-grade scores were more middling," the *New Yorker* reported in 2015. Since then, "gains in test scores at all levels have been relatively incremental; graduation rates have steadily increased, but they remain among the nation's worst."

Bush was done being governor, but he wasn't done with education. He became the leading evangelist for his brand of market-based, results-oriented schools. He created a new think tank named the Foundation for Excellence in Education (FEE! for short), then traveled the country preaching his pro-testing, pro-privatization gospel. Such a national effort wasn't cheap, but Bush was backed by some big-bucks contributors—the companies making lots of money off the government contracts that became available when a state switched to what Bush was touting.

Bush's longtime advocacy of testing ran into trouble, both nationally and in Florida, in 2014. Tea Party activists decried the part of Bush's plan that called for central government control over local school standards, a system known as Common Core. Meanwhile, Florida parents and school officials rebelled against Bush's system, calling for an end to all the testing. In 2015, the state dumped the FCAT and switched to a new test that had never been tried in Florida. A series of computer glitches repeatedly interrupted testing days, and by spring some of the largest school districts were canceling most if not all of their standardized tests. Just as Bush was warming up for his run for president, his signature achievement as governor had become about as popular in Florida as running barefoot down a hill covered in sandspurs.

The one part of Bush's educational legacy that's become the biggest success was the one that got him started. Charter schools have proved extremely popular. Heck, even Miami rapper Pitbull has one.

But they have also become a colossal headache for the school districts. I'm not just talking about the Palm Beach County charter school whose married principal was caught in a car with marijuana and an eighteen-year-old. When a cop opened the car door, the principal, caught with her shirt unbuttoned, quickly said she didn't know the teenager. The eighteen-year-old, meanwhile, told a different story—one that Debra Lafave would have recognized.

No, for the school districts the problem presented by the charter schools is much broader than one overly friendly principal. A newspaper investigation found that a lot of the charters were run by fly-by-night operators who went belly-up after a year or two, costing the school districts more than $1 million because the owners never returned any taxpayer money. The paper calculated that 119 charter schools had closed between 2008 and 2014, sending some fourteen thousand students back to the traditional public schools they'd been in before.

Among the charter schools that closed: the one Bush cofounded. It at last earned an A rating in 2007, then in 2008 tumbled down to a C just in time to shut down for good. What did the school in was not its rating. It was that it had gone $1 million into the red.

The most Florida aspect of these Florida charter schools is the way the law has been flipped on its head. The law requires the charter schools to be run by a nonprofit organization. Yet a majority of them—including Pitbull's—are run by a for-profit company called Academica. It's now one of the largest charter school management companies in the country, running charters from Georgia to California.

To slide around the law, Academica and its imitators create a nonprofit foundation to operate each school, and the foundation hires Academica to build the school, run the school, and hire principals and teachers to work at the school. Academica and its affiliates also serve as the schools' landlord, raking in millions in lease payments. Investigations have identified some of these deals as a conflict of interest, but Academica's officers and attorney deny it.

The charter school nonprofit switcheroo shouldn't be a surprise. After all, it's sort of what happened with the brilliant idea Florida legislators cooked up to guarantee Florida schools would always get enough money. It was an idea that was rooted in the basic Florida attitude toward everything involved in living here: namely, that it's all one big gamble.

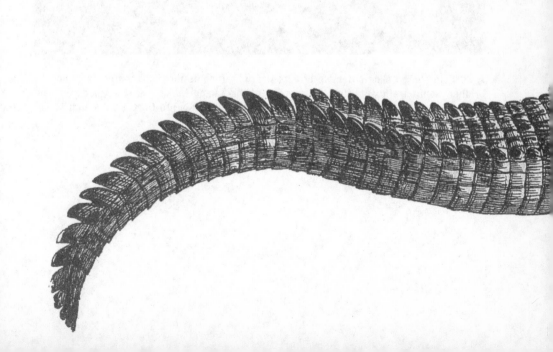

A St. Petersburg police detective arrests Henry Trafficante for running a bolita game. His brother, Santo Trafficante Jr., was the don of the Tampa Mafia and controlled gambling throughout much of Florida, as well as sharing the casinos in pre-Castro Cuba with Meyer Lansky. Photo courtesy of the *Tampa Bay Times*.

12

You Bet Your Life

Gambling is unknown among them.
——"Seminole Indians of Florida,"
report to Congress, 1921

Ah, Publix! The homegrown grocery chain hailed as one of the best things about Florida! The place with the deli subs that BuzzFeed raves about! The supermarket that says it's where shopping is a pleasure (and never mind about those racial and sexual discrimination lawsuits, or the occasional brawl involving the store manager, his wife, and his girlfriend). Also, it's the largest employee-owned company in the United States.

Ah, Publix! The place where so many deluded dreams are born, where so many of us Floridians stand in the line to buy Florida lottery tickets. Ah, scratch-off! Ah, Quick Pick! Ah, Powerball! Ah, shoot, I lost again.

I walked into my neighborhood Publix one night in 2012 and immediately spotted a man in the line for Powerball tickets who was far better dressed than the usual gamblers. The lottery line offers a cross section of the Sunshine State's poor to middle-class residents: young and old, fat and skinny, gay and straight, white, black, Hispanic, Asian, you name it. This guy had deeply bronzed skin, white hair, a classic blue blazer, expensive slacks, and tassel loafers. The other folks in line were chatting with him, snapping pictures of him with their phones.

"Hello, Governor," I said to ex-governor Charlie Crist, aka the Tan Man. He gave me his broadest smile, the one so bright it could be the bulb atop a lighthouse. When I asked what he was doing there, he reached for the oldest cliché possible: "You can't win if you don't play."

Someone else asked him what the state could do with the money if Florida itself won the jackpot. He shot back: "We could pay our teachers better!"

Ah, the irony. The justification for starting the Florida lottery in 1987 was to raise money for education—but it turned into a classic Florida shell game. Once the lottery money started pouring in, the legislature siphoned off money from the original education budget to spend it elsewhere. To make up the difference, local school boards would have to raise taxes, which in Florida is a no-no. Schools wound up worse off than before.

Lottery money that does go to education doesn't go to elementary, middle school, or high school classrooms. Instead, it's been primarily spent on college scholarships and school construction. Meanwhile, to assure everyone the games are honest, lottery officials hired as an inspector general a former cop once accused of (but never charged with) participating in a home invasion. Somehow he didn't catch that eighteen stores were selling tickets that produced a mathematically impossible number of winners. One player collected 568 times in fifteen months.

That's the Florida way, of course: Step right up and try your luck at a crooked game! Every Florida resident knows this is happening. Yet all we do is grumble about it, usually while standing in line to buy tickets.

Living in Florida is a daily gamble anyway, what with the sharks and sinkholes and lightning strikes. Thus it shouldn't be a surprise that Floridians are inclined to throw away—excuse me, *risk*—a lot of money on games of chance. In addition to the lottery, we've got horse racing and dog racing and jai alai. But bring up the idea of allowing casinos to set up here (a move backed by one part-time resident named Donald J. Trump), and listen to a lot of people start howling (including Jeb Bush). The voters have repeatedly shot that down.

Instead, we have cruise ships that take gamblers into international waters, where they can sail around and lose money playing slot machines, roulette, and baccarat all night, then return to port. Florida has more of these Cruises to Nowhere than any other state, and don't tell me that's not symbolic.

We Floridians have always had mixed emotions about gambling, condemning it even as we embrace it. Back before Florida became a state, all gambling was illegal, yet Floridians frequently entertained themselves by betting on horse races, dog fights, cock fights, cards, dice, and spinning wheels. There were times during that era, one historian noted, "when gambling seemed to overshadow all other illegal activity."

The legal system did little to discourage it. Grand juries might indict a score of gamblers, but seldom were they ever punished. Too many jurors were players.

In those days the state was infested with crooked faro dealers, toting their rigged layouts from town to town, fleecing the unwary and hustling away.

The itinerant gamblers tended to show up in a town anytime a crowd of suckers ripe for the plucking did. They always flocked to Tallahassee when the territorial legislature was in session.

The gambling bug didn't fly away after Florida became a state. Gambling became a way for Floridians to entertain tourists and separate them from their money. What could be more Floridian than that?

Gambling in Florida went from a trade practiced by shifty fly-by-nighters to a key part of the tourism industry thanks to Henry Flagler. To him, gambling was one more amenity for his well-heeled customers. As he worked his way down the coast, every time he built a new hotel, he also built both a church and a casino nearby. Now *there* was a man who knew how to hedge his bets.

In 1898, one of Flagler's pals, a Kentuckian named Col. Edward Riley "E.R." Bradley, and his brother John opened an opulent gambling casino near a Flagler hotel in Palm Beach. The casino offered an unparalleled cuisine as well as games of chance, yet by the end of the first year the Bradleys were ready to fold. One night, after a rather dull dinner party, as the tycoons were about to head for the gaming room, their wives clamored to accompany them. The Bradleys agreed to admit the women. Word got around and their business suddenly boomed. Before long their establishment became known as "the greatest gambling house that ever operated in this country."

Bradley's Beach Club had a few rules: No single women were allowed in, no one younger than twenty-five, and alcohol was sold only with meals. The most important rule: Nobody from Florida was allowed in. The colonel feared locals might testify in court about what they saw. Better to target the tycoons from up north taking their leisure at Flagler's resort, men who could afford to lose big.

The Beach Club ran for almost fifty years, longer than any other illegal casino in the country. Occasionally some ambitious prosecutor or policeman raided the joint. Inevitably, Bradley—who made generous contributions to local charities and politicians—was tipped off, so when the cops kicked in the door, the gambling tables had been folded away and the customers were sipping tea or dancing to the orchestra. Bradley didn't have to worry about nosy reporters poking around either, because he bought both local newspapers.

The casino didn't close until he died in 1945. Frequent visitor Joseph P. Kennedy lamented that Palm Beach had "lost its zipperoo," whatever that meant.

Bradley's casino wasn't the only ritzy Florida gambling establishment that the authorities ignored. Early in the 1920s, aviation pioneer Glenn Curtiss and cattleman James Bright created a new town called Hialeah. Their town offered water and electricity, a dance hall, a roller coaster, an official snake catcher (they built a tad close to the Everglades) and, to attract the suckers, gambling galore.

They opened America's first pari-mutuel greyhound track, following it with the nation's first jai alai fronton. Then, in 1925, they opened Hialeah Park, a one-mile track for horse racing. It went on to become an institution in the Sport of Kings. Seabiscuit raced for the first time at Hialeah, and there's a statue of Citation. In time it attracted everyone from Will Rogers to Frank Sinatra. Winston Churchill called the track "extraordinary."

The Hialeah track was badly damaged by the Great Miami Hurricane in 1926, but a few wealthy men—including Col. Bradley—stepped in, bought out its founders, and renovated the place. Among their changes: importing more than a hundred flamingos from Cuba to hang out by the infield lake, giving the track a particularly colorful touch (one that later showed up in the *Miami Vice* credits).

None of this was legal, of course. But in the depths of the Depression when Florida became desperate for revenue, the legislature voted to legalize wagering on horse and dog races so they could tax the proceeds.

Gov. Doyle Carlton said gamblers offered him a big bribe to sign the bill—$100,000. He refused, but it didn't matter. The legislature overrode his veto. Four years later they legalized betting on jai alai too, and for a while they even allowed slot machines. By 1937, there were twelve thousand slots ringing bells all over the state, yielding an estimated $60 million annually.

But the casinos, the horse tracks, the frontons—those were originally designed to appeal to the wealthy snowbirds. The games that filched pennies from the poor were the ones that really had an impact on the rest of the country, thanks in part to Florida's toughest writer.

Over the years, Florida has served as a refuge and a muse for plenty of writers—science fiction authors Piers Anthony, Jeff VanderMeer, and Hugh Howey; young adult authors Judy Blume and John Green; thriller writers Charles Willeford, Randy Wayne White, and Paul Levine; and modern novelists such as Edwidge Danticat, Lauren Groff, Meg Cabot, and Connie May Fowler.

When I say "Florida's toughest writer," you probably think I mean Hemingway, who loved to take a poke at a passing poet (sorry, Wallace Stevens!). Or you might think I mean Carl Hiaasen, who was a hard-nosed investigative reporter before he became a columnist and author.

It's neither. I believe the darling of the Harlem Renaissance, Zora Neale Hurston, could whup them both.

Hurston grew up in Eatonville, one of the few Florida towns back then with a black mayor and marshal. During the Depression, she traveled around the state collecting folklore for FDR's Works Progress Administration. She hit the phosphate mines, sawmills, and turpentine camps—places far from civilization. She knew that was where she'd find plenty of songs and stories, as well as plenty of trouble.

"All of these places have plenty of men and women who are fugitives from justice," she wrote. She found they were "quick to sunshine and quick to anger. Some little word, look, or gesture can move them either to love or to sticking a knife between your ribs." As a result, her life "was in danger several times."

Sometimes she packed a pistol, but mostly she relied on her quick wit. "If I had not learned how to take care of myself in these circumstances, I could have been maimed or killed," she wrote.

She'd drive into camp and tell people that she "was also a fugitive from justice, 'bootlegging.' They were hot behind me in Jacksonville and they wanted me in Miami. So I was hiding out. That sounded reasonable. Bootleggers always have cars. I was taken in."

From her research she brought back fresh reports about the way people really talked, including one word nobody had ever put in print before: "jook."

Florida has contributed some memorable phrases to the English language ("Don't Tase me, bro!", "the Cuban relatives", "Stand Your Ground"), but "jook," also known as "juke," is our greatest single-word contribution. Hurston's 1935 book *Mules and Men* was the first place the word was used in print, according to the *Oxford English Dictionary*. In her book's glossary, she defines a jook as "a fun house. Where they sing, dance, gamble, love, and compose 'blues' songs incidentally."

In a different essay, she expounded on the subject: "Jook is a word for a Negro pleasure house. It may mean a bawdy house. It may mean the house set apart . . . where the men and women dance, drink and gamble. Often, it is a combination of all these . . . Musically speaking, the Jook is the most important place in America."

Hurston loved hanging around jooks, watching the dancers grinding away in a dance called "jooking." She would sing along with the guitarist providing the music. She picked up a lot of folk songs that way—and occasionally something more.

"It was in a sawmill jook in Polk County that I almost got cut to death," she wrote. She was saved by a friend named Big Sweet, who happened to be gambling at a nearby table. The ensuing brawl involved women and men armed with "switch-blades, ice picks, and old-fashioned razors."

"Jook" expanded to mean any roadhouse. In 1939, the *WPA Guide to*

Florida (to which Hurston contributed) commented on one particular stretch of pavement: "Strung along the highway west of Jacksonville are many 'jooks' of the type found on the outskirts of almost all large Florida cities" in which "patrons . . . drink and dance to the music of a 'jook organ,' a nickel-in-the-slot, heavy-toned, electric phonograph." Thus we got the jukebox.

In 1942, Warner Bros. released a movie called *Juke Girl,* starring Ann Sheridan as a tough-talking dame who hangs out at a Florida roadhouse, and Ronald Reagan as a farmworker who becomes an Anglo Cesar Chavez. (Neither performance caught the attention of Oscar voters.)

Over time, "juke" expanded its meaning, becoming a sports term for dodging an opponent with your fancy footwork. More recently, it became a term for dancing around the truth and faking things. In the TV show *The Wire,* the cops talk about underreporting or misclassifying crimes to hide their failures, calling it "juking the stats." But I digress.

In the jook joints that Zora Neale Hurston visited, the gamblers played poker games called Florida-flip and Georgia skin, as well as one involving both cards and dice called Coon-can. But none of those games transformed the state like one played in the cities, the one they called "bolita," Spanish for "little balls."

In Cuba, the government ran bolita as a national lottery. Transplanted to Florida, bolita soon became our most pervasive—and persuasive—private industry.

In the 1880s, a casino owner named Manuel "El Gallego" Suarez introduced bolita in the Tampa enclave known as Ybor City, home to a lively mix of Spaniards, Cubans, and Italians. By 1927, Tampa had some three hundred bolita operations going. By the '30s, the bolita craze had hit Miami, Fort Lauderdale, Key West, and Jacksonville. By the '40s, it reached Daytona Beach, where the bolita bankers included NASCAR racing champ Smokey Purser.

You played it like this: A hundred balls, consecutively numbered, are tied into a sack and tossed around. Someone picks one ball from the sack. That's the winning number of the day. Payoffs, at least in the early days, could be as high as ninety-to-one.

Of course, this being Florida, the bolita throwers knew ways to rig the game. They could hollow out the ivory balls, putting cork in some to make them lighter and lead in the others to make them heavier. They might even paint several balls the same number.

You could buy your bolita ticket on the street from a passing ice cream vendor. Or you could buy it from a well-dressed dealer in a swanky casino where roulette and other games were played, a place where the bolita sack was made of velvet and tied with a red satin bow.

Ybor's biggest industry was rolling cigars, but bolita soon rivaled it. In the cigar factories, Cuban workers sipped strong coffee as they hand-rolled tobacco leaves into panatelas. The only diversion came courtesy of the lector who, as they worked, read aloud to them from Spanish-language newspapers and books. On payday, the workers walked out the gate and faced collectors at three tables awaiting their cut: *el lector, el cafetero,* and *el bolitero.*

The game's influence on Tampa's economy grew. Department stores sold "dream books" to interpret which numbers matched a player's nighttime visions—a cow meant x, a horse y, et cetera. A baker noticed his sales fell off one day a week and figured out it was because that was bolita day.

The Tampa bankers who controlled the games were Cuban and Spanish. The Italians specialized in bootlegging. Then Charlie Wall took over as Tampa's top bolita boss by consolidating, chasing away, or eliminating the independents. The black-sheep scion of an upper-crust Anglo family, Wall knew whom to pay off and whom to flatter. Anyone who defied him got a shotgun blast and a ride in a hearse.

Wall's ascension to power marked two major changes. One was that Ybor's immigrants, who previously had been discouraged from applying for citizenship, now were encouraged to become Americans so they could vote. Of course, they voted for whomever the bolita boys told them to vote for, giving Tampa's politicians yet another reason to kowtow to Wall. The second change was that between controlling minority voting blocks and bribing politicians, Wall launched a twenty-year period in which, experts have concluded, not a single Tampa election took place that wasn't as rigged as a faro wheel.

With Wall in charge of City Hall and the underworld, cops were happy to supplement their salaries and ignore bolita. They still made bolita busts from time to time. Sometimes they busted independents who were trying to evade Wall's influence. A raid made them run to Wall for protection.

More often, the bolita "raids" were strictly for show. Historian Gary Mormino interviewed one Ybor old-timer who boasted he'd been busted sixty times, yet he didn't have a record. Every few months, the police would call and ask him and a dozen other bolita boys to report to the station—in effect pulling a raid in reverse. When they showed up, the cops would tell them to hand over $100 as their "fine." The cop writing up the report would ask, "What name would you like to be arrested under?" The bolita boys would think up an alias, then go home. The next day's paper would dutifully report, "Police Arrest 13 in Bolita Raid" and list all the fake names. It was the Tampa version of juking the stats.

As Wall's fortune grew, his gaming interests grew to include Orlando and smaller towns nearby. The list of officials taking his orders reached to Tallahassee. But Wall's success attracted unwanted attention. In the '30s, the Italians muscled him out, backed by Mob bosses up north. Similar takeovers occurred throughout the state, installing Mafia dons as top dogs. It was just like when a town's mom-and-pop stores are pushed out by big retail chains, only with more bloodshed.

The man who eventually became Tampa's don, Santo Trafficante Jr., grew up in Florida but was dispatched by his father to study with Mob families up north, then to Mexico to learn about narcotics and smuggling. It was the underworld's version of an exchange program. By the time he took charge in the '50s, he was one of the most powerful gangsters in both America and Cuba.

Meanwhile, Florida cops continued accepting payoffs, albeit from a different source. Mobsters joked about their bought-and-paid-for Hillsborough County sheriff, Walter Heinrich, dubbing him "Cabeza de Melon"—in other words, melon head.

Some top cops did more than just look the other way. Broward County sheriff Walter Clark assigned his deputies to provide security for some of the Mob casinos. He assigned others to show up at closing time to escort the cash to the bank. The money rode in armored cars owned by the sheriff's brother. Meanwhile, Clark became part owner in a company that stocked Mob-connected bars with slot machines and (ahem) jukeboxes. He even sold bolita tickets out of his office.

When Fred Cone (the postmaster shooter) became governor in the late 1930s, someone asked him why he didn't stop the gambling in Miami.

"I will come down and personally close up gambling places so tight you can't stick a sewing needle through them, if and when the majority of people want it stopped," Cone said. However, he added, "The sentiment of the people is in favor of gambling."

A ministers' group and the Chamber of Commerce objected, but Cone knew what he was talking about. Miami mayor E. G. Sewall said, "I don't mind gambling as long as it's honest gambling without hoodlums and gangsters," not explaining how he could have one without the other.

In Broward, some good-government folks persuaded a judge to issue an injunction shutting down the Plantation, a big gambling hall in Hallandale. The Plantation was so popular that the owners had to rig up outdoor speakers so the crowds standing in the parking lot could hear the winning numbers. In addition to gambling, the Plantation routinely featured shows by such big-name performers as comic Joe E. Lewis and singer Sophie Tucker (today's equivalent would be performances by Louis C.K. and Rihanna). Now it appeared doomed.

The Plantation was affiliated with Miami mobster Meyer Lansky, a gnome-like man regarded as the brainiest guy in the Mafia. Lansky studied the wording of the injunction, then issued orders. The Plantation was torn down, and an exact duplicate was built on adjacent property not covered by the injunction. The gambling in the building now dubbed the Farm proceeded as if nothing had happened. Nobody tried shutting it down again.

By 1948, the number of Lansky-owned gambling interests in South Florida had hit fifty. Lansky planned to expand into Cuba. He had become friends with Cuban dictator Fulgencio Batista, who lived in exile in Daytona prior to returning home to seize power. Lansky's only rivals were the Trafficantes of Tampa, who also opened Cuban casinos.

By this time, gamblers had taken over even Florida's smaller resort towns, altering their breezy charm. Thriller writer John D. MacDonald, who'd recently settled in Florida, described the change in his 1950 novel, *The Brass Cupcake*: "A new group had taken over the beaches. Middle-aged ladies with puffy faces and granite eyes brought down whole stables of hundred-dollar call girls . . . Sleek little men with hand-blocked sport shirts strolled around and made with the Bogart hand gestures. Boom town, fun town, money town, rough town . . . Local eyes held a wearied acceptance. Tourist eyes had a brighter glaze, a hectic promise, a threat of excitement."

Military officials griped about the gambling to everyone from the local sheriff to the governor. Commanders complained that soldiers, sailors, and airmen were repeatedly fleeced, leaving wives and children to starve. If they got a response, it was poorly feigned ignorance.

"There's no gambling in this town—on Saturday night or any other night," the Monroe County sheriff insisted about Key West. Meanwhile, a block from city hall, a casino ran from 11:00 P.M. to 7:00 A.M. despite a town ordinance requiring all bars to close by 2:00 A.M. Its owner was the brother of a state legislator.

Bolita never caught on in the Panhandle the way it did elsewhere, but slot machines sprouted all over Pensacola, Fort Walton Beach, and Panama City, in bars, hotels, grocery stores, bus stations, laundries, gas stations, and at least one skating rink. They were in all the juke joints too. Just as in the big South Florida cities, the cops didn't see a thing. It was like alcohol during Prohibition: If the tourists wanted it, the tourists got it, no matter what the law said.

With the exception of Colonel Bradley's Palm Beach publications, Florida's newspapers repeatedly tried exposing the rackets. In 1912, a reporter for a

Jacksonville paper visited several Tampa bolita joints to document what went on—until his cover was blown and an angry crowd knocked him to his knees. Cops intervened, saving his life but also charging him with illegally carrying a weapon. His story identified Charlie Wall as controlling both bolita and the politicians, and labeled Tampa "the most wicked city in the United States." In the 1930s, the *St. Petersburg Times* ran stories quoting gamblers saying they never worried about being shut down because so many people were making money.

These newspaper reports attracted little attention until 1949. That's when reporters at the *Tampa Morning Tribune* blew the lid off gambling statewide. They got hold of documents showing how many slot machine owners paid a federal tax on their machines, and they were able to identify who paid the tax and in what counties. They ran stories on each region. They reported that gambling was going strong in Jacksonville, home of Gov. Fuller Warren, and that Fort Walton Beach had so much gambling going on that a reporter "could hear the chips rattle from the main street."

What made the *Tribune* stories more potent was that they fueled the Kefauver committee hearings. Folksy Tennessee senator Estes Kefauver had created the group he chaired—officially known as the United States Senate Special Committee to Investigate Crime in Interstate Commerce—to boost his national profile so he could run for president someday (he did, and he lost). The five senators on the panel focused exclusively on gambling, never asking about prostitution, narcotics, loan-sharking, leg breaking, fraud, or anything else the Mob was involved in.

Kefauver's committee visited fourteen cities in fifteen months. Their first stop was Miami, where they found gambling everywhere they looked, from restaurants to cigar stands. In addition to putting bookies and gangsters on the hot seat, the committee poked into who got paid protection money.

The Dade County sheriff could not explain how his personal fortune had grown from $2,500 when he took office in 1944 to more than $75,000 in 1950. The testimony of Broward's Sheriff Clark, a gregarious good old boy, was even better. Clark admitted he was a partner in a bolita operation worth more than $750,000. He didn't see a problem with that, or with never raiding a single casino.

"You have never known that there was gambling in those places?" Kefauver asked.

"Rumors, but no actual evidence on it," Clark replied. "I never had any complaints that they were gambling."

Clark, whose major campaign donors were two brothers named Lansky, explained that he took a "liberal" approach to enforcing the law. Pressed to define the term "liberal," Clark said, "Well, I am not going around snooping in private businesses and homes."

In Tampa, the committee took testimony from Charlie Wall, retired but happy to reminisce about the good old days when he was boss. He all but drew the committee an organizational chart of how gangsters ran the town. (Five years later, he was found lying on his bedroom floor with his throat slit from ear to ear. On his bedside table, a book called *Crime in America* by Estes Kefauver.)

Tampa mobsters testified about payoffs to the sheriff, the town constable, the police chief, the state attorney, even Mayor Curtis Hixon. One told of driving his boss over to Hixon's house and waiting outside while the two men discussed business. (Hixon once told a police lieutenant who was his bagman that he didn't see anything wrong with taking payoffs of up to $100,000 "as long as there's no greed or killings or no scandals.")

In the end, only the sheriff got in trouble. For the others, it was as if the testimony evaporated into thin air the moment it was spoken. Not only did they face no legal consequences, but, as one historian pointed out, Hixon now has a lovely waterfront park in downtown Tampa named for him.

Two of the three biggest names on Kefauver's Florida subpoena list were Lansky and Trafficante. Lansky didn't show up until the hearings moved to New York, then replied to nearly every question by pleading the Fifth. Trafficante didn't bother to respond and faced no penalty, perhaps because of his close friendship with Florida's U.S. Sen. George Smathers, a frequent visitor to his Havana casino.

The final big name was really big: Gov. Fuller Warren.

Warren may not have been the dumbest governor Florida ever had, but I'd say he's in the top five. He was a handsome man known for his spellbinding oratory, but when he ran for governor he believed the job to be primarily ceremonial.

He found out otherwise in the worst way possible. Right after he was sworn in, his predecessor informed him the state was broke, wished him good luck, and left.

After that, pretty much everything Warren touched blew up in his face. His solution for refilling the treasury was a business tax that violated his own campaign promises and angered every CEO in the state. Soon his relations with the legislature soured, and his selections for state agency jobs turned out to be either incompetent or crooked.

Warren did do one thing no other Florida governor has ever done: He wrote a book while in office. It was titled (without a trace of irony) *How to*

Win in Politics. In it, he urged any office seeker giving a speech to always "speak loudly" and "gesticulate wildly." Also, he said, don't skimp on the adjectives: "Don't just call an opponent a 'mean man.' Fulminate in stentorian tones that 'he is a snarling, snapping, hissing monstrosity.'"

Upon receiving Kefauver's subpoena, Warren snarled, snapped, and hissed. He refused to testify and accused Kefauver, a fellow Democrat, of being a "headline-hungry hypocrite" who had "perverted and prostituted the chairmanship of the Senate crime investigating committee to promote himself for president." Warren was right, but the fact was, Kefauver had the goods on him.

When Warren ran for governor in 1948, he signed a statement that said his campaign had received only $12,241 in contributions and spent slightly less. In fact, the committee learned that Warren had a trio of backers who had put up $450,000 to $500,000, allowing him to run radio ads his opponents could not afford. The trio was Charles V. Griffin, a citrus magnate; Louis Wolfson, the tycoon who would later bribe a Supreme Court justice; and a Miami dog track operator named William Johnston.

After Warren took office, these three often asked him for favors he felt obliged to grant, such as letting them pick who would head up various agencies. A South Florida antigambling group asked Warren to investigate four of Johnston's dog tracks that seemed shady. The governor said no, which the Kefauver committee found suspicious.

Warren proclaimed his innocence. As for those secret donations, he said he "knew nothing of who contributed or how much," adding, "I had no part in handling the financial part of the campaign. I could hardly keep up with my speaking engagements."

Nobody believed him. Then Warren made things worse. When he ran for office, he had promised to suspend any law enforcement official who went easy on gambling. But when the Kefauver committee showed that a lot of police and prosecutors failed to enforce gambling laws, Warren dragged his feet. At last, after months of criticism, he suspended five sheriffs the committee had identified as being on the pad. But one of them he replaced with the man's own son-in-law, and three others he quickly reinstated.

Derisive laughter at his ineptness echoed around the state. "Only Fuller Warren would pull a stunt like that!" people snorted.

Legislators moved to impeach him, but it was a halfhearted effort that failed by a wide margin. There's no telling how many of the legislators who voted against impeachment were equally indebted to gangsters.

To top it all off, *Collier's* magazine ran a story laying out the Kefauver committee's evidence and accusing Warren of being in league with the gamblers. He sued for libel, demanding $1 million in damages, but ultimately settled. The settlement was secret, but the fact that Warren paid court costs should tell you who prevailed.

When Warren's term as governor ended, the author of *How to Win in Politics* never won another election.

The Kefauver hearings made plain to a nation what a cesspool Florida had become. It was one thing to know that you could bet on bolita regardless of what the law said. It was quite another to see the curtain pulled back to expose the army of bent-nose mobsters, corrupt cops, and crooked politicians running the show. What tourist would want to venture into such a place?

The state's business leaders pushed for a real crackdown on gambling, and they got it. Among those busted in a wide-ranging 1955 raid on bolita dealers were Santo Trafficante Jr. and his brother, Henry. An undercover St. Petersburg cop wore a bulky wire recording device under a trench coat, catching Henry on tape bribing him with cash, a suit, a case of whiskey, even a new car. When Henry was busted, the look he gave a newspaper photographer could have been bottled and sold as rat poison.

Gambling was driven underground, but it didn't go away. It would eventually come roaring back as a major tourist attraction—with the blessing, and perhaps an assist, from a Miami mobster.

The Native Americans who killed Ponce de León with a poison arrow were called Calusa. The arrival of white settlers and their diseases soon wiped out them out. Meanwhile, settlers moving into other parts of the South chased out the tribes who lived there. Some of them fled into the Florida swamps and became the Seminoles.

Led by the charismatic Osceola, they learned the terrain well, enabling them to defeat the U.S. Army repeatedly. They are the only tribe that never surrendered.

Yet it's hard to eat military victory. The Everglades where Osceola's tribe once thrived was soon ditched and drained. As their world changed, they had a hard time coping. White families didn't waste much worry on the Seminoles, regarding them as illiterate savages.

Consider what occurred in 1891 in Lee County. The county set up a school for both white and Seminole children, with the promise the county would pay for the white kids and a missionary group would pay for the Seminoles. When none of the Seminole children showed up, the teacher gave the white students Indian names and stuck the missionaries with the whole bill.

In the early twentieth century, the federal government coaxed some of the Seminoles out of the swamps and onto scattered reservations by helping them set up small cattle ranches. Meanwhile, the surrounding towns vied to be chosen as the location of the Indian agent's office because that would guarantee a constant stream of Seminoles visiting in their colorful garb, acting as a living tourist attraction.

Florida's white residents could have learned a thing or two from the Seminoles. Their marriages lasted much longer, the Indian Agency wrote in a 1921 report to Congress, and the women were "quite independent." The report added: "Probably no people on earth have a higher standard of morality . . . Gambling is unknown among them."

Once the Tamiami Trail sliced through their reservations, some Seminoles made and sold crafts to tourists while others exhibited animals and wrestled alligators. But even the Seminoles who worked also relied on handouts from the Bureau of Indian Affairs.

Then, in 1976, tribal chairman Howard Tommie figured out the tribe could make money off the white man's vices. As a sovereign nation, the tribe was not subject to the laws that governed the rest of the country. Tommie opened a shop selling cigarettes cheaper than anywhere else because the Seminoles didn't have to pay taxes. Nicotine addicts flocked to the reservation.

What happened next remains a subject of disagreement. One version of the story says that white business investors approached Tommie about opening a bingo hall offering bigger prizes than Florida law allowed. That would attract gamblers from all over.

"The toughest part of building a bingo hall was to line up investors to take a chance, because no Indians had ever done this before," Tommie said in a 2004 interview. The plan—Tommie called it "a sweetheart deal"—dictated that the investors would keep all the profits up to $3 million, then share whatever was over that amount with the tribe.

At that point, Tommie gave up his chairmanship to become majority partner in the bingo hall's management company without investing any of his own money. He bought an expensive waterfront home and mostly dropped out of sight.

Another version says Tommie nodded his head a lot but did nothing with the bingo hall proposal. Instead, the guy who got the tribe into the gambling business was Tommie's successor, Jim Billie. That's the version Billie tells.

Billie is a classic Florida character—profane, charismatic, as wild and unpredictable as a rattler full of Red Bull. He was born at a roadside chimp farm. He wrestled gators, which was how he lost part of a finger. He served two tours in Vietnam, got a cosmetology license, worked at a lawn-care business, and cut some country albums. His second wife was once charged with assaulting his mistress. He killed an endangered Florida panther and ate its heart—part of a ritual, he said, to become a medicine man. When he was prosecuted, he won acquittal by questioning whether the panther was really a panther—although if it wasn't, that would seem to nullify his medicine man qualifications.

What is established fact is that in 1979, Billie was elected to succeed Tommie as chairman, and he changed the management agreement so the tribe got 55 percent of the bingo hall's profits.

Within months, the tribe's first high-stakes bingo hall—a one-story concrete block building—opened on the Hollywood reservation, much to the dismay of Broward County sheriff Bob Butterworth (the future attorney general). An ex-judge with a face like a basset hound, Butterworth vowed to padlock the place and arrest everyone.

Instead, the tribe sued him, winning an injunction that allowed the hall to open on schedule offering jackpots of up to $2,000. The suit went to the U.S. Supreme Court, and the tribe won. Soon it was offering $100,000 jackpots and the place was jammed.

Seminole Tribe of Florida v. Butterworth kicked the door open for every tribe to build casinos, creating America's lucrative Indian gaming industry. By the time the Seminoles' original bingo hall turned twenty-five in 2004, some 225 Indian tribes nationwide had gaming facilities, raking in $16 billion annually. The Seminoles were making $320 million a year, and distributing $42,000 a year to each of the tribe's three thousand members.

Money changed the Seminoles. Young ones moved off the reservation and into the cities. They didn't want to wrestle alligators now, prompting one Seminole village to post an ad for non-Indians willing to risk life and limb. When tribal members shopped for major purchases such as cars, they dressed like whites and didn't mention their real names until the deal was done. Otherwise the price would be jacked up.

Another Florida tribe, the Miccosukee, spent their casino-generated cash on suing anyone who was polluting their homeland in the Everglades. The Seminole tribal leaders, on the other hand, blew theirs on luxury cars, breast implants, and Super Bowl tickets.

Still, everyone agreed the tribe was better off than back when they were starving. Florida's state government was better off too, because the Seminoles agreed to pay the state millions in exchange for permission to offer slot machines, blackjack, baccarat, and chemin de fer.

So why did Sheriff Butterworth oppose this free-enterprise solution to helping the impoverished Seminoles? Because, he explained, "We always knew the Mob was there."

The management company that pitched the bingo hall idea, Seminole Management Associates, was run by men with ties to Pittsburgh's LaRocca crime family. A 1992 Pennsylvania Crime Commission report noted that one of them started the company with $1.2 million from a Miami dog track partner whom the commission identified as a "close personal associate of Meyer Lansky." The report said the entire bingo operation had been "set up with the help of . . . Meyer Lansky."

Billie has said he obtained Lansky's approval of the bingo hall, as well as South Florida's Catholic archbishop, convincing them that the tribe would not compete with their operations. The tribe's archivist says Lansky did more than give his blessing—he loaned the tribe $3 million when the banks would not. A tribal newspaper reporter who has written several profiles of Billie says that when a rumor circulated that the Justice Department was still trying to put Lansky away, Billie said, "I hope they get him, because then I wouldn't have to pay him back."

Lansky, by then, was an old man in ill health. The Mafia was under fire and in decline. Santo Trafficante Jr. was telling congressional committees how he'd helped the CIA try to assassinate Castro, meanwhile denying he had anything to do with killing JFK. The other old bosses Lansky knew were dead or dying. Lansky claimed to be retired, spending his time walking his dogs and playing cards while under FBI surveillance.

Did he nevertheless have a hand in creating a whole new gambling industry, one that could yield big profits for whoever managed the tribal casinos? I asked the tribe's longtime attorney, Jim Shore, if Lansky had bankrolled the bingo hall. Shore, who was once shot by a gunman who has never been caught, gave me an enigmatic smile and said, "I don't think so—but I think he was in the neighborhood."

The Seminole bingo hall proved to be a big success. Billie expanded gambling to the tribe's other reservations, including one in Tampa that local officials thought would be a tribal museum. The tribe had pulled a fast one that Lansky would appreciate, building a Hard Rock Hotel and Casino and putting the museum *inside* it.

But odd things happened with the casinos' cash flow. Sometimes the same people won multiple jackpots on the same game. One gambler beat the slots twenty-two times. Five officers on the tribe's own police force reported suspicions that someone was skimming. They were all fired.

In 1997, the National Indian Gaming Commission, after conducting its own investigation, voided the Seminoles' contract with Seminole Management. The company handled it just like Lansky did the Plantation. They set up a company with a new name and went back to doing what they did before. Finally, under pressure from the gaming commission, the tribe bought out the management contract for $60 million.

Billie, in a long 2006 interview with *St. Petersburg Times* reporters, sounded a lot like Sheriff Clark facing the Kefauver committee.

"Are you satisfied that there has never been any skimming or problems of that sort in the casinos?" one reporter asked.

"That I can't answer 'cause I don't know," Billie replied. "As far as I know, my percentage of money has always been comin' to the Tribe."

By then, Billie was making $300,000 a year—more than the governor—and living like a Fortune 500 CEO. He had a Mercedes, a forty-seven-foot yacht, a $9 million Falcon 50 jet, and three helicopters. He flew all over, meeting dignitaries and making deals. Reality show star and future presidential front-runner Donald Trump, who badly wanted in on the Indian gaming business, even made him one of the judges for the Miss Universe pageant—all for naught.

Billie's wheeling and dealing led to trouble. In 2002, a federal grand jury indicted three former tribal officials on charges they embezzled $2.7 million and funneled it to an offshore Internet gambling site. A judge threw out the indictments after Billie testified the tribal officials were following his orders.

After an extensive audit, the other four members of the tribal council voted unanimously to oust Billie as chairman. They said he had lied repeatedly to the tribe and treated it the way a dictator would.

What really got the council riled up was Billie's testimony in federal court he had funneled $250,000 in Seminole funds into a Nicaraguan hotel that was bought by two of his ex-employees—then gave them $80,000 to pay for their battling *against* the tribe for control of the hotel. They were also unhappy about an employee who sued, saying he'd given her $100,000 in phony sick time after he'd gotten her pregnant, made her abort the baby, and then fired her. (She later dropped the suit.)

Eight years later, though, all was forgiven and Billie won reelection. That gave him a much bigger stage on which to strut. In 2006, while he was out of power, the tribe closed on its biggest deal ever, buying the Hard Rock chain for $965 million. With its acquisition of the chain's 145 restaurants, plus hotels, casinos, and performance venues, the tribe's reach now stretches to forty-five countries. The tribe also got the Hard Rock's collection of guitars and other rock'n'roll memorabilia. For a change, the once impoverished Indians owned artifacts cherished by the white man.

That's the Florida way, flipping things around and producing ironies galore, turning yesterday's losers into today's winners (at least until the next hand is dealt).

Perhaps that's why Florida was the ideal spot for launching the biggest gamble in history.

Looking north on Canova Beach in Brevard County in 1929, all you could see was gloriously empty beach. By 1960, this land would be completely transformed. Photo by Herman Gunter. Photo courtesy of State Archives of Florida.

13

Space Invaders

It is probably the highest point in southern Florida, its base being washed by the head waters of the chief rivers . . . By its position, its dryness, its rocky soil mixed with sandy alluvium, it appears to me to possess every condition desirable for the success of our experiment.

—*From the Earth to the Moon* by Jules Verne (1867)

Florida politicians expend a lot of energy fussing about the federal government. It's so awful, so intrusive, so bossy! Taxes are too high! The EPA is trying to take our property rights! Congress is out of control! The president takes too many vacations! The Supreme Court is full of activist judges! Wouldn't we all be better off if the earth just opened up and swallowed Washington?

Every time I hear that kind of talk, it cracks me up. Those same politicians are the first to howl if someone suggests cutting federal price supports for Florida's sugar crop or federal flood insurance subsidies for high-priced waterfront homes.

Florida is America's Welfare Queen. It receives more federal funds than any other state, both in total dollars and per capita. Adding up programs ranging from Homeland Security to Social Security, Florida got more than $577 billion in the 2011 fiscal year, which works out to some $30,000 per Florida resident. The second-place state, Texas, trails us with a mere $294 billion.

Some of that money is well spent, but a lot of it rates as grade A pork brought home by our congressional delegation. People joke about what body part Florida's shape resembles. Perhaps the most accurate comparison, given how much we depend on government largesse, is a teat.

The federal government has been feeding Florida's economy for decades. During the Depression, with the real estate boom a distant memory, Florida was in a world of hurt. Franklin D. Roosevelt's New Deal programs—the Civilian Conservation Corps, the Works Progress Administration, and so forth—kept Floridians from starving.

Federal funding established farmers' markets to save agriculture. The feds bought thousands of acres for national forests and preserves that, in the decades to come, would draw ecotourists interested in hiking, canoeing, and watching migrating butterflies. Florida's earliest state parks were built by CCC workers. One, Highlands Hammock, has a CCC museum to honor its creators.

The Florida city hardest hit by the Depression was Key West, which had already lost its Navy base and cigar industry. City hall declared bankruptcy, so the Federal Emergency Relief Agency took charge. Eighty percent of the populace was put to work cleaning the streets, renovating hotels, and sprucing up the city. Federal officials recommended Key West focus on a new industry: tourism. That's been its main economic driver ever since.

Florida got the chance to pay that all back when the Japanese bombed Pearl Harbor in December 1941. The first American soldier to earn a Congressional Medal of Honor in World War II hailed from Florida: Alexander "Sandy" Nininger Jr., twenty-six, of Fort Lauderdale, who in January 1942, during the siege of Bataan, killed at least fifty Japanese soldiers with grenades, his rifle, and his bayonet before being gunned down himself.

The end of the war had a Florida angle too. Paul Tibbets Jr., who piloted the B-29 that dropped the A-bomb on Hiroshima in 1945, grew up in Florida. As a boy, he was selected to ride in an open-cockpit biplane over the Hialeah horse track and toss out Baby Ruth candy bars attached to tiny parachutes.

"From that day on," his biography says, "Paul knew he had to fly."

During the war, scientists decided Orlando was the ideal place to test a new insecticide called DDT. It did a great job of killing off roaches and mosquitoes. Soon airplanes and trucks were squirting the stuff all over the state—and killing off a lot more than bugs. In 1945, long before Rachel Carson wrote her cautionary book *Silent Spring,* the *Tampa Morning Tribune* reported that ducks were "dying by the hundreds" around MacDill Air Force Base, and "federal authorities believe the mass deaths have been caused by DDT." It took Carson's book and years of repeated demonstrations of harm to persuade the feds to ban DDT in 1972.

Overall, though, what the war did for Florida would prove to be even more significant than what Florida did for the war. Thousands of new defense-related jobs opened up, offering big paychecks at new shipyards in Tampa, Miami,

Jacksonville, and Pensacola, and on construction jobs building or expanding military bases.

Military leaders liked Florida's generally mild weather. The wide range of landscapes, from swampy to sandy, seemed ideal for training new soldiers. Florida's Camp Blanding became the largest military installation east of the Mississippi, turning nearby Starke from a dusty crossroads into a neon-lit, people-packed boomtown.

Along the state's coasts, hotels that had been dying for lack of tourists were now filled with fresh recruits, billeted there by Uncle Sam as a quick way to provide shelter. Imagine being an Iowa farm boy, joining the Army to fight Hitler, and being shipped off to bivouac amid the splendor of the Breakers in Palm Beach or the Don Cesar on St. Petersburg Beach. A lot of soldiers liked what they saw in Florida. Some fell in love with the beaches and weather. Some fell in love with Florida girls. Several cities set up women's groups to cater to the servicemen, including one in St. Petersburg with the pun-ishing name of "Bomb-A-Dears."

After the war ended, these enchanted ex-GIs returned to Florida, ready to stroll through paradise without a full pack. Thanks to the generosity of the federal GI loan program, they built or bought houses here, paving the way for a massive postwar real estate boom.

Meanwhile, some military bases became municipal airports (including Miami International, Florida's largest), while others became spring-training baseball sites. Some remained military bases, continuing to pump federal dollars into Florida's economy.

The most significant change the feds made in Florida, though, involved a small naval base on the Atlantic coast.

The Banana River Naval Air Station was built on the eve of World War II. The windswept promontory where it was located had once been the haunt of pirates and privateers. Just off its lonely coast is where the last naval battle of the Revolutionary War was fought.

Not much had happened in Brevard County since then. The beaches of Merritt Island were difficult to reach by land, so few settlers tried. That meant that when the war came along, there were miles of undeveloped land for the military to put to use. Soon little old Banana River had added everything from Navy blimps to German prisoners of war to antisubmarine patrols to its mission.

When the war ended, Banana River was headed for a shutdown—until a cemetery in Mexico blew up.

The U.S. Air Force had been testing missiles by firing them off from White Sands, New Mexico. One day, one strayed off course and obliterated a Juarez graveyard. Mexican officials complained, and the Air Force scrambled to find a new missile launch site.

Banana River was perfect. The weather was mostly good. Few people lived nearby. The site was close enough to the equator for zooming missiles to take advantage of Earth's rotation for a little extra speed.

Banana River became the Joint Long Range Proving Ground, with the missiles rocketing over the Atlantic, far from any politically sensitive cemeteries. The government began condemning private land in the scattered seashore settlement north of Canova Beach to make more room for missile tests at what was now Patrick Air Force Base.

Then, in 1957, the Russians launched Sputnik. As that metal basketball orbited Earth for twenty-one days, Americans flipped. Suddenly everyone was asking why we let the Commies beat us to space.

Congress created a new agency to enable the United States to catch up. In 1958, the National Aeronautics and Space Administration was born, and it soon took over the old missile site and a lot more land nearby in an area that had for centuries been known by the alliterative name Cape Canaveral. Then JFK became president and vowed the United States would put a man on the moon by the end of the decade.

In his 1867 novel *From the Earth to the Moon,* Jules Verne had correctly predicted the United States would shoot a moon rocket off from Florida because of its proximity to the equator, but he'd selected a spot near Tampa. He was off by more than one hundred miles from Cape Canaveral, where the homes of the remaining fishermen and farmers were now being torn down by space invaders intent on launching things into the wild blue yonder.

First came *Explorer I,* which lifted off from Cape Canaveral atop a modified V-2 rocket on January, 31, 1958. The *Explorer* did more than just circle Earth and stop, like Sputnik I. Its onboard scientific equipment documented the existence of radiation zones encircling Earth that were shaped by the planet's magnetic field—the Van Allen radiation belts.

To stay ahead of the Russians, NASA needed scientists and engineers, fast. They came flooding into sleepy Brevard County from all over. There were buzz-cut defense contractors, stiff-backed military men, and heavily accented Germans who had worked on the Nazis' V2 rockets. NASA also needed construction crews to build its launch pads, gantries and, eventually, the largest one-story building in the world, the Vehicle Assembly Building—525 feet tall and 716 feet long—where the rockets were put together. To design its launch center, NASA hired architect Charles Luckman, who also designed Meyer Lansky and Bugsy Siegel's famous Flamingo Hotel in Las Vegas.

Thanks to the influx of high-IQ rocket scientists and blue-collar builders, Brevard County's population zoomed from 23,000 in 1950 to more than 111,000 in 1960. That's more than a fivefold increase, and mostly in the last three years of the decade.

Suddenly Brevard needed more roads, schools, churches, stores, and everything else. Nobody had time to plan anything. Nobody thought about the long term. Crews threw together buildings as fast as possible and moved on to the next site.

So many new people had poured in that even with the locals renting out rooms, some recent arrivals wound up sleeping in their cars, or worse. When county work crews began installing a giant concrete pipe to bring potable water to the cape, they would knock off for the day and leave the pipe sitting by the roadside. In the morning, the crews would come back to work to discover people sleeping in the pipes.

Most NASA employees lived on the mainland, and the only way for them to get to work out at the cape was via a two-lane road with shoulders of soft sand. Anyone who veered off the pavement bogged down. When a NASA employee had a flat tire, he'd change it the middle of the road, stalling traffic behind him for miles. To file traffic reports, a local radio station employed a reporter on a mule because the mule could handle the sand.

The new arrivals didn't always get along with the locals. They had such different backgrounds.

"Cape engineers thought they were smarter than everybody here. That filtered down to their kids," one longtime local resident recalled years later. "They made a lot more money than the locals."

The locals jacked up prices for tires, food, and other essentials, figuring the space cases could afford it. Meanwhile, a fresh contingent of hustlers moved into Brevard, looking to make a fast buck off the NASA crowd.

"The beach mushroomed and became sheathed in schlock," writer Herbert Hiller reported. "Everything was built quick and short-term. Motels in Cocoa Beach and Titusville flashed neon rockets and dancing girls. Inside, sequined cuties danced and did more. Motel Row became Sin Strip . . . Saturnalia topped Saturn."

Between the long hours at work at the Cape and the temptations offered by Sin Strip, Brevard soon had one of the highest divorce rates in the country. Then, when NASA brought its first class of astronauts to Florida, they treated Cape Canaveral as, in the words of Tom Wolfe, "a paradise of Flying and Drinking and Drinking and Driving."

Still, thanks to NASA, Florida's reputation as a haven for gangsters faded, the racketeers replaced by rocketeers. With every news story about NASA, the state basked in the luster of Kennedy's New Frontier. Titusville declared itself "the City of Tomorrow." A new town was built named Satellite Beach. The region dubbed itself "the Space Coast." Forget the past—Florida was all about the Fuuuuutuuuure!

When NASA started shooting astronauts into orbit—Alan Shepard, Scott Carpenter, John Glenn, and the rest—spectators showed up to watch. At first it was a few NASA employees and their families, but soon there were outsiders who brought binoculars, cameras, and a gaping curiosity. They were fascinated by the spectacle of a giant rocket roaring off the launch pad, with its occupants sitting in a little tin can on top, waiting to see if it would explode.

While the space program kept everyone looking up, they should have been looking around. NASA's impact was much broader than just giving the nation a new set of heroes and lending Florida a new tourist attraction. The science behind the space shots spun off everything from new techniques for cleaning up pollution to the spread of those automatic teller machines that Florida crooks are constantly trying to uproot and carry away.

NASA's presence also created some space-related weirdness. There was the couple who stole some moon rocks and put them under their bed in an Orlando hotel room so they could have "sex on the moon." Their would-be rock buyers turned out to be undercover FBI agents who quickly brought them back to Earth.

I must also mention the UFO sightings. In 1965, a retired roller rink music composer named John Frank Reeves claimed he'd encountered a space alien in the woods near Brooksville—the first to ever make such a claim. Reeves said the alien had invited him to inspect his spacecraft and also handed over some sheets of paper covered with odd hieroglyphics.

A second alien encounter led to his taking a ride to the dark side of the moon and reporting that Earth, when seen from that perspective, is shaped like an oval. A third led to a trip to Venus, where he was given the cure for cancer, he said.

Among the UFO believer community, Reeves was called the Dean of American UFO Contactees. Among his neighbors, he was called "nuts," especially after he flunked a *Life* magazine lie detector test. Nevertheless, Reeves proudly posted a sign on his lawn that said FLYING SAUCER AREA. HOME OF JOHN F. REEVES. In his backyard he built a full-size replica of the first UFO he saw, complete with flashing red and white lights that alarmed many a passing motorist.

A more believable UFO story—at least at first—came from the community of Gulf Breeze near Pensacola. A local builder named Edward Walters reported spotting a spaceship shaped like a top hovering above the road in front of his house. He snapped photos until a bright blue light hit him and lifted him in the air, and he heard a voice say, "Don't worry. We won't harm you."

The photos seemed genuine. Walters's story spurred reports of other UFO sightings around the area. He passed two lie detector tests and wrote a book called *The Gulf Breeze Sightings: The Most Astounding Multiple Sightings of UFOs in U.S. History.* But in 1990, when Walters sold his house, the new owner discovered a nine-inch UFO model that looked exactly like the one in Walters's photos. Walters defended himself by pointing out, "Only a fool would leave behind such a piece of evidence," but that failed to convince the public he wasn't trying to fool them.

Because President Kennedy had pledged to put a man on the moon, that was the space program's main focus. The Florida space program was so identified with him that after his death, the space center became the Kennedy Space Center, and Cape Canaveral—one of the oldest place names in the country—was changed for a while to Cape Kennedy.

As NASA geared up for the Apollo 11 launch to fulfill Kennedy's pledge, its workforce at the cape peaked at 26,500 people. On July 19, 1969, the Saturn rocket carrying Neil Armstrong, Buzz Aldrin, and Michael Collins thundered into the sky for the rendezvous that Verne had predicted during the Civil War. To cover the biggest story in human history, seventeen hundred reporters from fifty-six countries had gathered at the cape. Meanwhile, jamming the beaches and highways were an estimated one million spectators, the largest crowd to ever witness a launch.

When Armstrong hopped down the ladder to the lunar surface and spoke his famous words about "one small step for man," I was just a kid. My parents let me stay up late to watch the grainy images on our TV. I had trouble grasping how these pictures had been beamed from the moon outside our window straight down to our living room. Then the Apollo 11 astronauts came home to be greeted by President Nixon, his face frozen with that deathly rictus that showed he was trying, really trying, to grin.

After that, NASA's sense of mission dropped off. Everyone in Brevard County found out what every coal miner and millworker in America knows: It's not so great living in a company town, even if your company is out of this world. The whole town's fortunes rise and fall on what that one company does. A year after the moon landing, the workforce was cut to fifteen thousand employees. By 1975, it had fallen to a mere eight thousand.

Things got so bad in Brevard that some unemployed rocket scientists took jobs pumping gas. "Families left the area," *Florida Today* reported. "People tell stories of some leaving their keys at their front door on the way out of town."

Fortunately, in 1971, a big new employer opened right down the road from the Kennedy Space Center—one that redefined what a "City of Tomorrow" looked like.

Rewind to November 22, 1963, that fateful date in American history.

Walt Disney and a handful of trusted advisers boarded an airplane borrowed from Miami TV entertainer Arthur Godfrey and took off from the Tampa airport. They flew to the Orlando area so Disney could see a vast alligator-infested swamp. Walt had already rejected Niagara Falls, St. Louis, and Washington, D.C., for the East Coast version of Disneyland. Now, gazing down at the swamp, Walt said, "That's it."

The swamp didn't bother him. What he liked was the pavement nearby: Interstate 4, then under construction, which would connect Interstate 75 on the Gulf coast with Interstate 95 on the Atlantic coast; and Florida's Turnpike, which ran north–south, crossing I-4 heading for Miami.

"The freeway routes, they bisect here," he explained.

When the plane landed, people were weeping in the streets. That's when Disney and his entourage found out that Kennedy had been killed in Dallas. The New Frontier was over, but that didn't affect Walt's vision for Florida.

Building a theme park like Disneyland bored him. He'd done it already. He had to build this second one, though, to attract East Coast residents, something Disneyland in California had been unable to accomplish.

No, what had Walt jazzed up was his other, bolder plan. He wanted to create a real City of Tomorrow—not like the one in Titusville, but one that actually did look to the future. He already had a name: Experimental Prototype Community of Tomorrow, EPCOT for short. It would be a showplace for the most advanced technologies. He called it "the most exciting and challenging assignment we've ever tackled at Walt Disney Productions."

The first challenge: buying the land without anyone finding out. If word leaked that Disney was interested in a big chunk of Florida land, the price would skyrocket. Disney consulted his New York attorney, William "Wild Bill" Donovan, who during World War II had headed up the Office of Strategic Services, the predecessor of today's Central Intelligence Agency. Donovan steered Disney to an OSS buddy of his in Miami, a chain-smoking lawyer named Paul Helliwell who had been the head of American intelligence operations in Europe. Since then, Helliwell had been involved in everything from financing the Bay of Pigs invasion to helping the CIA connect with mobsters such as Santo Trafficante Jr. He also ran a bank or two that loaned money to people who might or might not be involved in drug smuggling. He was, in short, a guy who knew how to keep his mouth shut.

Does it seem strange to you that the beloved figure of Walt Disney would wind up working with a guy tied to the CIA, drugs, Cuban revolutionaries, and the Mafia? Does that odd juxtaposition make you feel uncomfortable? In Florida, we call that feeling "Tuesday."

Helliwell arranged for Disney to buy twenty-seven thousand acres in Orange and Osceola Counties, his identity cloaked by several phony corporations. (Later some of those companies' names would adorn the fake storefronts that line Disney World's Main Street USA.)

Some of the land had been subdivided for a development that never got off the ground, probably because the ground was so soggy. Other parcels were occupied by people who weren't keen on selling. One elderly couple had a hundred-year-old log cabin, sweet-smelling citrus groves, flocks of turkeys, and a lake where they could regularly catch twelve-pound bass. The land looked "just like the Lord made it," the woman later told historian Richard E. Foglesong. So when the buyers showed up, "We kept saying, 'No, no, no, no.'" Eventually, though, they sold Disney's phony company the land they'd originally bought for $45,000, collecting $194,000 and moving to North Carolina with some regret.

Disney now owned a landmass twice the size of Manhattan that also happened to be 75 percent underwater during the summer. That's why Disney was able to acquire it for just $5 million. Central Florida businesspeople noticed that some mysterious entity had gobbled a chunk of property. Speculation ran rampant. Was it a defense contractor? A manufacturer?

The *Orlando Sentinel* duly recorded the transactions and the rumors. Meanwhile, Helliwell tipped off the publisher, who agreed to keep it secret from even his own staff.

At the time, Disney's PR folks regularly paid for reporters to fly out to California, visit Disneyland, and hobnob with the Great Visionary. The reporters were usually too starstruck to ask tough questions. But in October 1965, the PR folks included on one such junket Emily Bavar, editor of the *Sentinel*'s Sunday magazine and nobody's fool. When Disney sat down with the reporters, Bavar asked him point-blank: "Mr. Disney, are you buying all that land in Orlando?"

Disney sputtered a no-comment that confirmed her suspicions. Trying to cover his flub, Disney gave her several reasons why Florida would be a bad location for a theme park—but then, as if he couldn't stop himself, he systematically knocked down his own arguments.

Bavar wrote a story that toppled the façade of Helliwell's Potemkin corporations. "Girl Reporter Convinced by Walt Disney" said the 1A headline over the story by Bavar, who was forty-five.

Disney's staff hastily arranged a press conference with Florida Gov. Haydon Burns, who until then had been kept in the dark. Burns officially announced the project, telling the crowd of about five hundred people that Disney would build "the greatest attraction yet known in the history of Florida."

Exactly what that attraction might be, Disney kept vague. He said it would be bigger and better than Disneyland. He only briefly addressed the part he really cared about: "I would like to be part of building a model city, a City of Tomorrow, you might say, because I don't believe in going out to this blue-sky stuff that architects do. I believe that people still want to live like human beings."

People across the state wondered: What was the big deal about another roadside attraction? Between 1946 and 1954, more than thirty new Florida tourist attractions had thrown open their gates and cranked up the ballyhoo. There were jungle gardens with employees dressed as Tarzan and Jane, pirate coves where the staff all said "Arrrrr!" and Western towns with regular Main Street shootouts—anything to drag in the tourists and get them to open their wallets. When I was a kid, I was struck by how many attractions ended in the semi-aquatic suffix "-arium"—Gulfarium, Seaquarium, Swamparium. What was one more "-arium"?

Although Disney was vague in public, in private he knew exactly what he wanted, and he picked the people he thought qualified to carry it out. At the top of his list was William Potter, a retired Army Corps of Engineers general who had run the technical side of the New York World's Fair. Disney dispatched Potter to visit labs and factories all over, with an eye toward incorporating their latest discoveries into EPCOT.

"The idea was that here the people of the world . . . would see and experience what industry was about to develop, or thinking about developing, to put new products into use," Potter explained later. "[Disney's] idea was to expose not only our great industries but our great philosophies of life to foreign nations and people in the United States."

However, Walt had some less progressive ideas concerning the land that looked "just like the Lord made it." When he surveyed the cypress trees and dark water he now owned, he was not pleased.

"No, no, this won't do," he announced. "Can you change it?"

The water had to be blue, he said, to match the color in his imagination. With enough money, his engineers assured him, it could be whatever color he wanted.

Before they were done, Disney's workers had built forty miles of drainage canals, eighteen miles of levees, and thirteen water-control structures. Everything was hidden—the canals, for instance, disguised as meandering streams. All the dredging yielded enough fill dirt to raise the theme park twelve feet, making it less likely to flood and also creating space for underground utility tunnels that the employees could use as secret passageways.

To Potter, Disney was a creative genius, someone who could look at swampy land and tell everyone how to turn it into something sleek and futuristic. Walt had another quality that undercut his brilliance, though. He was a nicotine fiend, addicted to smoking little cigars—and it was killing him. In November 1966, he had part of one lung removed. Disney's PR folks claimed he was just dealing with an old polo injury. A month later, he was dead at age sixty-five, and not from polo.

Walt's death was, for his company, a disaster. He had written down virtually none of his plans for the property. Like the blue water in the brown lakes, EPCOT existed mostly in his head. There was talk that without Walt at the helm, his corporation might fold.

The job of rescuing it fell to his brother Roy, seventy-three, who before Walt's death had been contemplating retirement. Despite sharing a last name and a similar upbringing, the brothers could not have been more different. Walt was a creative guy with money to burn. Roy was a hard-headed businessman trying to save his company.

Under Roy, the Florida project—now to be called Walt Disney World, to honor his brother—took on a different focus. He couldn't see EPCOT being the moneymaker the company needed, so the part with the rides, the Magic Kingdom, would be the main attraction. As for EPCOT, it would never be a real "city" the way Walt had envisioned—but people in Florida didn't need to know that just yet. Instead, EPCOT would become leverage with the politicians—an ironic outcome, given Walt's true intentions.

On Walt's desk when he died lay a memo from Helliwell outlining the legal ramifications of creating a new city. He foresaw a big problem: EPCOT's residents. They'd want a say in the way their city was run. They would want elections.

On the memo, anywhere Helliwell mentioned "elections," Walt had written "NO" in large red letters. Wherever Helliwell mentioned "permanent residents," Walt crossed it out and wrote "temporary residents/tourists." Walt wanted a city of the future, but he had no interest in citizens of the future if it meant giving up control.

Four days after Walt's death, Helliwell stood up in front of some legislators to tell them that his late client had wanted nothing more than to build an experimental city. To make Walt's dream come true, Helliwell said, the company needed to charter two municipalities. That part, he said, was still being drafted.

Two months later, he unveiled the specifics. In a nine-hundred-seat theater in Winter Park, Helliwell, Roy Disney, and other Disney executives in effect dictated their terms to newly elected Gov. Claude Kirk, his cabinet, and half the legislature. The Disney execs needed a theater because that allowed them to deploy their secret weapon: a movie clip of their dead genius.

In the movie, Walt talked briefly about a Magic Kingdom ten times as big as Disneyland, then brought up his dream of "starting from scratch on virgin land and building a special kind of new community." He called it "a living blueprint for the future," where "everything . . . will be dedicated to the happiness of the people." Well, everything but the right to vote, but nobody from Disney mentioned that part.

To make it happen, the Disney executives said, they needed a lot of things—new highway interchanges, a wider I-4, bonding authority, special trademark protection, and those two municipalities, which would be known as Bay Lake and EPCOT. But what was most important was creating something called the Reedy Creek Improvement District that would cover all of Disney's twenty-seven thousand acres. The Disney execs made it sound like this was no big deal, yet Reedy Creek would be a governmental entity the likes of which Florida had never before seen.

The legislature reacted to Disney's demands the way the woodland creatures did to Cinderella needing a fancy dress: They did everything they could to give the company what it wanted. All of the Disney-related bills passed in twelve days and Kirk signed them. Later, when it was too late, one of the lawmakers admitted that he hadn't really read the Reedy Creek Improvement District bill thoroughly. Once he saw how it worked out, he regarded it as "one of the worst things that ever happened" in Florida. Why? "Because it gave them too many powers."

He's not alone in that opinion.

"Never before or since has such outlandish dominion been given to a private corporation," Carl Hiaasen wrote. "Disney runs its own utilities. It administers its own planning and zoning. It composes its own building codes and employs its own inspectors. It maintains its own fire department . . . Florida's starstruck lawmakers didn't stop there. They also gave Disney's puppet government the authority to build its own international airport and even its own nuclear power plant—neither of which the company has needed . . . yet."

As for those two "cities," the "residents" are Disney execs and their families.

And while Florida's Sunshine Law applies to city and county and state governments, the Reedy Creek government meets in the shadows.

The flip side to Disney's autonomy is that it's not responsible for what it spawned outside its own borders—the sclerotic traffic, the loss of farmland, the sprawl of T-shirt shops and strip malls, the rise of a minimum-wage majority who work service industry jobs and barely scrape by. Local governments must grapple with all that without any help from the House of Mouse.

Disney opened the Magic Kingdom in 1971, and eventually opened EPCOT in 1982. It looked nothing like what Walt had described. It wasn't a City of Tomorrow. It was just another theme park, offering a scaled-down Eiffel Tower and Taj Mahal and Disney-fied versions of international cuisine. The only way where you can see what EPCOT should have been is if you go to Tomorrowland in the Magic Kingdom and ride the Blue Line, a slow-moving tram that circles through several of the rides and the gift shop. It passes a scale model of the original EPCOT, with churches and schools and other features that were never built.

Don't get me wrong. As a parent, I'm glad the Magic Kingdom is just ninety minutes from my doorstep. My kids have enjoyed every ride or event we've ever tried there, from Buzz Lightyear's Space Ranger Spin in Tomorrowland to battling Darth Vader as part of the Jedi Training Academy in Disney Hollywood.

They even learned about patience at theme parks. One of them recently informed me that among his classmates, "doing a Disney" is a phrase that means "finding you're in a long line full of twists and turns." (To avoid "doing a Disney," some wealthy New Yorkers paid disabled people from Florida to lead their tour groups through the park, so they could take advantage of Disney's practice of giving handicapped visitors a separate, faster entrance to rides. After newspapers blew the whistle, Disney stopped it.)

As a homeowner, though, I have to say I'm glad Disney is no closer to me than ninety minutes away. I wouldn't want to live anywhere near the car-clogged region that now boasts six of America's eight most popular theme parks.

"Show me a mayor in the United States who wouldn't love to have Disney . . . as a neighbor," said the mayor of Orlando on the theme park's tenth anniversary in 1981. Just nine years later, though, in 1990, he moved to North Carolina "to get away from all the traffic."

Everyone wanted some of those Disney dollars—even NASA, which began offering tours of Cape Canaveral. Brevard's towns advertised to the Disney throngs that they had the nearest beach. As its moon landings stopped and its space shuttles blew up, the space center built a Shuttle Launch Experience ride for tourists, as well as something called an Astronaut Training Experience at the Astronaut Hall of Fame, all part of the Kennedy Space Center Visitor Complex. Instead of attracting visitors with actual space shots, NASA tries drawing visitors with fake experiences that make them feel like they are the ones in space.

Sometimes—even in Florida—reality overwhelms fantasy. Disney World is known for its fakery—its fake trees that look real, its fake buildings that disguise their true functions its fake presidents who are just as stiff as the real thing. In the late 1980s, though, Disney tried putting real animals in a venue called Discovery Island. The island had lemurs, giant tortoises, flamingos, hornbills, kookaburras, trumpeter swans, and scarlet ibises.

For a while it was also home to the most endangered bird in America, the dusky seaside sparrow. The little bird used to thrive in marshes north of Cape Canaveral's launch pads, but its habitat had been all but wiped out by the NASA-driven growth there, the new roads that Walt Disney liked so much, and state efforts to control mosquitoes.

Disney volunteered to oversee a last-ditch captive-breeding program to save the species. Unfortunately, by the time biologists went looking for sparrows to breed, they found only five males. The last dusky seaside sparrow died at Discovery Island in 1988, the last bird species on the federal endangered list to go extinct.

What Discovery Island had in abundance were vultures. They pooped on everything, tore up vinyl seats, stole the tortoises' food, and regurgitated all over. Attempts to drive them away with fireworks and helicopters failed. This was something Disney could not control. Other birds became a nuisance too—falcons, hawks, and owls attacked the show pigeons. Meanwhile, two native bird species, egrets and ibises, defecated too much and made too much noise, Disney officials concluded.

Disney got a federal permit to trap one hundred of the vultures and relocate them far from Discovery Island. What happened next was like something out of *The Lord of the Flies*.

Seventy-two vultures were captured and crammed into an unventilated shed big enough for only three of them. Some died. Two employees beat some of the trapped vultures to death, jotting logbook entries that said, "Found 3 or 4 dead vultures. I guess you wouldn't know how they got that way." Workers tried shooting the hawks with a .22 caliber rifle. This was all illegal. One employee later told state investigators that they had not sought government permission to kill any of the birds because "it was company policy that there should not be a permit or request for a permit in a public file that indicated that Walt Disney World Co. had requested a permit to kill animals."

In 1990, Disney paid $95,000 to make its Discovery Island animal cruelty charges go away. It shuttered the attraction and today the place remains abandoned, its buildings slowly being overtaken by nature—the real nature, the kind that Disney has figured out how to contain and market at nearby Animal Kingdom.

In the mid-1990s, Disney finally built a real city with real people in it. It didn't look like a City of Tomorrow but like the Small Town of Yesterday. That was the idea—to recreate the tin-roofed, picket-fenced ambience of a small town next door to the world's greatest theme park. They called it Celebration. The governing body for the town is a community development district, just like in the Villages, which means voting is based on how much land you own. Disney owns the most so it still controls the town. Walt would be proud.

But not even Disney can control human nature. In 2010, homes in Celebration were going into foreclosure. The town experienced its first murder—a fifty-eight-year-old teacher bludgeoned to death—as well as its first suicide after a police standoff. Not much celebrating went on in Celebration that year, because everything got a little too real.

Trying to figure out what's real and what's not is an essential skill for Floridians, and especially Florida journalists. And creating our *own* false fronts has had an impact all over the world.

Soldiers from Company E of the Ninth Infantry read newspapers in camp during training in Tampa for the Spanish-American War, 1898. Photo courtesy of State Archives of Florida.

14

See You in the Funny Papers

Reading the news in Florida resembles scanning through . . . a
list of the more unbelievable urban legends.

—Jason Marc Harris, "Absurdist Narratives in the
Sunshine State: Comic, Criminal, Folkloric,
and Fantastic Escapades in the Swamps
and Suburbs of Florida"

Florida's journalistic fraternity has a deep, dark secret. Lean in close
and I'll reveal it to you. Ready? Here it is:

Covering news in Florida is . . . *fun.* SHHH!!! Don't tell anyone!

It's a blast to be a reporter in Florida. Every beat you cover offers an opportunity for wackiness. Politics? "Florida Senate candidate admits to sacrificing
goat, drinking its blood." Courts? "Breast implant leak delays congressman's
wife's bigamy trial." Local government? "Man the lifeboats! Ocoee city hall
is sinking." Cops? "Felon wields sword, guitar in bloody tattoo-shop attack."
The mother lode is my beat, the environment—pythons battling alligators,
bears hanging out in hot tubs, sea cucumbers dwindling because they're
supposedly an aphrodisiac, etc.

Even the most innocuous story you write can turn out to have a Florida
twist. A simple story on a truck overturning can turn into "Shark Dies in
Crash on Florida Interstate." In 2013, a photo of a screaming Miami Heat fan
flipping off player Joachim Noah for being ejected went viral. The fan turned
out to be a millionaire widow who'd been accused of (though never charged
with) killing her fourth husband in a case that involved a three-hundred-
pound psychic and a male stripper named Tiger.

My reporter friends who have worked in Florida and moved away tell me they miss it terribly. They miss the sunshine and beaches, of course, but what they really miss is the steady flow of weird stories. They miss them the way an ex-smoker misses nicotine. Whenever a weird Florida story hits the national news, they look around at their gaping newsroom colleagues and say, "Oh, yeah. That's Florida." Often they say it wistfully.

What few people realize, though, is that without one Florida newspaper, the world would not have a crucial journalistic technique, one that has proved essential to our fast-paced, heavily aggregated online meme creators.

I am speaking here of the great storytelling innovation known as the listicle.

This goes back to NASA's arrival in Cape Canaveral. When the rising tide of slide-rule-toting engineers turned into a pocket-protector-wearing human tsunami, one newspaper editor from frigid South Dakota watched with great interest.

The editor's name was Al Neuharth. He stood five foot seven, if he stretched. He was a self-professed SOB, the kind of guy who would screw over a friend and expect the friend to say thanks for the learning experience. He invariably dressed in black, white, and gray. People who worked for him said that when he showed up in his sharkskin suit, you couldn't tell where the shark left off and Al began.

At the *Miami Herald,* Neuharth was in charge of reporters covering state news, and the big story in Florida then was the space program. Neuharth visited the Space Coast as often as possible to hobnob with astronauts and NASA bigwigs. He listened to what people talked about. As Brevard County swelled up like the world's biggest water balloon, he could see possibilities that his peers could not.

Neuharth went to Jim Knight, the general manager of the *Herald.* Brevard had nothing but local weeklies or afternoon papers, he said. Out-of-town morning papers like the *Herald* and the *Orlando Sentinel* covered Brevard, but from an outsider's perspective. The *Herald* should start a new morning daily in Brevard, he said, one backed by the *Herald*'s resources but headquartered in the Space Coast.

Knight laughed. He pointed out that the *Herald* was doing fine financially without taking on such a big risk. Neuharth dropped the idea—temporarily. He went to the *Herald*'s sister paper in Detroit for a while, then was hired away by a chain called Gannett. Almost from the moment he set foot in Gannett's corporate offices, he was talking up his Brevard idea.

"During the interviewing process," Neuharth recalled later, "I had told [the CEO] that I had a strong interest in and knowledge of the state of Florida, and that Gannett ought to be in Florida."

The CEO said Gannett had tried repeatedly to buy Florida newspapers but never with success.

"Well," Neuharth told him, "maybe you should start one."

While Neuharth thought this was a great idea, history was against him. Since the end of World War II, only one new newspaper had been success-fully launched in America—*Newsday* on Long Island. Still, he managed to convince the CEO to let him try.

First he hit the publishers of the local papers, telling them about Gannett's plans and then saying, "We hope you won't get hurt." The prospect of com-peting with a big chain was enough to convince them to sell to Gannett.

Meanwhile, Neuharth commissioned pollster Lou Harris to produce a study of potential subscribers. The results showed what he'd expected. They were "from all over the country, some from all over the world," he said. "Most of them were well-educated [and] . . . their interests went well beyond the boundaries of Cocoa or Titusville or Melbourne or wherever they happened to be living."

Those potential readers wanted "a more sophisticated daily newspaper that would emphasize heavily space coverage," Neuharth said. They also wanted "news from beyond the Space Coast, coverage in Florida, the U.S. generally, and around the world." And most important, they didn't have a lot of time to spend reading long stories. Neuharth knew what to do.

The newspaper that debuted on March 21, 1966, didn't look like the gray-faced papers then circulating everywhere else. It had been designed to be "a breezy-looking paper," Neuharth said, "breezy in content and appearance." The colors jumped out at you. The comics page was in color too, a first for the nation. As for the content, the stories were jazzy and tended to be short.

"It was designed to appeal to those who were in a hurry," Neuharth said.

To veteran journalists, the new paper looked and read like a print version of the TV news. It even carried a TV show's name: *Today*.

Neuharth accused the editor who dreamed up the name of ripping off NBC's morning talk show. The guy insisted he had been out drinking until dawn, and as he staggered home, the name popped into his head. Whether stolen from TV or a drunkard's dream, Neuharth liked it. What he liked even better was what the designers did with the idea, adding Saturn's rings to the O and the slogan "Florida's Space Age Newspaper."

The new paper, *Cocoa Today* (renamed *Florida Today* in 1985) became a circulation and advertising smash. Within two years, it was making money and pushing out the Orlando and Miami papers. This unlikely triumph fueled Neuharth's already mammoth ego. In the *Today* lobby, he enshrined a bust of the newspaper's founder, i.e., himself. His reporting staff, resentful of his skinflint tendency toward their needs compared to his lavish spending on his own whims, would sneak over to the bust at night and tape pennies to its eyes.

Now living on the beach in Cocoa in a house known to the staff as "Pumpkin Center," Neuharth was delighted at his baby's success—but he wasn't done. He wanted to create another paper, this one on a national scale. He took control of Gannett as CEO in 1973. By the end of that decade, he had set plans in motion for what he'd code-named NN, for "New Newspaper." His critics said it stood for "Neuharth's Nonsense."

Neuharth picked a team of young executives to brainstorm about the NN and installed them in Cocoa Beach in a building five blocks from Pumpkin Center. He picked that spot so he could keep an eye on their progress, and for another reason.

"I wanted them to be where *Florida Today* reminded them of the success of a new newspaper and where they could see how it was done," he explained, adding, "I wanted them in the shadows of the launch pad at Kennedy Space Center, where I think there is more vision per square mile than anywhere on Earth."

Is it any surprise that Neuharth's second paper looked a lot like his first?

The first *USA Today*—unveiled in a 1982 ceremony that featured President Ronald Reagan—had the same jazzy colors, the same breezy style, the same addiction to brevity as its Sunshine State predecessor. It had some of the same staffers. The headquarters for what they called "the Nation's Newspaper" even boasted another bust of Neuharth. The reporters still taped coins to its eyes, but now they were quarters.

"A lot of that Florida background and experience . . . helped us make it work at *USA Today*," Neuharth said.

USA Today spurred a wholesale change in the look and content of newspapers around the country—and more. Press critic Jack Shafer noted that *USA Today* contained "so many of the visual motifs that would become common on homepages a decade later when the Web really got rolling that you've got to suppress the urge to click and scroll."

Neuharth's newspaper even altered people's reading habits. "It seems to me that the short attention span of the reader has become a self-fulfilling thing. *USA Today* made the reader what he is," Choire Sicha, a *Gawker* editor who founded the site The Awl, said. Web sites have become "an experience of looking, not of reading . . . numbers in huge type, pictures, polls. Databits. Postliterate!"

Much has been made of how Neuharth dictated that the lead story on the first issue of *USA Today* would not be a big plane crash, but rather would focus on the car wreck that killed Princess Grace of Monaco or, as the headline called her, "America's Princess."

What's often overlooked is what was in the bottom left-hand corner of that page: a box called "USA Snapshots." That first Snapshot featured a bar graph showing retirement costs in major cities. It didn't go with anything else on the page—just floated out there on its own, clinging to the edge of 1A.

What was it doing there? The Snapshot was a colorful way to snag the readers' interest without burdening them with a lot of information. Sometimes it was a poll, sometimes a set of statistics. Often it had a headline that included the word "we" or "our," in an overly folksy attempt at inclusiveness. It was, in short, a listicle before we knew the word. Someone dubbed it a "charticle," which is pretty close.

The weirdly random nature of these Snapshots inspired plenty of spoofs. The satirical Web site The Onion created a "Statshot" with such titles as "Where Are We Scoring Our Heroin?" and "What Are We Hoping and Praying No One Ever Finds Out About?"

Miami Herald humor columnist Dave Barry, who won a Pulitzer for getting the word "booger" into print more than any other journalist, brought up the Snapshot when he interviewed Neuharth about his memoir, *Confessions of an S.O.B.* Barry noted that "the book is written in Neuharth-*USA Today* style, meaning it:

1. Has short sentences and short paragraphs.
2. Has lots of lists.
3. Is aimed at the average person.
4. Or reasonably bright fish."

Neuharth bragged that his paper was superior to all others, including Barry's own, where Neuharth used to work.

"There are more facts in *USA Today* than in *The Miami Herald* or *The New York Times*," Neuharth said, which Barry wrote was "probably true. Although *The Times'* facts tend to involve issues such as Lebanon. Whereas a lot of the *USA Today* facts concern things like What Flavor Gum We're Chewing."

My colleagues and I used to joke about *USA Today* winning the Pulitzer for "best investigative paragraph," but I think we were overlooking the paper's very real influence on American journalism, creating something people would read no matter how odd or disconnected to the news it might seem.

But *USA Today* is still not the most influential Florida-spawned paper ever.

Sometimes the stories we cover do more than go viral. Sometimes they affect the course of history.

In 1988, Colorado senator Gary Hart was the front-runner for the Democratic nomination for president. Hart had been the subject of repeated rumors about womanizing, rumors that Hart denied. In one interview Hart even challenged reporters to check up on him.

"Follow me around," he said. "I'm serious. If anybody wants to put a tail on me, go ahead. They'd be very bored." It must have seemed a safe thing to say, because back then most reporters considered Hart's personal life off-limits.

Meanwhile, though, *Miami Herald* political reporter Tom Fiedler had gotten a tip that Hart was cheating on his wife with a Miami woman, someone the senator had met during a yacht trip to Bimini. His tipster was a costume designer who had been on the boat for a party. She said Hart's new girlfriend had confessed the affair to her, and even shown her a photo of her with the senator. Fielder went after the story with every resource the *Herald* could muster.

Was this really a story? Yes—not for the infidelity but for the lying. American presidents had lied about Vietnam, about Watergate, about swapping arms for hostages. Now here came a politician who portrayed himself as an alternative to those lying politicians. Yet he displayed what reporters regarded as a pattern of subtly shading the truth about aspects of his life—shaving a year off his age, for instance. If he was a liar regarding his infidelity, then his whole campaign was a fraud.

Five *Herald* reporters staked out Hart's Washington town house and spotted the blond woman Fiedler had heard about. Her name was Donna Rice. She was sort of an actress (she had appeared in one episode of *Miami Vice*) and a model (a photo of her showing off J. C. Penney's latest swimsuit design would later turn up on the cover of *Paris Match*). She appeared to be spending the night with Hart while the senator's wife was in Denver.

When the *Herald* reporters confronted Hart in an alley, he didn't help his cause. They asked if the woman was in his house, and he replied, "She may or may not be." They asked if he was denying that he met her on a yacht.

"I'm not denying anything," Hart said heatedly. He was trying not to lie, but his evasions sounded desperate.

After the *Herald* story broke, Hart denied having any "personal relationship" with Rice, or even that she had spent the night with him. But then it turned out the yacht was called *Monkey Business,* and the *National Enquirer* published a photo of Rice sitting on Hart's lap on the dock near the boat, with Hart wearing a shirt that said MONKEY BUSINESS CREW. It ran a story too, headlined, "Gary Hart Asked Me to Marry Him," but that didn't have nearly the impact as what the paper billed as "Exclusive Photos of Fun-Filled Weekend in the Bahamas." When that issue hit the nation's supermarket checkout counters, Hart's campaign sank like a leaky rowboat.

From then on, candidates' private lives were fair game for everyone looking for a scandal. Instead of calling them "personal," such probes by journalists and politicians became inquiries into "character." Without the *Miami Herald* chasing Hart down an alley, there might never have been an effort to impeach President Bill Clinton for lying about his affair with a White House intern, an impeachment led by a Georgia congressman who was at that moment cheating on his wife too.

But that's not my point. My point is that whenever this story is told, the role of the *National Enquirer* usually gets short shrift, which I believe is a mistake. Why? For two reasons: (1) That picture is what really shut down Hart, and (2) the *Enquirer* was a Florida newspaper.

This is where I'd like to point out that Florida is now the center of the modern media universe. A lot of people think it's New York, home of the *New York Times* and the *Wall Street Journal*. Others contend it's California, because of all the movies and TV shows there. Nope. It's Palm Beach County, Florida.

Exhibit A in my case for Palm Beach involves a round mound of sound known as Rush Hudson Limbaugh III. Limbaugh, the most popular syndicated radio show host in America, left his home in New York to relocate to a palatial waterfront estate in Palm Beach in 1996. He's been broadcasting from a Florida studio ever since, reaching hundreds of millions of fans who call themselves Dittoheads.

"One of the great things about your show is it's broadcast in the Sunshine State, for which a whole lot of Floridians are very grateful, including me," Jeb Bush told Limbaugh in 2008.

Limbaugh's presence has encouraged lesser lights of the right-wing chattering class to settle nearby: Lou Dobbs, Dick Morris, Conrad Black, and Ann Coulter all landed in Palm Beach (where Coulter once got in trouble for voting in the wrong precinct, then blamed election officials for her error). Matt Drudge and his ugly but essential Web site settled in the Miami area. Christopher Ruddy planted his Newsmax magazine and Web site in West Palm Beach and started laying plans to take on Fox in the TV realm. The presence of so many conservative pundits prompted the *New York Times* to dub the area "the Right Coast."

(Some other big names got started in Florida and then departed: Glenn Beck first tried his hand at talk radio on a Tampa station, and long before he became MSNBC's "Morning Joe," Joe Scarborough was a rock'n'roll-loving congressman from Pensacola.)

So why did Limbaugh land in Florida? Blame the Big Apple. According to his biographer, Limbaugh hated the decade he spent living in New York. He kept vying to join the ranks of the media elite there, but never was able to get past the velvet rope. The place was expensive, thanks in part to a state income tax. Because of the traffic and the parking, he had to either hire a chauffeur or walk to go anywhere (and given his girth, he wasn't much for walking). He kept hoping people would recognize him, but in New York that seldom happened.

"When strangers did recognize him," his biographer wrote, "they were often rude."

Palm Beach, on the other hand, seemed like a GOP-designed paradise. Plenty of the wealthy people who lived there were fans, so he was frequently saluted by Dittoheads. In such a carcentric state, he could drive all over in his $450,000 Maybach 57S or one of his six other expensive rides. Given the usually balmy weather, he could even leave the top down. And thanks to Gov. Hardee's handiwork in the 1920s, Florida charged no state income tax.

Five homes stand on Limbaugh's waterfront estate. The main one, in which he lives, measures twenty-four thousand square feet and includes gleaming cherrywood floors, handwoven oriental carpets, and a mahogany-paneled library. By the time Limbaugh gets home from a hard day in his studio, his staff has lit scented candles for him to enjoy, as he gazes upon the life-size oil painting of himself hanging on the wall of the main staircase.

Limbaugh has always boasted that he has "talent on loan from God," but once he moved to Florida it has sometimes seemed as if God was initiating repossession proceedings. First he went deaf, an ironic fate for a man whose entire career is built on the spoken word. He couldn't even hear his own voice. A cochlear implant helped, although he says he now finds many common sounds irritating. When he's not performing, "I crave silence, blessed silence because anything other than speech is just noise."

Then he and his third wife split up. Limbaugh and the former aerobics instructor lived in separate houses on his estate for years (an advantage to having several homes in one spot) before they at last divorced.

Then came the ultimate humiliation: Limbaugh, who had once sneered at drug abusers, was busted for abusing painkillers, his shame splashed in newspapers across the country.

And for that he could blame Palm Beach County's other major media star, my Exhibit B for Palm Beach being the center of the media universe: the *National Enquirer.*

The scandal sheet paid Limbaugh's supplier, a member of his household staff, to spill the dirt. Every step that followed—charges by the state attorney's office, probation, and rehab—was played up by the *Enquirer.*

Limbaugh bounced back, of course. His listeners forgave him. The funny part is, he'd wanted to be treated as a celebrity. He got what he'd wished for.

Like Limbaugh, the *Enquirer* originally tried to make it in New York. Its owner, Generoso Pope Jr., was the son of New York's sand and gravel king. Thanks to his father's connections, Pope's godfather was Frank Costello, head of the Luciano crime family. Those connections unfortunately attracted the FBI, and Pope's dad wound up convicted of racketeering.

For a time Pope, who graduated from the Massachusetts Institute of Technology with a degree in mechanical engineering, ran an Italian-language newspaper owned by his father. Then he spent a little while working for the CIA in its psychological warfare section. He told people later that he didn't like it. He had bigger plans. He quit and borrowed thousands of dollars from his godfather and bought a struggling newspaper, the *New York Enquirer.*

Then he set about completely remaking it. He cut down its size from broadsheet to tabloid, made its stories shorter (long before Al Neuharth came along), and focused on blood, gore, sex, and celebrities. In 1954, he unveiled his true ambition, changing his tabloid's name to the *National Enquirer.*

His greatest innovation wasn't the name, though. It was in realizing that corner stores and newsstands were no longer the best places to peddle his papers. Americans were moving into the suburbs and shopping at supermarkets. Pope went after supermarket executives, offering a deal they could not turn down: He'd sell at least half the papers he put in the store. If he didn't, he'd pay the store owner the difference.

To guarantee he'd never have to pay, he put his paper on a specially designed rack that would sit right by the store's checkout, exactly at eye level with the customers waiting in line—right where the garish front pages could grab their attention. When the *Enquirer* started selling in the supermarkets in the late 1960s, Pope was rolling in revenue.

In 1969, Pope got in his car and drove down I-95 to Florida, where he had already built his paper's national printing plant. He liked what he saw, and by 1971 he had moved his newspaper's headquarters there. He picked a nondescript two-story brick building sitting in a quiet Palm Beach County fishing town called Lantana, where the only other industry was a culvert manufacturer.

Soon the *Enquirer* became Lantana's largest employer, and Pope became the town's most prominent citizen. He gave generously to the Little League and local charities, and every year spent $1 million on what he swore was the biggest Christmas party in the world, featuring not just Santa but also an Elvis impersonator and toy trains and toy flying saucers and the grandest 150-foot Christmas tree his staff could find, decorated with every light and bit of tinsel they could locate.

Pope changed Lantana and its surrounding area forever. To staff his tabloid, he hired dozens of Fleet Street veterans, creating a colony of United Kingdom ex-pats amid the palm trees—Aussies, Kiwis, South Africans, Irish, and Scots as well as British. Pope wasn't shy about firing reporters too. The Fleet Streeters, now suntanned and determined to stay where it was warm, would just shrug and go to work for one of the other scandal sheets that had followed the *Enquirer* to the area now being called Tabloid Valley. Or they would get back on the *Enquirer* payroll as freelancers, using assumed names so Pope wouldn't know.

Although Pope was the King of Lantana, he didn't live there. Like Limbaugh, he bought a waterfront estate—not in tony Palm Beach but in nearby Manalapan. He drove an old Impala and spent six days a week at the Lantana office. On Saturdays, he'd show up wearing swim trunks, a T-shirt, and flip-flops.

Why move his whole operation to Florida? One source says it was to get out from under Frank Costello's influence ("Uncle Frank" liked to visit the newsroom once a week, an event that usually left the staff quivering). Another suggests the move came about because Pope hated unions and Florida is a right-to-work state. My theory is that he was trying to get out from under his father's shadow and find a place with cheap land prices for even waterfront property.

From his Florida newsroom, the soft-spoken but autocratic Pope dispatched reporters to every corner of the globe. He sent them to climb a Himalayan mountain and interview people who claimed to have seen the Yeti. He sent them to the Soviet Union, where officials were happy to talk about their paranormal experimentation. He sent one reporter to a series of would-be Shangri-las, searching for a modern Utopia, a search that cost some $100,000 and did not yield a single published story because no location measured up to Pope's expectations. He even sent a reporter to steal Henry Kissinger's garbage off the sidewalk and sort through it for state secrets.

Pope didn't mind spending money to score the stories that sold papers. He paid his reporters and editors far better salaries than they had ever made at stodgier, more mainstream publications. He was happy to spend big bucks buying stories from disgruntled movie stars' assistants, waiters in fancy restaurants who had witnessed a celebrity meltdown, even autopsy photos sold by crooked coroners. In 1978, when Elvis Presley died, the *Enquirer* ran a front-page photo of the King in his coffin and sold seven million copies, an all-time circulation record. The photo, shot by one of Presley's relatives in exchange for $18,000, was flown by private jet to Lantana, where the chief of police provided security as an official company car whisked it from the airport to Pope's waiting hands.

Pope's little Florida paper nailed plenty of political figures, including presidential candidate John Edwards (child out of wedlock) and Rev. Jesse Jackson (ditto). During the O. J. Simpson murder case, the *Enquirer* ran photos of Simpson wearing the same kind of shoes that left footprints at the crime scene, and broke the story that he'd written a book called *If I Did It.*

To me, the greatest thing Pope ever did was a little bit of recycling. Around 1979, the *Enquirer* switched from black-and-white presses to color, but Pope was loath to just junk the old equipment. Instead he created a new black-and-white tabloid called the *Weekly World News.*

Florida has a hall of fame called Great Floridians, and it includes everyone from Juan Ponce de León to golfer Bubba Watson along with a bunch of politicians and football coaches. But there's a glaring omission among those ranks: Eddie Clontz, who spent twenty years as editor of the *Weekly World News,* making it the wildest collection of screaming headlines in journalism history.

With Clontz at the helm, the *Weekly World News* reported stories nobody else would, stories revealing that a dozen U.S. senators were from another planet, that the lost continent of Atlantis had turned up near Buffalo, New York, and that a "bat boy" had been discovered living in a West Virginia cave.

Unlike most editors, Clontz always advised his staff not to be too skeptical.

"Never question yourself out of a good story," he would say.

"I think every journalist in the United States secretly envied Eddie Clontz. I did," *Washington Post* humor columnist Gene Weingarten told me. "Here was a man who simply refused, as a matter of principle, to allow truth to get in the way of a great story."

A tenth-grade dropout from North Carolina, Clontz was working on a clam boat when he joined friends on a tour of the *St. Petersburg Times–Evening Independent* newsroom. Watching people writing cutlines and laying out pages, Clontz thought, "Geez, I could do that." So he talked his way onto the staff of the afternoon *Evening Independent.*

Then, in 1981, he hired on to run Pope's little tabloid, which up until then had been filled with revamped *Enquirer* stories. Clontz had spent some time studying the history of sensational newspaper reporting, and he remade the paper into what he called "the last true tabloid in America," with barely believable tales like: "Blind Man Regains Sight and Dumps Ugly Wife!" and "3-Breasted Woman, 3-Armed Man Have 3-Legged Baby!"

In an era when other newspapers were firing reporters who made up stories, Clontz stood out as an editor unashamed of publishing fiction in a paper whose name included "News."

"We don't know whether the stories are true, and we don't really care," Clontz said. "When we inform people, it's usually an accident."

Sometimes the stories supposedly occurred in Florida: "Half-Human, Half-Fish Are Washing Up in Florida!" the *WWN* reported. "Half-Human, Half-Alligator Eats Six Campers in Florida!" it reported another time. One front-pager claimed gators measuring sixty feet long had been sighted in the Everglades. Another claimed that manatees were fighting back against their biggest human threat: "Gentle Sea Cows Attack Boozing Boaters!" (I saw that one clipped out and posted on the wall at the Save the Manatee Club headquarters in Maitland.)

More often, the stories originated from as far away as possible. University of Florida journalism professor Mike Foley, who had worked with Clontz at the *Evening Independent,* recalled visiting his old colleague when the *News* staff was trying to track down a story about a woman in California who had accidentally crushed her child by sitting on him. No one in California could confirm it.

"Finally, Eddie wrote, 'Dateline, Bolivia,' and said, 'Write it and print it,'" Foley said.

Clontz often wrote the weekly "Ed Anger" opinion column, which was so vitriolic that it made Limbaugh sound like St. Francis of Assisi. (Ed Anger's solution for school shootings? Arm every student so they could all shoot back.)

He took great care with the outlandish headlines. When his staff planned to run a cover story about the face of Satan being photographed floating above Washington, D.C., Clontz ordered the headline changed.

"Make it 'Face of Satan Seen Over U.S. Capitol!' Now make it bigger. Remember, we need to catch the reader in a couple of seconds. Bigger. Bigger. Good." Then he said the subhead should be "Has the Devil escaped from Hell?"

By going over the top, the little tabloid climbed into the readers' hearts. The *Weekly World News* became a pop icon, with TV shows such as *The X-Files* and movies such as *Men in Black* suggesting that its craziest stories were true. The tale of Bat Boy became an off-Broadway musical. In 1992, when the *News* announced that a visiting space alien had endorsed Bill Clinton, incumbent President George Bush said he was disappointed to lose such a supporter.

Clontz's biggest scoop began with an anonymous letter from a reader claiming he'd spotted Elvis stuffing his face with a triple cheeseburger at a Burger King in Michigan, rather than lying a-moldering in the grave. Clontz saw possibilities.

"Hey," Clontz said to an editor named Joe West, "let's do an 'Elvis is alive' story."

"Hell no," West replied. "Who's going to believe that crap?"

"Maybe a million people," Clontz predicted.

That issue, bearing the headline, "Elvis Is Alive—That Was a Double in My Coffin!" became the first *Weekly World News* to sell one million copies. It spawned a running gag in the *News* as the paper periodically checked in with Elvis to see what new adventures he'd had. It also spawned a pop culture meme that inspired movies, cartoons, TV gags, even a song. "Elvis is Everywhere," by Mojo Nixon and Skid Roper, suggested that not only was the King still around, but he was behind some of the great mysteries of the universe, such as the Bermuda Triangle.

In 1993, Weingarten phoned Clontz to pass along a suggestion from Dave Barry that the *News* should now report that Elvis had just died, this time for real.

"I could hear the wheels turning," Weingarten recalled. "Eddie knew this would end a cottage industry of tabloid Elvis-still-lives articles, basically cripple the franchise—but, man, what a story!"

A few weeks later the story hit the stands: "Elvis Dead At 58."

"It was a huge scoop," Weingarten said. Time passed, and then the *News* "exclusively learned sometime later that reports of Elvis's death were a hoax. And they were back in the Elvis business."

Meanwhile, the *Enquirer* made a bid for respectability, breaking legitimate stories amid talk of a Pulitzer nomination. When *Time* magazine named *Enquirer* editor Steve Coz one of its most influential Americans in 2007, Coz had no illusions about his paper's true influence.

"Every single network, every single magazine in America has gone more celebrity," Coz said. "That's the *Enquirer*'s influence, whether you like it or don't like it."

That these two scrappy little tabloids could wield such outsized power over the news diet being fed to the public seems not just remarkable but astounding—unless of course you subscribe to the theory that Pope never really quit the CIA's psychological warfare unit, and his screaming headlines and celebrity focus were actually experiments in government propaganda and rumor control.

Naaaaaaaaaaah, nobody would believe that story.

These days, while Elvis may still be alive, Eddie Clontz is dead (and, worse, his obituary revealed that his real first name was Harold). Generoso Pope Jr. died too, and his tabloid empire was swallowed by a big corporation that moved it back to New York. The *National Enquirer*'s Lantana HQ is now a charter school, and the *Weekly World News* is an online publication only, no longer offering gasp-inducing entertainment to bored shoppers waiting for the checker to ring up their ramen noodles.

Instead, they have to content themselves with perusing all the sex-related magazine story teases from *Cosmopolitan,* the cleavage-baring starlet photos on the front of *People* and *Us Weekly,* the acres of flat midriffs and perky but-tocks on the exercise mags with names like *Glutes.*

To Floridians, though, those sights are nothing special. We see that much flesh every day. Because this is a sun-soaker's paradise, Florida can seem virtu-ally saturated in S-E-X. You might even call us the Sinshine State.

A stripper accused of showing too much skin during a performance gives Pinellas County Judge David Demers a good look at the evidence for the defense, namely that her panties are far too large to expose the area that is forbidden, 1983. Photo by Jim Damaske. Photo courtesy of Jim Damaske.

15

The Sinshine State

The principal thing that most tourists do is loaf in the sun,
usually with as few clothes on as the law permits.
—FRANK PARKER STOCKBRIDGE AND JOHN HOLLIDAY PERRY,
SO THIS IS FLORIDA, 1938

One afternoon when I was at my office, a young woman called and said
she worked for a network morning show.

"They're starting a weird news segment," she said, "and I hear you write
about weird stuff, and I wondered if you had any story ideas for me."

"Lady," I said, "this is Florida. We get that kind of stuff every day. Just
read the papers!"

Her call got me thinking about the essential elements of Florida Weird,
and how they might be combined to create the Ultimate Weird Florida Story.
I drew up a list of common elements, including these points:

- Nudity is not essential, but it is recommended ("Florida Man Tasered
  After Naked Marriage Proposal at Wrong House").
- The presence of an animal helps, especially an alligator, whether large
  or small ("Alligator Crashes UF Students' Lake Alice Picnic"). Some
  sort of big snake is good ("Missing King Cobra Snake Found Under
  Dryer"). Monkeys are an old standby ("Monkey on Loose in Florida
  Steals Mail, Hearts"). Llamas are the new hotness ("Four Llamas In-
  volved in Florida Car Crash").
- The participation of Florida's many sex-industry workers tends to

boost the story's visibility ("Stripper, Boyfriend and 72-Year-Old Meth Suspect Busted in Stolen Car").

- You'd be amazed how many stories there are about sexual encounters gone horribly awry ("A night of drinking resulted in a wild ride, sex behind the wheel, a gun to the head, a crash and a 26-year-old Port Charlotte woman under arrest" is one of the best Florida story openers ever). You'd also be amazed at how great the mug shots tend to be.
- Note that said sexual encounter does *not* have to involve a couple ("DUI Driver with Sex Toy in Tush Rear-Ends Other Driver" is the classic, although I also like "Man Arrested for Blow-Up Doll Orgy in Parked Lincoln Town Car").

Why do sex and sin play such a huge role in wacky Florida stories? Blame the weather, for starters. As *So This Is Florida* noted, the state is so hot for so much of the year that people tend to strip down as far as they dare. This is especially true for our tourists from colder climes, such as those pale and overweight European guys who think a size XS T-shirt and Speedos are proper attire for Disney.

Some folks go all the way nude. We've got only one beach that's legally certified for nude sunbathing—Haulover Beach in Miami—but at least nine more, from the Panhandle to the Keys, where tradition says your birthday suit is your swimsuit.

Nudity is not confined to the dunes. We've got plenty of nudist resorts, including one near Kissimmee that maintains the American Nudist Research Library, and one on the Suwannee River run by the Bare Buns Bikers. Pasco County is widely known for its nudist resorts. One of my favorite Florida stories involved a woman staying at a Pasco resort who went for a nude swim in a lake. She was attacked by an alligator, and saved by her equally nude husband, thus fulfilling two of the categories on my top ten list.

Even the most mundane activities become newsworthy when they involve a nudist colony. My friend Corky says one of his best reporting assignments was covering a Land O' Lakes Naturist Volunteer Fire Department drill: "The old coots emerged from their trailers wearing hats and boots and nothing else and yelling, 'Grab your hoses!'"

The proliferation of these resorts has led to lots of nudists moving here full time. Many were assisted by a nudist-friendly real estate agent, who then got his own reality TV show. If there were Emmy awards for artful cropping, that show would have won them all.

Pasco's greatest contribution to sex-related Florida headlines involved something beyond nudity. I am speaking here of the Hall of Fame headline from

2010, "Fetish Model Indicted in Pasco Sex Party Slaying" by my friend Molly Moorhead. The victim, a biker who owned a tattoo parlor, was found on a massage table, stabbed to death, and then his head, crushed by a sledgehammer. The model had help from her boyfriend, a porn actor and sometime DJ, although she was married to someone else. Reading the story felt like playing Florida Mad Libs.

Because of our tourists, Florida offers a lot of strip joints—fifty in the Miami area, another thirty or so in Tampa, smaller numbers in other towns. They provide us with a lot of story fodder.

In 1983, Clearwater police busted some strippers for showing too much of what their mamas gave them. In court, one dancer bent over to show the judge that her panties were too big to expose much skin. As a photographer snapped the photo, the judge quickly dismissed the case.

In 1996, a man sued a Clearwater strip joint claiming that when performer Tawny Peaks thrust her size 69HH breasts at his face, he suffered a neck injury. The case landed on *The People's Court,* where the judge—former New York City mayor Ed Koch—ruled for Ms. Peaks.

The most reliable newsmaker in Tampa is strip club magnate Joe Redner, credited by some with inventing the lap dance. Redner even ran for mayor (he lost). Before the 2012 Republican National Convention, the *New York Times* and the *New York Daily News* both wrote about how Tampa's legion of strippers was salivating at having so many Grand Old Partiers in town. Afterward, Redner admitted his strippers found the convention a bit of a bust.

Even our restaurants try to be sexy. The first Hooters opened in Clearwater in 1983, featuring the combo of Buffalo wings, beer, and waitresses in tight T-shirts and tiny orange shorts. Three years later, the first Hooters Girl, Lynne Austin, became *Playboy*'s Miss July, giving the chain national publicity. By 2014, Hooters had 412 restaurants in 27 countries, and entendre-heavy imitators had sprung up all over, creating a trend called "breastaurants." Yet what once seemed titillating now seems tame. In 2015, one of my colleagues reported that Hooters was now considered a "family restaurant."

Still, sex is all around us in Florida—even in the air, in the form of lovebugs, those euphemistically named invasive insects that flitter around joined together, male to female, too blissed-out to avoid being splatted by passing vehicles. Lovebugs are more than just a stimulant to the state's car-washing industry. They are a challenge to parents whose curious children ask why those bugs are stuck together. My best response came out as: "Uhhhh, one is giving the other a piggyback ride!"

In Florida, sex is money. Our tourism industry has been using sex as a weapon since Carl Fisher lined up bathing beauties on Miami Beach for photos to send the Northern papers. Across the state, St. Petersburg's publicity agent invented a Purity League to "complain" to the mayor about all the scantily clad women at the beach in the winter. The Northern papers ate it up. "Protect Our Husbands from the Wiles of the 'Sea Vamps'" read a *Pittsburgh Press* headline above a story with lots of pictures of "vamps."

"The human form is divine," the mayor, a bachelor, declared, "and judging from some of the bathers I have seen, a divinity shaped their ends for they are certainly well shaped."

It's not difficult to draw a direct line from those 1920s sales gimmicks to modern-day Panama City Beach hotels enticing spring breakers by promising the "world's largest & longest keg party, Wet T-shirt Contest, and Wet Jockey Short Contest."

Florida tourism ads of the 1980s featured a flirty blond lifeguard who purred, "The rules are different here." The implication was that there were no rules at all, that Florida was the place to fulfill your wildest desires and never fear the consequences.

Alas, consequences do occur. Just ask the guy visiting Orlando on his honeymoon who got busted trying to hire a prostitute who was an undercover cop. Or the couple, ages sixty-eight and forty-nine, who were caught having sex in the middle of a town square at the Villages. Or the Philadelphia weatherman vacationing in Miami whose bid for a threesome with two Latvian women he met in a bar led to him being lured into a swanky nightclub where he was drugged and ran up a charge of $48,000 on his American Express card. This eventually led to the indictment of seventeen people connected to the Russian mob. The nightclub owner got twelve years in prison, while the mobster who organized the racket got only three because he agreed to testify for the government. As for the weatherman, he lost his job.

Even people who aren't looking for a kinky time can be ensnared in Florida's sex games. The prime example: the New Jersey woman who in 2013 sued a posh South Beach hotel. She said a gang of ten high-priced prostitutes had assaulted her in the lobby. They took one look at her and figured she was a competitor horning in on their turf.

However that case turns out, I sincerely hope the Jersey lady will get a makeover. Perhaps she can borrow a look from the woman credited with setting the stage for America's sexual revolution.

Bettie Page grew up in Tennessee, graduated from Peabody College, and tried, briefly, to be a teacher. It didn't work out.

"I couldn't control my students," she said, "especially the boys."

When she moved to New York she met a cop who was an amateur photographer. He helped her assemble a portfolio of cheesecake shots. A year later, she was posing for photos and the occasional stag film in spike heels and bondage gear, sold via mail order. Pictures of the raven-banged Page ran in nudge-nudge men's magazines with names like *Wink, Eyeful,* and *Titter.* Occasionally they spelled her name right.

Bettie's big break came on a trip to Florida. She hired herself out to local photographers shooting bikini-clad girls for postcards. One now-famous postcard, shot by Hans Hannau, showed her flashing her naughty-girl-next-door smile as a stuffed alligator appeared to snap at her rear. The caption: "Wow! We alligators do have fun in Florida!"

Then, thanks to a local newspaper columnist, Bettie met a photographer named Linnea Yeager. Nobody called her "Linnea." She had dubbed herself "Bunny," after a character Rita Hayworth played in the movies.

Bunny, who stood five foot ten and measured 36-25-37, had been crowned Queen of Miami, the Cheesecake Queen, and (best of all) Miss Trailer Coach of Dade County. She had posed for cheesecake photos herself, then decided she'd make more money behind the camera. Bunny knew how to talk to the models. She knew how to use Florida's bright and sometimes brutal sunshine to light her photos. She also knew how to sew, creating skimpy outfits for her shots.

She dressed Bettie in a leopard-print getup and took her out to the Africa USA theme park in Boca Raton. She posed her with a pair of cheetahs, plus some chimpanzees and zebras. She even had her swing from a tree limb, a knife in her teeth. Bettie, Queen of the Jungle! The wholesome but curvaceous Wild Woman of Florida! The sunlight brought out a more playful aspect of Bettie's sex appeal that had been obscured in her fetish-dungeon shots.

Bunny and Bettie were the perfect pairing of photographer and subject. Bunny shot a thousand pictures of Bettie, seeing in her a model who could exhibit a charismatic personality in any setting or costume—or no costume at all.

"When I told her I thought I might want to photograph her nude, she said, 'Funny, I sunbathe nude and I have a tan like this all over,'" Bunny recalled years later. "And she did, everywhere, even behind her knees and all the places you wouldn't think."

She posed a winking Bettie kneeling down to hang an ornament on a Christmas tree, wearing a Santa hat and nothing else. She sold that photo to a hot new magazine called *Playboy.* Hugh Hefner paid $100 to make Bettie Page one of his first—and most memorable—centerfolds.

Bettie's *Playboy* debut in 1955 sent her career in a new direction, exposing her sunny smile and other assets to a wider audience. She was named Miss Pinup of the World. Big-money offers poured in for modeling jobs, and her career took off.

By 1957, she had had enough. She hung up her stilettos and walked away, until a revival of interest in her in the 1990s brought her, reluctantly, back into the spotlight. By the time she died in 2008, a *TV Guide* poll had named her the "ultimate sex goddess."

Bunny Yeager, meanwhile, parlayed her work with Bettie Page into a long and lucrative photography career. She shot more *Playboy* centerfolds. She published a book on how she took her own cheesecake photos, even including sewing advice. When she died, her *New York Times* obituary declared that she was "widely credited with helping turn the erotic pinup—long a murky enterprise in every sense of the word—into high photographic art."

In other words, just as Linnea had transformed herself into Bunny, so she had also made her fantasy of becoming a world-renowned photographer come true too. How Florida is that?

Florida tries to cater to every possible fantasy. I wasn't kidding about the convocations of furries. They congregate near the theme parks, for obvious reasons.

Florida helped to thrust weird sex into national prominence in 1972 with the inexplicably successful porn film *Deep Throat,* financed by the Mafia and filmed at several locations around Miami. Two of its most notorious scenes were shot in a mansion owned by a man described in the local press as "bon vivant Baron Joseph 'Sepy' De Bicske Dobronyi." Over the years, guests who partied at his oddly configured home included Errol Flynn, Nat King Cole, John Wayne, and Raquel Welch.

Deep Throat starred Linda Lovelace as a woman whose G-spot is located near her esophagus—a completely believable medical condition to the men who bought tickets. The sixty-two-minute amateur hour was shot for $23,000 and made an estimated $600 million.

Before the movie, Lovelace had been Linda Borman, daughter of a retired cop. One day while she was sunbathing at a beachside condo, she was spotted by producer-pimp Chuck Traynor. Thanks to him she acquired a new last name, a new boyfriend (Traynor), and stardom. She was interviewed by Johnny Carson on *The Tonight Show,* appeared on the cover of *Esquire,* and posed for *Playboy.* (Eight years later she became an antiporn crusader.)

Deep Throat precipitated what one cultural critic called "a great national tie-loosening. It was a dirty movie, but it made a clean hit on the American psyche: Nothing was ever the same again."

After my call from the network news person, I quizzed some friends and col-leagues about what was the weirdest Florida story of all time. We winnowed the possibilities to three finalists. The winner, selected by me, was the ulti-mate in Florida sex scandals.

Let's start with the ads. They were far from discreet. "FROSTED BLONDE. Great tan, hot body, very sexual, turquoise eyes, romantic & sensual, seeking generous, affluent executive male for day/evening interludes. Fun loving & hot. Enclose business card."

Plenty of men answered that 1991 ad—so many that the thirty-three-year-old Tamarac woman who placed it, Kathy Willets, raked in $2,000 a week.

Then her husband fouled everything up.

Jeffrey Willets, forty-one, had persuaded his wife to quit her office job and become a stripper, and he had no problem with her taking up the oldest pro-fession, even meeting customers in the couple's own bedroom. He would hide in the closet and peep through the slats, jotting notes about how much clients paid, how long they stayed, and what sort of kinks they preferred.

One client seemed to be getting too cozy with Mrs. Willets. Jealous, Mr. Willets left a threatening message on the man's answering machine. The client called the cops, and everything unraveled. You see, Willets was him-self a cop—a Broward County sheriff's deputy for seventeen years. He'd fallen for Kathy while giving her a ticket and left his first wife for her. Now, thanks to a vengeful john, he was arrested for making a living as a pimp, then fired. His wife was busted for prostitution.

That might have been the end of it, except for Willets's legal pad list of clients. A prosecutor told reporters, "You'd probably find almost every pro-fession going, from advertising to zookeepers, with the possible exception of Buddhist monk." It also turned out that Willets had been videotaping his wife's amorous encounters.

Afraid the client list and videos would become public, several men, using the pseudonym John Doe, sued to keep everything secret. Clever entrepre-neurs peddled T-shirts proclaiming I'M NOT ON THE LIST. The question of making the list public went all the way to the Florida Supreme Court, which ruled that the men gave up their privacy by participating in a criminal act.

The biggest name on the list turned out to be Doug Danziger, Fort Lauder-dale's vice mayor. Danziger had built his political reputation on trying to close down nude bars and porn shops. He denied knowing Kathy Willets—a grainy video proved him a liar—but he resigned anyway, citing "personal reasons."

The couple hired a flamboyant attorney named Ellis Rubin, who played the media like a Stradivarius. Rubin contended Kathy Willets was driven to prostitution by nymphomania. And how had she become a nymphomaniac? It was, Rubin said, a side effect of taking the antidepressant Prozac—the same medication that Gov. Lawton Chiles was taking, although apparently with no similar symptoms.

Rubin said that because of Kathy Willets's insatiable appetite, her husband suffered from impotence. Thus their bordello operation was, in fact, couples therapy.

Rubin's laughable defense attracted international notice. Kathy Willets appeared on all the tabloid TV shows, posed for *Playboy,* and became, as the *Sun-Sentinel* put it, "America's sweet tart."

The "nympho defense" was never aired in a trial. The couple pleaded guilty and served time. When they got out, they cashed in on their notoriety by going into the porn business. Mrs. Willets tells me they're still married. She bills herself on Twitter as "Fla's Naughty Nympho."

What I like about the Naughty Nympho story is that just when you thought the story had gotten as weird as it could get, it got weirder. If there had been an alligator involved, then this would definitely be the Ultimate Florida Story, but it's probably about as close as we can get.

The Naughty Nympho is far from the only sex scandal in Florida history. As I mentioned, we've had legislators caught with prostitutes. We've had politicians caught propositioning cops in restrooms. We had a closeted congressman caught sending smutty texts to underage pages.

So many Florida ministers have succumbed to the temptations of the flesh that one newspaper compiled a top ten list. Two of them, though, shook up parishioners across the country.

One was the Rev. Henry Lyons, an African American minister from St. Petersburg who served as president of the National Baptist Convention, the largest black religious denomination in America. Lyons, a dynamic pulpit pounder, was equally adept at schmoozing with white corporate execs.

One day his wife, Deborah, spotted some expensive gifts in the trunk of their Mercedes. When those gifts didn't turn up under the Christmas tree, she wondered what he was up to.

That led to her discovery that he'd bought a house, which led her to discover the house was a gift for his mistress—a house she then torched in a jealous fury. She wrecked her car on the way home, at which point the cops got involved. When one of my colleagues called Mrs. Lyons to ask what happened, she said she'd merely dropped a cigarette and the fire was an accident. The reporter, a heavy smoker, replied, "Oh? What brand do you smoke?" She couldn't name one.

A lengthy newspaper investigation followed, which turned up more mistresses and exposed how Lyons had defrauded his denomination's corporate partners and spent the money on himself and his women. He wound up behind bars. His wife got probation for arson, then divorced him.

Lyons's fall was dramatic, but not as dramatic as that of Jim Bakker, a white televangelist who headed up a North Carolina–based ministry called PTL, which at various times stood for Praise the Lord and People That Love. The elfin Bakker and his overly made-up wife, Tammy Faye, traveled in private jets and rode in limos. They built a five-hundred-room hotel with a water park. *The Jim and Tammy Faye Show* beamed their smiling faces—and Tammy Faye's warbling voice—to millions of followers eager to fork over their money. The Bakkers were so rich that they air-conditioned their doghouse because Tammy Faye worried that her dog, Snuggles, was getting too warm.

But Bakker wanted something more, something that brought him to Florida. One December afternoon in 1981, in room 538 of the Sheraton Sand Key Resort on Clearwater Beach, he had sex with a twenty-year-old woman who was not named Tammy Faye and did not wear makeup by the pound. The woman was promised $265,000 to keep quiet, but by then PTL was having cash flow problems, so she got just $20,000.

Charlotte Observer reporters had spent years digging into the Bakkers' shady finances. In 1987, the paper trumpeted the story on the Sheraton tryst, naming the woman involved as Jessica Hahn. Bakker went on TV and announced he was resigning his ministry because he had sinned—but said he'd been tempted by a woman who "knew all the tricks of the trade."

Actually, Hahn was a church secretary who had been a virgin prior to her Florida tryst. A B-list evangelist she knew had invited her to fly down for what she thought would be a chance to see Bakker filming a telethon. Instead, she said she was given some wine containing a drug, then coerced into having sex with both Bakker and the other evangelist.

The Bakkers slid downhill fast. For a while they tried broadcasting from a run-down Orlando shopping center. Bakker said he liked Florida because "it's a place where it seems like everyone's welcome . . . I believe there's great religious tolerance here."

Bakker ended up divorced, disgraced, and convicted of fraud for his fundraising shenanigans. Hahn, meanwhile, posed for *Playboy* (Hefner totally owes Florida, don't you think?).

But what I always liked about this story was what happened at the Sheraton Sand Key. People all over the world began calling the hotel to book a night in room 538. They wanted to buy the sheets, the blanket, the towels. Radio DJs asked if they could broadcast their shows from inside the infamous Florida hotel room. People trekked there just to gawk at the door, as if it had become an antireligious shrine. Perhaps the management should change the number to 666.

Protestants aren't the only ones involved in sexcapades. In 2009, two Irish priests assigned to an upscale Delray Beach parish were convicted of grand theft in the worst case of embezzlement in the U.S. Catholic Church's history.

Police said the pair—one in his eighties, one in his sixties—stole more than $8 million from the offering plates and spent it on gambling junkets to Vegas and the Bahamas, on buying real estate, as well as on their much younger girlfriends. It was the biggest scandal to hit the Palm Beach diocese since allegations of sexual abuse led to the resignations of two bishops.

You might think, based on all the nudity and the sex and the scandals, that people in Florida are not at all religious. You would be wrong.

Floridians frequently feel stirrings of strong religious belief, especially when one of the many disasters that constantly threaten us finally occurs. When a hurricane roars through the land, we drop to our knees. When floods wash away our homes, we seek the comfort of the church. In 1998, when wildfires ravaged so much of Florida that forty thousand people were forced to evacuate, Gov. Chiles said, "I hope you will join me and pray for rain." And the rains came.

Then, when the crisis is over, everyone goes back to doing what they'd done before. The truth is, a lot of Floridians don't think too much about what's going to happen in the hereafter, or in the next twenty years (think coastal development versus climate change) or even what might happen next week. We're too busy angling for a fast buck in the here and now.

For those of us who are concerned about the hereafter, though, Florida offers plenty of choices for belief systems. Jim Bakker was right about how tolerant we are. In my neighborhood of brick streets and quaint bungalows, for instance, there is a Quaker meetinghouse, a small Buddhist center, and a white-columned home that contains a commune full of people who appear to believe the Amish are a tad too modern. We also have a neighbor who's covered a car bumper to bumper in Hello Kitty stickers, although I'm not sure that counts as *religious* devotion.

The Spaniards who landed in Florida conducted the first Catholic mass in North America. Ever since establishing that biblical beachhead, religion has swept across the state—albeit, in a Florida kind of way. In other words, we have religions and antireligions from every column of the menu.

Take what happened in bucolic Bradford County after a group called the Community Men's Fellowship put up a Ten Commandments monument at the county courthouse. An atheists' group sued to have it removed. Court-ordered mediation followed, leading to a very Floridian solution: The atheists could put up a monument too.

In June 2013, two hundred people crowded into downtown (if you can call it that) Starke to witness the unveiling of the first public marker in the nation dedicated to atheism (it resembled a fancy bench). I think the agnostics were supposed to get a monument too but weren't sure whether they needed one.

The big city has its religious quirks too. In Miami, so many defendants facing charges at the county courthouse are believers in Santeria that the maintenance crew set up a special group called the "Voodoo Squad." Their job is to clean up the gruesome animal sacrifices that have been left around the building overnight to influence pending cases.

Sometimes the voodoo creeps indoors. A Miami lawyer I know was startled during a trial when someone with the other side blew white powder all over him. It wasn't cocaine or anthrax, just a Santeria ritual.

"It looks like white talcum powder," he said. "If someone throws it on you and you're in a blue suit, it looks like you've got the worst case of dandruff in the Western Hemisphere."

I have to admit that not everyone is so blasé about Santeria. When Oba Ernesto Pichardo opened his Church of the Lukumi Babalu Aye in the city of Hialeah, city commissioners passed an ordinance forbidding animal sacrifice. Pichardo sued over that 1987 ordinance. The case went to the U.S. Supreme Court, which voted 9–0 for Pichardo. Animal sacrifice, the court said, is protected by the First Amendment.

That ruling has had an unusual side effect involving one of Florida's strangest animal invaders, the giant African land snail, GALS for short. GALS grow up to seven inches long, and their reproductive potential is stunning. Each snail is a hermaphrodite, meaning it contains both female and male reproductive organs. They can lay about twelve hundred eggs each year. Wherever they go, they leave a smelly trail of excrement. If the weather is too dry, they can bury themselves in the dirt until the rain returns, then come back up out of the ground like zombies clawing their way out of the grave. They are as destructive as a Looney Tunes Tasmanian devil set on super slo-mo.

They gobble at least five hundred different types of plants, but that's not all.

They can cause structural damage to plaster and stucco by chewing on houses. They also carry a parasitic nematode that can give humans meningitis.

I saw some GALS in a government lab in Miami where they were kept under lock and key. Sure, any jailbreak would be slooooooow, but GALS are such a threat that the rules say they have to be locked away.

"We're paranoid about them escaping," explained the scientist holding one up for me to examine. It was so big it covered her gloved hand. I leaned in to stare at it. It stared back, its eye stalks popping up and down like little pistons.

So how did these GALS get to Florida? They were smuggled in by followers of a religion called Ifa Orisha, which is similar to Santeria except Santeria came out of Cuba, while Ifa Orisha originated in Africa. One Ifa Orisha follower flew from Nigeria to Miami with some snails hidden under her dress, according to investigators. Can you imagine being on that plane, in the next seat over, wondering why the lady's dress kept undulating?

Florida officials said the group's leader persuaded his followers to drink the snails' mucus as part of a "healing ritual" that instead made them ill. Meanwhile his little backyard colony proliferated like *Star Trek*'s Tribbles and spread across Miami-Dade.

Florida has spent millions tracking down and killing these snails, even going to the trouble of training dogs to sniff out their excretions. (New slogan: "Florida: The Only State with Snail-Sniffing Dogs!") But they've never prosecuted the Ifa Orisha leader or any of his followers.

Why? Because of the Supreme Court ruling, Pichardo told me. The government knows it must tread lightly in any case involving animal sacrifice. The snail drinkers had no bad intent, he contended, and thus should not be charged, no matter how much trouble they caused.

Pichardo said his own church steers clear of GALS. "We do use some Florida land snails in a very few, very limited rituals," he said, "but they are never consumed."

Even if you just stick to the mainstream denominations, we've got a dizzying array of variations on Christianity in Florida.

In addition to the usual Baptists, Presbyterians, Lutherans, and others, we've got Christian swingers who swear their alternative lifestyle is a good way to reach sinners in need of a savior. We've also got Christian nudists who held a convention at a nudist resort. I don't know if any preachers showed up—but if they did, would they be the men *not* of the cloth?

If Floridians aren't busy worshipping God or the devil, they are blaming them for their problems. In 1968, a Lake Worth man who had been injured in what his insurance company labeled "an act of God" sued "God & Co." as well as twenty-two local religious institutions.

"If he brings the Principal Defendant into court," said one reverend, "I'll be glad to come and testify for Him."

On the flip side, in 2001 the mayor of Inglis, a town of fourteen hundred north of Tampa, wrote out a proclamation that banned Satan from her city. Mayor Carolyn Risher said she had been inspired by 9/11 to kick the devil out.

"Be it known from this day forward that Satan, ruler of darkness, giver of evil, destroyer of what is good and just, is not now, nor ever again will be, a part of this town of Inglis," the mayor wrote.

She made five copies on official letterhead, putting four in fence posts at the corners of town. The fifth she hung on her office wall amid pictures of Elvis and *The Last Supper*.

There was talk of impeaching her, but when she ran for reelection she won easily. More than two hundred reporters worldwide did stories on Inglis, the most publicity the town has ever gotten. Three years later, the police chief claimed that crime was down and arrests up, and credited "the Big Man Upstairs."

The guy who lost the mayor's race scoffed, "Our drunks still drink, our hookers still hook, and truckers still ride like the devil up and down the highway. People are going to sin, plain and simple. No proclamation is going to stop that."

I have to admit that some religions have rubbed Floridians the wrong way.

When people on ultraritzy Star Island in Miami Beach saw the Egyptian Coptic Church take over a waterfront mansion and advocate smoking dope as a religious ritual, they objected, and the local prosecutor swung into action. Florida's supreme court ended up telling the Copts: Sorry, dudes, you're wrong. The weed's got to go.

Floridians were willing to put up with anti-Islam preacher Terry Jones barbecuing a Qur'an at his Dove World Outreach Center in Gainesville in 2011. But when he did it again a year later, the local fire department cited his church for violating fire ordinances.

In 2014, the state agency in charge of the Capitol let a religious group called the Florida Prayer Network put up a traditional Christmas nativity scene along with a menorah. The agency then had to give its blessing to other groups' displays, including:

- a Festivus Pole made of Pabst Blue Ribbon cans, in homage to the fake holiday invented on the TV show *Seinfeld*
- a statue by the Church of the Flying Spaghetti Monster, which protests the teaching of creationism and which featured what a newspaper described as "a googly-eyed blob of noodles grasping two meatballs"
- a diorama by the satirical Satanic Temple, a mocker of all religions, which featured an angel falling into a pit of fire

The sight of the Satanic Temple display right before Christmas upset one staunch Catholic lady so much that she attacked it. However, prosecutors later dropped all charges against her because nobody could prove she damaged the thing.

Still, I would argue that we're the most tolerant people in the country, because we tolerate the oddest religion of all, the Church of Scientology. How odd? It was allegedly founded by aliens and its world spiritual headquarters is the same Clearwater hotel where Mick Jagger and Keith Richards wrote "Satisfaction."

Its real founder, science-fiction author L. Ron Hubbard, chose Clearwater because he loved boats and wanted a waterfront home in a warm climate near a big airport. Clearwater filled the bill—plus of course there was that word "clear," which is the state that every Scientologist strives to attain.

Like Walt Disney acquiring land for his park, Scientology acquired the hotel under a phony name in 1975—then, unlike Disney, it launched a stealth campaign to take control of the whole city, which involved discrediting anyone who might stand in the way. When Clearwater Mayor Gabe Cazares, one of the area's few prominent Hispanics, questioned the church's sneaky pete real estate purchases, its lockstep mind-set, and the way its security guards marched around armed with billy clubs and Mace, church members staged a phony hit-and-run accident and tried to smear him with a fabricated sex scandal, to no avail.

Two *St. Petersburg Times* reporters won a Pulitzer in 1980 for a fourteen-part series outlining Scientology's skulduggery. They too became targets as the church tried repeatedly to get them fired and in tax trouble.

By 1993, church leaders had bombarded the IRS with so many lawsuits and unflattering ads that it stopped classifying Scientology as a commercial enterprise and restored its religious tax exemption. Now that it was respectable (although no less ruthless), Florida politicians and businesspeople found fewer reasons to duck the church. After all, it had bought up tons of property around Clearwater's downtown (sort of like what a commercial enterprise would do).

By the end of the following decade, Scientology owned twenty-one buildings downtown, soon encircling the venerable Baptist Church. The Clearwater congregation included fourteen hundred white-uniformed employees whose presence made visitors wonder if it wasn't a Navy base. More than six thousand followers of the church had moved there too. The church even sponsored its own Boy Scout troop.

"You can't separate Salt Lake City and the Mormons, and you can't separate Clearwater and Scientology," one church member building a condo boasted.

In 2013, the church opened a new $50 million headquarters, an event that attracted big-name Scientologists John Travolta and Tom Cruise. But by then the church was in a PR tailspin. Some of the church's Hollywood stars had jumped ship, as had some of its leaders. Several went on the record with *Times* reporters about how Hubbard's hand-picked successor, David Miscavige, liked to beat up underlings and sucker the faithful into buying junk they didn't need. (That last part, at least, sounded very Floridian.) Those revelations led to an award-winning book by Lawrence Wright called *Going Clear,* then an HBO documentary.

Travolta and Cruise are not the biggest names to visit Florida on a religion-related purpose, though. For that we must go back to the Depression, to the guy I like to call "the Gator Hollerer."

Imagine you're canoeing down the Hillsborough River in the '30s. You see gators and turtles galore. You hear a voice, shouting. It's shouting so fast that it's like listening to machine-gun fire. You can make out a few words, like "God" and "sinners" and "Jesus" and "saves." You wonder who could be raising such a ruckus.

Then you round a bend and see a spindly college boy waving his arms and yelling at the cypress trees at the edge of the river, shaking his finger at alligators on the bank. You move on, figuring him for another Florida nutjob. Who would waste time preaching to gators?

He was a Carolina farm boy known among his family as Billy Frank. In January 1937, he showed up on the campus of the Florida Bible Institute in Temple Terrace, near Tampa—a small, unaccredited school housed in what was once a hotel.

Young Billy Frank found the place quite exotic, with its creamy pink stucco and tiled roofs. Wrapped around the building was an eighteen-hole golf course that ran along the banks of the Hillsborough River. All of it had been built as an exclusive country club during the '20s land boom. When the boom went bust, so did the project, which made it available for an off-brand Bible college to pick up cheap. Most of the houses around it stood unoccupied too. You could drive for miles without seeing another person.

In addition to teaching preachers, the college rented rooms in the hotel to visiting clergymen, mostly Northerners who headed south when the weather turned cold. The students did double duty, taking Bible classes as well as working as the hotel staff and occasionally caddying at the golf course. To Billy Frank this was a vast improvement over his last seminary, a damp and chilly place in Tennessee full of rules he found too restrictive. He wrote his mother, "I love it here."

At Easter, the dean of men asked Billy Frank to accompany him to a Central Florida conference. While there, someone asked the dean to deliver a sermon at a church in the tiny town of Bostwick.

"No," he said, "Billy is going to preach."

Billy Frank's jaw dropped. He had a repertoire of four sermons, mostly lifted from other preachers' writings. Despite his extensive practice yelling at gators, he had never before preached to a human congregation. He spent the night studying and praying and the next day practiced his four sermons. At last it was time.

"The meeting room was small, with a potbellied iron stove near the front to take chill off that cold, windy night," he recalled decades later. "The song leader, who chewed tobacco, had to go to the door every so often to spit outside . . . The congregation of about forty included ranchers and cowboys in overalls and their women in cotton-wash dresses."

When he walked up to the pulpit, perspiration sprang up on his skin despite the chill. "I launched into sermon number one," he said. "It seemed to be over almost as soon as I got started, so I added number two. And number three. And eventually number four. Then I sat down."

He glanced as his watch and was horrified to discover that he had been talking for just eight minutes. He'd shouted out his four sermons so fast that he was done almost as soon as he'd begun.

Nevertheless, the young seminary student survived this debacle. He honed his technique by preaching everywhere he got a chance—in Tampa's jail, to a truly captive audience; in the trailer parks, where he could talk to hundreds of tin-can tourists stopping over for the winter; and on street corners, where he'd harangue passersby he spotted coming out of the bars. He'd thunder to the crowd that they were sinners and needed salvation. He'd tell them about how God had condemned them to hell, then sent Jesus to take their punishment and offer them a spot in heaven.

Remember, this was when Tampa was full of corrupt politicians, cops, and bolita kingpins. If ever there was a town oozing with sin, this was it.

But Billy Frank wasn't sure he wanted to be a preacher. By night he paced Temple Terrace's empty streets, or wandered through the golf course, trying to figure out his future. One moonstruck night in 1938, he dropped to his knees on a golf course green and sobbed, "O God, if you want me to serve you, I will."

He saw no heaven-sent sign, yet "in my spirit I knew I had been called to the ministry," wrote the man the world would come to know as Billy Graham, the greatest evangelist in history.

He was baptized in a Florida lake and ordained by a group of country preachers. Twelve years after that disastrous first sermon in Florida, Billy Graham catapulted to national fame thanks to an eight-week tent meeting in Los Angeles that drew thousands. He launched a radio show called *The Hour of Decision* that became a TV program. He preached to millions, wrote more than a score of books, took his crusade to venues around the globe, and met with every president from Harry Truman through George W. Bush. When Jeb Bush—a Catholic—was sworn in as Florida's governor, Billy Graham, a Baptist, came back to say a prayer for him. (Over the years people criticized Graham for hobnobbing with politicians. I figure he just got so used to hanging out with pea-brained reptiles that he missed their company and this was the nearest equivalent.)

There's been only one preacher with a bigger reputation than Billy Graham who spent time in Florida. Instead of praying with him, though, we had him arrested.

White segregationists try to prevent black swimmers from integrating a "whites only" beach during a "wade-in," while police officers use their clubs. St. Augustine, 1964. Photo courtesy of State Archives of Florida.

16

Confederacy of Dunces

He was too much for them to stomach, for he challenged the
code itself: he acted like a white man.
— Larry Goodwyn, "Anarchy in St. Augustine,"
Harper's, January 1965

No city in Florida embraces the past with as much ardor as St. Augustine, the oldest continuously occupied city in the United States. History is its biggest industry. They don't just have one statue of their founder, Pedro Menéndez de Avilés, but two. Every February they have a black-tie gala to celebrate his birthday, and every September they reenact his 1565 landing (but not his massacre of the French Huguenots).

Everywhere you turn, the city has set up attractions to milk money from the history-minded, although—this being Florida—a lot of the attractions only *look* authentic. Hordes of gawking tourists and raucous schoolkids troop through St. Augustine's streets to watch the (pretend) guards patrolling Castillo de San Marcos, to fire the (fake) cannon at the Pirate & Treasure Museum, to sip from the (phony) Fountain of Youth.

A few years ago, I rode along as an adult chaperone on a bus full of chattering children touring "the Ancient City" (ancient for America, anyway). I found the evening Ghost Tour quite entertaining, particularly the part about the 1876 funeral of the first bishop of Florida, whose metal coffin had been left in the heat too long and thus, during the eulogy, his corpse exploded all over the rich and powerful folks in the front pews.

My kid, meanwhile, went gaga for the Ripley's Believe It or Not Museum, with its shrunken heads and sly salute to gurners. For me, the most unbelievable thing about it is that it's housed in a hotel once owned by Marjorie Kinnan Rawlings, Pulitzer-winning author of *The Yearling*.

To my surprise, the tour skipped two things that I thought would be sure-fire St. Augustine attractions—authentic ones too.

One was the Florida School for the Deaf and Blind, a state-sponsored institution that for decades has taught handicapped children how to adapt to the world. Their most famous student was a young boy born in Georgia. His family moved to Florida and enrolled him in the taxpayer-supported school. There he learned about music, its ability to speak the things you couldn't say plainly, to make you feel and to move. He learned to play the piano, among other instruments.

Florida has produced a lot of musical talent—bebop giant Cannonball Adderley, rapper Flo Rida, rocker Tom Petty, the boy bands of O-town, and more—but nobody had a bigger impact than that student, Ray Charles Robinson. After he left St. Augustine to play Florida's Chitlin' Circuit and cut his first records, he would drop his last name and become Ray Charles, the genius who would change the sound of American popular music.

The other thing I had wanted to see was more mundane yet even more important: a set of brick steps, the sole remaining part of an old motel torn down years ago.

Those treasured steps are a part of St. Augustine's history that its residents have only recently begun to come to grips with—a painfully real, painfully violent episode from which the city has yet to fully recover, although the nation continues to reap its benefits.

On July 2, 1964, Congress passed and President Lyndon Johnson signed into law the Civil Rights Act. The act's sweeping provisions prohibit discrimination in public places, provide for the integration of schools and other public facilities, and declare employment discrimination to be illegal. That law would not have passed Congress had it not been for the blood that was shed during violent protests at St. Augustine.

The best person to tell the story is Dr. Robert Hayling, the African-American man saluted by *Harper's* in its story on anarchy in the Ancient City. He was then in his thirties, a dentist who served both black and white patients, Hayling spearheaded the St. Augustine protests. He's the one who launched the sit-ins, brought Martin Luther King Jr. to town to stand on those steps, and paid the price for his crusade when he was captured by the Ku Klux Klan.

When I talked to him, the firebrand was in his eighties, a soft-spoken, white-haired man with a sharp mind and a mischievous smile. He had out-lived almost everyone from those days—the racists who beat him, the sheriff who sided with the thugs, the mayor who was convinced he and all the other marchers were Communists.

But he still had vivid memories of them. He remembered, in particular, the day he met with the city's leading white businessman, bank president and former mayor H. E. Wolfe. Fuming with frustration, Wolfe demanded that Hayling explain what the city must do to end the protests chasing away the tourists.

"He asked what it would take to satisfy me," Hayling recalled, "and I said, 'Let me be an ordinary citizen.'"

These days a lot of people—even people in Florida—do not consider Florida to be part of the South. Sure, it's below the Mason-Dixon Line, but just try finding some collard greens in Boca Raton.

Yet until the 1970s, people in the North considered Florida as Southern as Jeff Davis's underpants. People in Florida did not disagree. Among Florida's sixty-seven counties, there is one called Dixie and another named for Robert E. Lee. (A painting of the dour old general hangs in the county commission chambers, staring down at the commissioners as if they disappoint him.) Several Florida cities have monuments to the Confederate dead, and until recently a Jacksonville school bore the name of Nathan Bedford Forrest, the Confederate general who helped launch the Ku Klux Klan.

When I was growing up in Pensacola in the 1960s and '70s, Rebel flags were as common as blue jeans. I even had a miniature one that I'd gotten at the state fair. Because I was young and hazy on history, I thought it was from something called the "Rebel-lutionary War."

I vividly remember my eighth-grade social studies teacher trotting out the old claim that the Civil War was actually fought over states' rights, not slavery. That set off such furious eye rolling by our future valedictorian that I thought she'd snap an optic nerve.

"Yeah," she told the teacher in a voice drenched in teenage sarcasm, "it was about the states' rights . . . to let all the white people keep their slaves!"

A disagreement over the Civil War led to a riot at one Pensacola school during the nation's bicentennial. Although Escambia High School had desegregated in 1969, Escambia had kept the nickname "Rebels" and still flew the Rebel flag at sporting events and school assemblies while the band played "Dixie." Black students complained, and their parents went to court.

A federal judge ruled that the nickname and flag were "racially irritating," and barred their use. That annoyed white students and their parents, and drew in some politicians trolling for votes. A gospel-singing ex-cop legislator named R. W. "Smokey" Peaden was quoted using the N-word and saying he was so irritated by black people that he'd like to grab a machine gun and cut them down. After the quote appeared in print, Peaden said he was just joking about that, heh-heh. He didn't fool anyone.

A year later, an appeals court overturned the ruling. The school board chose to let the student body vote on their nickname. "Rebels" failed to get enough votes.

The day after that 1976 election, a mob of angry white students tried to hoist a Rebel flag on the school's flagpole. Black students blocked them, and violence erupted. The riot left four students shot and thirty injured, a hundred windows smashed, trophy cases damaged, clocks clobbered. Someone even ripped out a water pipe, flooding part of the building.

While the riot was going on, Peaden showed up, thinking he could cajole the white students into settling down by offering to get their old nickname reinstated. They ignored him and kept smashing windows. In the weeks that followed, school board members found crosses burning on their lawns, and someone torched Peaden's house.

The Florida National Guard acted as hall monitors for the remainder of the school year. By 1977, things had finally quieted down. Escambia's students decided that they'd rather be known as the "Gators." Apparently, no Florida State fans objected.

As for Peaden, he announced he was running for sheriff on a law and order ticket. Instead he went to federal prison. Turned out he'd financed his campaign by running a cocaine ring.

Still, Florida's multicultural history sets it apart from the rest of the South. Ponce de León's 1513 expedition included a free black conquistador, Juan Garrido. He left behind no portraits, but I picture him as Cleavon Little from *Blazing Saddles,* riding along behind his diminutive leader with a sardonic smile on his face, muttering about how ridiculous it was to invade a tropical land dressed in metal clothing.

Later on, the Spanish governor of St. Augustine liberated more slaves than anyone else this side of Abe Lincoln. Under Spanish law, slaves who converted to Catholicism must be declared free. Slaves fled plantations across the South to reach St. Augustine, undergo a convenient conversion, and be freed. Many then settled in St. Augustine, opening businesses and some even marrying white settlers. Others chose to live apart. In the 1730s, they created the first free black settlement in North America, Gracia Real de Santa Teresa de Mose, aka Fort Mose.

It didn't last long. In 1740, Georgia's British governor, James Oglethorpe, was so fed up about the fleeing slaves that he led an invasion of Florida. Fort Mose's militia ran, letting Oglethorpe take the fort. But then it counter-attacked, retaking the fort in the most violent battle of what historians call the War of Jenkins' Ear. (I'm not making that up. There was a British smuggler named Jenkins, and the Spanish cut off his ear, which he then displayed in Parliament, eventually sparking a war between Britain and Spain.) When the English eventually retook Florida from the Spanish via negotiation, though, slavery was reinstated.

Florida being Florida, we backed the wrong side of the Revolutionary War, remaining loyal to the British while the other colonies fought for life, liberty, and that Florida specialty, the pursuit of happiness. When the Civil War arrived, Florida did it again, dispatching troops to fight the Yankees and die in far-off battlefields. Florida's most valuable contribution to the war was providing cattle and salt to the Confederacy, which, as we soon learned, couldn't pay for it.

A few minor battles played out here. I once took my kids to a Civil War reenactment called the Brooksville Raid that featured cannons booming, a Gatling gun going rat-a-tat, and rifle volleys that didn't appear to hit anyone. Before the battle, I talked to my kids about why we were rooting for the visitors in blue instead of the home team. Afterward, they told me the best part was when the Yankees blew up the Rebels' outhouse.

The closest thing to a major battle fought here was in 1864 at Olustee, near Lake City. A ragtag Rebel group turned back the Union's attempt to march on Tallahassee, leaving it the only Southern capital not captured. Olustee is memorable for three things: the three regiments of black Union troops (the same ones featured in the movie *Glory*) who fought bravely there, the savagery of the battle between white and black troops, and the contemptible things the Confederates did to the wounded black soldiers after the battle.

"A young officer was standing in the road in front of me," a Confederate captain wrote about the aftermath, "and I asked him, 'What is the meaning of all this firing I hear going on?' His reply to me was, 'Shooting niggers, Sir. I have tried to make the boys desist but I can't control them.'"

Fast-forward to the present day, to the Olustee Battlefield, Florida's first state historic site, donated by the United Daughters of the Confederacy. A monument built in 1912 commemorates the Rebels who died, but there's no salute to the Union's honored dead. In 2013, the Sons of Union Veterans proposed building a monument saluting the Northern soldiers. A public hearing drew about one hundred.

"Passions ran high," one newspaper reported, "at one point erupting in a spontaneous chorus of 'Dixie' led by a black man, H. K. Edgerton, who called Union soldiers rapists and wielded his large Confederate flag like a conductor's baton as the audience sang."

Edgerton is not alone. In 2008, a black Jacksonville city councilwoman named Glorious Johnson made headlines for attending a gathering of the Sons of the Confederacy and leading the group in singing "Dixie."

The councilwoman, a Republican—the party of Lincoln!—said she had learned about the Civil War and the Rebel flag by talking to the group. She informed reporters, "This flag is not a flag of hate, but a flag about heritage and history."

That would be news to the black soldiers killed after Olustee.

Once the South lost and Gov. Milton shot himself, Florida underwent Reconstruction along with its Southern neighbors. Plenty of its resentful whites joined the nascent Klan. It remained a pervasive terror here for a century, despite the efforts of a Florida writer named Stetson Kennedy to expose its secrets with newspaper stories and a book called *I Rode With the Ku Klux Klan*.

Attempts by black Floridians to exercise the same rights as whites were literally beaten back. In 1920, a black man named Moses Norman attempted to vote in Ocoee. Before long, hundreds of outraged whites had poured into town and burned down the home of every black family, who had by then hidden in nearby citrus groves. The NAACP estimates between thirty and sixty people were killed. One black man who fired back at a white mob attacking his home was shot, hanged, then shot again. The census counted 495 black people living in Ocoee in 1920. The 1930 census counted 2. The 1940 census counted zero. In the 1960s, a sign posted at the town limits said, DOGS AND NEGROES NOT WELCOME.

About two years after the Ocoee Massacre, another eruption occurred, this time in rural Levy County in a town called Rosewood. The town had a handful of white property owners but most of Rosewood was owned by blacks. Nearby stood the lily-white town of Sumner. On New Year's Day 1923, a white woman in Sumner accused a black man from Rosewood of rape. Later investigations suggested she concocted this lie to hide an affair, but at the time the merest whisper about a black man attacking a white woman had the same explosive capacity as an atom bomb.

A white mob formed in Sumner and headed for Rosewood. One of the first black men they captured there, they interrogated by hanging him. When they didn't like the answers he gave, they shot him and left his bullet-riddled body still swinging from a limb. By the time the violence was over, Rosewood had been wiped off the map—and, for the most part, from the history books.

Nearly sixty years later, a *St. Petersburg Times* reporter named Gary Moore visited Cedar Key to do a travel story on the island community. As he read through the town's history, he learned that it owed its existence to a railroad built by black workers. But as he strolled around, Moore saw no black residents. He began asking why. At last someone told him about Rosewood.

Moore wound up with something much more powerful than a travel story. His 1982 exposé led to the state paying more than $2 million in reparations to Rosewood's survivors and descendants. Later on, a movie version somehow contrived an upbeat ending.

If you drive to Cedar Key now, along the roadside you might see a historic marker for Rosewood. You might not, though, because it's been repeatedly dragged off, shot up, or otherwise defaced. It is the most frequently replaced historical marker in Florida.

Another Moore bears a different distinction in Florida's civil rights history. In the 1940s, Harry T. Moore was kicking up a fuss, registering thousands of black voters and writing countless letters to the white authorities complaining about lynchings and other horrors. Someone dubbed him "the most hated black man in Florida."

On Christmas Eve 1951, someone bombed his house in Mims. Harry T. Moore died in the explosion, his wife, Harriette, a few days later. They were the first civil rights martyrs in U.S. history. Their murderers were never charged.

When the civil rights movement began stirring in earnest in the '50s, Florida's black residents took action just like African Americans in Alabama, Georgia, and Mississippi. Tallahassee had its own bus boycott in 1956 organized by students at the historically black Florida A&M University. Despite cross burnings and other violence, they stuck to it, and by the summer of 1957, Tallahassee had abolished whites-only seating in its buses.

On the Fourth of July 1961, Fort Lauderdale civil rights activists joined hands, walked onto a whites-only beach, and waded into the Atlantic. White swimmers ran out of the water, as if fearful their skin might be tainted by waterborne contact with the protesters. Fifteen minutes later, police showed up and arrested the protesters, but the "wade-ins" continued for six weeks. Finally a court ruled that all the beaches had to be open to everyone.

Other than a single attempt at a lunch-counter sit-in in 1950, St. Augustine's black residents appeared unable to attack the city's ongoing segregation—until Dr. Robert Hayling arrived.

Hayling grew up in Florida, but not St. Augustine. That made the difference. Blacks who grew up in St. Augustine accepted segregation as something they didn't like but were reluctant to challenge. Hayling hailed from Tallahassee, where his father taught at Florida A&M. His summer jobs included trimming shrubbery around Florida's old Capitol. After a stint as a lieutenant in the Air Force, he earned his dentistry degree, married his college sweetheart, and headed for St. Augustine, where an older black dentist was retiring.

As Hayling drove around in his red Volkswagen convertible, what he saw baffled him. He saw black and white men who had been working side by side for weeks aboard a shrimp boat step onto a dock and go opposite directions as if they were strangers. He noticed the city's sole black employee was a patrolman who was not allowed to wear a uniform. He wondered why white patients who didn't balk at letting him stick his fingers in their mouths would refuse to let him eat where they ate. Longtime black and white residents were accustomed to such segregated circumstances. Hayling was not.

In 1963, St. Augustine began gearing up for its four hundredth birthday the following year, an event sure to attract droves of tourists. Merchants "wondered can we get enough cash registers in town to hold all the money that's going to come in," local historian David Nolan told me.

When Hayling heard that the city hoped to get $350,000 from the federal government to pay for the party, he saw a chance to change things. But every time he tried, he hit a solid wall of white resistance.

When Hayling and his fellow activists threatened to picket an upcoming luncheon honoring Vice President Johnson because it included no blacks, two all-black tables were put in—as far as possible from the white tables.

When he requested a forum where city officials would listen to black residents' grievances, it turned out to be an empty room with a tape recorder that they knew no one would ever listen to.

When he dispatched well-dressed teenagers—adults feared losing their jobs—to start sit-ins at restaurants and get arrested, a judge sent four kids to adult prison for long sentences. Their crime was asking a waitress for a hamburger and a Coke. The judge's unjust sentence sparked such widespread consternation among St. Augustine's black population that the protests and sit-ins at last began drawing hundreds of grown-ups.

A reporter from *Harper's* described what Hayling encountered while meeting with the city's white leaders: "One white representative . . . read from a pamphlet in which he substituted the word 'nigger' for Negro each time it appeared. Dr. Hayling protested, and when one white person present suggested to the white leader that he might, in the interests of harmony, use the correct form, he did so." Later, "Dr. Hayling wryly remarked that the meeting 'at least accomplished one thing—one of us has learned a new word.'"

The next day, Hayling received the first phone calls threatening his life.

Hayling was no Harry T. Moore. He had no interest in being a martyr. He was a military man familiar with firearms. When a reporter asked him how he would respond if someone fired at him, the response attributed to him was, "Shoot first and ask questions later." Hayling said he was misquoted, but this early form of Stand Your Ground did not go over well with the city's white establishment, or with the NAACP, which regarded Hayling as too radical.

To Sheriff L. O. Davis—one of Hayling's patients but not his friend—Hayling was just a rabble-rouser with no following. The dentist was one of a handful of malcontents "muttering and fussing around," he told an interviewer in the 1970s.

But what Hayling and his cohorts were doing had riled up enough white-power terrorists—there really is no other word for them—that they poured in from around the country, spoiling for a fight. They firebombed houses, beat the marchers, drove around shooting at anything that could be a target. They shot into Hayling's house, missing his family but killing his dog. Hayling hustled his wife and children to Tallahassee to keep them safe, then went back alone.

"Some said I didn't have enough sense to know how much danger I was in," Hayling told me, chuckling.

One night in September 1963, Hayling got wind of a big Klan rally outside town. He and three other men drove out on a back road hoping to spy on the group. Instead they were caught and dragged into the middle of a cross burning. Furious Klansman beat them with wrenches and chains. When the Klan realized one victim was a dentist, they made sure to break one of Hayling's hands, as well as knocking out eleven teeth.

Women in the crowd were yelling, "Castrate the bastards!" Instead, Sheriff Davis showed up and shut everything down. Four Klansmen were charged in the beatings but acquitted. Because a Klansman claimed Hayling had a gun, he was convicted of assault and fined $100.

Hayling repeatedly appealed for help from the national movement leaders, but he was too radical for some, too ready to fight. Finally, in spring 1964, Martin Luther King Jr. and the Southern Christian Leadership Conference said yes.

Soon King's fiery aide Hosea Williams was leading marchers through downtown into what was still called "the Slave Market." The marchers sang hymns and held hands as crowds of jeering rednecks threw rocks, bricks, and bottles, even attacking newsmen covering the march.

At one march, another of King's aides, the coolly analytical Andrew Young, tried talking to some of the angry whites lining their route. Someone hit him from behind with a blackjack. As Young fell to the ground, the crowd kicked him repeatedly. Police stood by and did nothing.

"St. Augustine turned out to be the SCLC's most violent and bloody campaign," Young wrote years later. When King arrived, he rented a beach home—which someone burned to the ground.

The sheriff arrested hundreds of marchers at a time, cramming them into his overcrowded jail. The SCLC sued, and a federal judge ruled that they had a right to march without interference. That ruling set a precedent for similar protests throughout the South. It also led to the judge being ostracized by every white person he knew.

Every march and sit-in of the SCLC campaign was choreographed to bolster the argument for passing the Civil Rights Act. First proposed by President Kennedy before his assassination, the bill had been held up in the Senate by a long filibuster.

King and his aides wanted the protests in St. Augustine to remind everyone of why the bill was needed. The upheaval there had begun garnering widespread news coverage. If the dunces opposing him had been smarter, they would have ended the brutality until the story faded and the bill failed. Instead they became even more violent, and so nuns and rabbis and liberal white protesters drove down to join the throng of marchers, fueling the fire.

During one sit-in, those arrested included the seventy-two-year-old mother of the governor of Massachusetts, a very proper Boston Brahmin named Mary Peabody. That made headlines across the country. She appeared on NBC's *Today* show to denounce St. Augustine as a town festering with violence and hate—not what the business community wanted a national TV audience to hear. The mayor demanded, and got, equal time to claim that she was just taking "the word of a local Negro dentist about conditions," and his city had had no racial problems until all those outsiders showed up.

The protests became more creative. A group of black and white students in swim trunks tried to integrate a whites-only beach, a copy of Fort Lauderdale's successful wade-ins. Angry whites beat them, and then state troopers waded in with their nightsticks and beat both sides.

"There was blood in the water," Hayling recalled.

King tried to get a meal at the Monson Motor Lodge. Owner Jimmy Brock refused to even let him in. While standing on the Monson's brick steps—the steps still standing in St. Augustine today—King was handcuffed and hauled off to jail, making St. Augustine one of only three American cities to bust the future Nobel Peace Prize winner.

Later he told a reporter that St. Augustine was "the most lawless city I've ever been in. I've never seen this kind of wide-open violence."

Then a group of white and black protesters held a swim-in by jumping into the Monson's pool. Brock, outraged, grabbed a jug of muriatic acid, normally used for cleaning the tile, and poured it into the pool to drive them out. His act was captured by network and wire service photographers. If the concept of "going viral" had existed in the 1960s, that would have been an apt description of what happened.

After that, the eighty-three-day filibuster ended, Congress approved the bill, and LBJ hurriedly signed it into law.

To test it, Young took a group to the Monson for lunch. A nervous waitress seated them, took their orders, and served their food without incident. That night, the racists firebombed the restaurant to show their displeasure.

The SCLC declared victory, packed up, and headed for the next battlefield needing big-name generals. But the fight in St. Augustine wasn't over. Businesses fearful of facing the same fiery fate as the Monson refused to follow the law. Hayling's group had to sue them individually to force them to comply.

In 1965, Hayling left town, moving his family to South Florida to start over.

"I stayed as long as I could," he said.

Other African-American families abandoned St. Augustine as well. Now that they had seen their white neighbors' true nature, they couldn't abide the place any longer.

The city they left behind was economically crippled. One estimate said the bad publicity cost St. Augustine $5 million in tourism revenue. Rebuilding the city's image took years—and during that time, no one wanted to talk about its role in the Civil Rights Act. When David Nolan moved there in the 1970s, he asked about it and "was quietly taken aside and told, 'You must never mention the name of Martin Luther King.'"

When the Monson Motor Lodge was torn down in 2003 to make room for a Hilton, Nolan and other preservationists argued for saving it. An official repeatedly insisted the site had no historical significance. The best they could do was to preserve the steps where King was cuffed.

Attitudes began to change in 2007, Nolan said. Young returned to St. Augustine to show a documentary he'd made on what had happened there. The viewers included young people who hadn't known their town's story.

"People came out of it with tears in their eyes," Nolan said. Afterward, the city named the spot where Young was knocked senseless Andrew Young Crossing and began posting signs marking where protests occurred.

On July 2, 2014, the fiftieth anniversary of the Civil Rights Act, the city's newest tourist attraction opened: a civil rights museum. The city offered no financial support, so private donors got it started. Its location: the eight-room building that had housed Hayling's family and dental practice.

Hayling headlined the festivities. Changing attitudes had led to the once reviled dentist being showered with accolades. But when I talked to him, he saw little progress in the city he fought so hard to change. Instead of one black policeman, there were none. Unlike in many Southern cities, there were no African American officeholders. The *St. Augustine Record* ran a series about the fiftieth anniversary of the riots, and online commenters complained that the newspaper should stop dredging up awful memories.

The Civil Rights Act, though, was a success.

"Now I can get in my car . . . and drive to St. Augustine, and along the way I can go into a restaurant or a gas station and use the bathroom," he said. "And when I get to St. Augustine, I can at least go in and have a hamburger and a Coke."

Such victories are important. By the time the Civil Rights Act had passed, a group originally launched to harass Florida's black activists had turned its attention to a minority far more vulnerable to persecution.

A 1964 meeting of the Florida Legislative Investigative Committee, aka the Johns Committee, Florida's answer to Joe McCarthy. Its ironic nickname came from its staunchest advocate, Sen. Charley Johns, the man in the glasses in the foreground. Photo courtesy of State Archives of Florida.

17

The Friends of Emma Jones

I don't really like Florida . . . I want to go where I have a chance. I don't have a chance here.
—*RUBYFRUIT JUNGLE* BY RITA MAE BROWN, WHO WAS
OUSTED FROM THE UNIVERSITY OF FLORIDA

As with its boom-and-bust economy, some Florida news events repeat like a sun-drenched version of *Groundhog Day*. New residents are shocked, unaware that this has happened before. Veteran Floridians shake their heads that the problem still isn't fixed.

One repetitive cycle involves children getting lost in the state's foster child system. Children disappear, or are found dead from abuse. The foster parents turn out to have criminal records or intentions or both. Their case workers turn out to be slackers who never checked on them. Someone goes to prison. Someone else resigns. Everyone agrees how awful it is—and then the news fades until the next crisis.

In 2002, a particularly horrific missing-child case led to the arrest of two women who claimed to be the girl's grandmother and great-aunt. They were in fact not related to her at all but had collected $14,000 in state money for her foster care after the girl disappeared. The girl's body was never found, but one of the women would eventually be convicted of kidnapping her. The case prompted the head of the Department of Children and Families to resign and the legislature to pass new laws, which I believe were all titled "The Shutting the Barn Door After the Horse Is Gone Act."

Shortly after the women were arrested, a group of Panhandle lawmakers visited Gov. Jeb Bush at his office in the Capitol. Bush bragged to them that investigators had briefed him on what he called "the juicy details." He implied they were not sisters but rather a lesbian couple.

"As [one woman] was being arrested," Bush said, "she told her co-workers, 'Tell my wife I've been arrested.' The wife is the 'grandmother,' and the aunt is the husband." He used his fingers to make air quotes around the word "grandmother."

"Bet you don't get *that* in Pensacola," Bush added.

When I heard this story, I could see two things wrong with Bush's statement. One was that a reporter for the *Pensacola News Journal* had accompanied the lawmakers and, unbeknownst to Bush, was transcribing every word he said. Her story, which was published statewide, would show a side of Bush seldom exposed to the public—the snarky frat boy gossiping as a way to show off, instead of being the responsible executive, looking for ways to fix a flawed state agency that repeatedly lost or killed children. He later issued a halfhearted apology.

The other, bigger problem was Bush's ignorance about Pensacola. For years, Pensacola Beach has been the center of the biggest gay and lesbian Memorial Day gathering in the South, drawing an estimated sixty thousand people from across the country for four days of swimming, snorkeling, live music, costume contests, boat parties, and beach house get-downs, turning the Redneck Riviera into the Gay Riviera.

Pensacola has had an active gay community since at least the '50s, thanks to the presence of the Pensacola Naval Air Station and, about an hour away, Hurlburt Air Field and Eglin Air Force Base. Gather so many soldiers, sailors, and airmen together, and statistics say that some will be gay. That plus the many isolated beaches attracted gay men from as far away as New Orleans and Birmingham for secluded weekends.

But in the '50s, homosexual activity in Pensacola was, as one writer put it, as repressed as it was rampant. Shore patrol cops would sometimes follow sailors to the site of their assignations and bust everyone. Police made regular arrests among the men who gathered at Wayside Park for anonymous sex. Meanwhile, postal authorities were on the lookout for single men receiving packages in brown paper wrappers.

And in Tallahassee, there was the all-seeing eye of the Florida Legislative Investigative Committee, better known as the Johns Committee.

Remember when I said that in Florida, tragedy often wears the mask of comedy? That pretty well sums up the Johns Committee. Its ridiculously appropriate name, its ludicrous tactics, its thoroughly appropriate ending—it's easy to laugh at the whole mean-spirited, misguided enterprise. But if you do, you may not notice the terrible price paid by a lot of innocent people.

Start with the man who gave it its name. Charley Johns may not have been the worst governor Florida ever had, but he was about the homeliest. Horn-rim specs, thinning hair, thin lips, ears that threatened to become wings on a windy day, crooked teeth, jowly cheeks—he was definitely not one of those pretty boy politicians.

Johns grew up in rural Starke and started his own insurance company. First elected to the legislature in 1934, by 1953 he was Senate president. Then the governor died of a heart attack mere months after taking office. Back then, Florida had no lieutenant governor—instead, the president of the Senate became governor. Thrust into a job for which he was woefully unprepared, Johns repeatedly ticked off the people who'd gotten the dead governor elected. In the special election that followed, they backed LeRoy Collins, a wavy-haired progressive legislator from Tallahassee.

When Johns and Collins had a televised debate, Collins grinned and laid on the aw-shucks drawl and mopped the floor with his sputtering opponent. Collins won the election, becoming one of Florida's greatest governors. Johns went back to the Senate after just fifteen months, a most unhappy man.

This was around the time of the Tallahassee bus boycott, when state officials regarded civil rights activists as part of the Communist conspiracy intent on bringing down America. Based on this cockeyed theory, state legislators in 1956 approved the formation of the Florida Legislative Investigative Committee, modeled on Sen. Joe McCarthy's House Un-American Activities Committee.

The committee, chaired by Johns, was supposed to investigate the ties between Florida NAACP chapters and the Communist Party. To do that, the Johns Committee subpoenaed NAACP officials to testify and bring along lists of members. That way the committee could compare the membership list with the names of known pinkos. NAACP officials refused and went to court to block the committee from getting their records. One NAACP official, a minister from Miami, proclaimed how much he loved America and then walked out on the committee hearing, much to the members' dismay.

The way the committee had been set up, it had to justify its existence to the legislature every year for its charter to be renewed. Once the fight against the NAACP became mired in the courts (which would ultimately rule for the NAACP), the committee needed a new target, maybe one with a little less grit.

There are different versions of how the committee picked its next target. One story says the idea came from Johns, after his son complained of "effeminate" teachers at the University of Florida. Whatever the reason, the committee went after suspected homosexuals in the state's educational system, on the grounds that sexual perversion and political perversion were both dire threats to the American way of life.

The committee's investigators set up surveillance in the men's room of the Alachua County courthouse, a place known as a pickup spot for men wanting anonymous sex. If this happened today, headline writers would have a field day: "Johns Committee Hunts for Johns in John."

The investigators pulled in teachers and students—and traveling salesmen, blue-collar workers, you name it. If the committee members had been paying attention, they might have drawn a conclusion about the prevalence of homosexuality in society, based on the wide variety of their detainees, but it didn't register.

Instead of holding open hearings the way they had with civil rights activists, the committee members met their latest targets in motel rooms. A tape recorder would be set up by the bed, and the investigators or committee members or Johns himself would threaten the horrified subject: Answer our questions here, or we'll drag you into a public forum and then everyone will know your secrets. Usually they talked.

One witness did challenge the committee members to explain their purpose. The committee's attorney snapped, "Well, we don't explain the purpose of this committee to anybody."

Hundreds of witnesses surrendered to Johns Committee pressure, first at the University of Florida, then at other schools. The interrogations went into excruciating detail about the witnesses' sex lives, often exposing the questioners' own ignorance. Sometimes they seemed confused about the definition of "homosexual," conflating it with any sexual practice that didn't involve the missionary position—even the ones involving people of different genders. At one point an investigator asked a gay man, "Have you ever thought of having homosexual relations with a woman just to find out what it's all about?"

Occasionally, the committee did uncover actual crimes—for instance, a Brevard County principal who admitted fondling boys at his elementary school—and then took no action to stop it. An investigator questioned a dozen inmates at a state prison for women, hearing testimony about Tampa cops extorting sex from suspected lesbians and stag shows a judge put on for the benefit of FBI agents. The investigator didn't care about that. He wanted more details about a reform school gym teacher who had short hair and drove a convertible and thus might be a lesbian. The committee even hired a black-haired bartender from Pensacola with a felony conviction for writing bad checks, paying her $450 a month to hang around bowling alleys and seduce lesbians, bringing them back to a hotel where they would be coerced into answering questions.

Despite—or rather, because of—its ignorance, the committee cut a swath through the universities like the one Sherman cut through Georgia. It branded scores of teachers and students as homosexuals and thus a threat to the state, getting them fired from their jobs or expelled from their colleges. One University of Florida professor, Sigmund Dietrich, reacted to his outing and firing by attempting suicide. He failed.

"I was guilty of breaking conventions," he wrote to a friend. "I was guilty of not measuring up to what I was supposed to have been."

Among the students ousted for being gay: Rita Mae Brown, whose high school scores had earned her a scholarship to the University of Florida. Brown wasn't expelled, but she was subjected to so much official harassment that she got the message and left. Her unceremonious departure was especially remarkable because she had been considered among the elite. She'd even wangled an invitation to serve as "governor for a day" in Tallahassee. Her UF experience became fodder for her landmark 1973 novel *Rubyfruit Jungle.*

Anyone who opposed the committee could become a target. Its investigators searched for Communist connections involving the publisher of the *St. Petersburg Times,* which had run editorials questioning its work. They couldn't find any. When an *Orlando Sentinel* columnist dared criticize the committee in print, it struck back. Its investigators paid a female convict to lure the columnist, a recovering alcoholic, to a motel room, ostensibly because she needed help to combat her own drinking problem. She met him at the door in a robe that was open to the waist—and then in mid-seduction, the cops burst in and charged him with violating an archaic law against oral sex. He was convicted and lost his job and, eventually, his marriage. He would be the only person targeted by the Johns Committee who was charged with a crime.

In 1964, to show off all that they had learned after nine years of investigating, the committee members and staff put together a report called *Homosexuality and Citizenship in Florida.* This was to be the committee's crowning achievement, a demonstration of how deeply it had plumbed the depths of Floridian depravity. The staff director said it would be a "definitive report, factual in nature, and complete in its descriptions."

This is where the story takes such a classic Floridian twist that, in a way, it's an even better example of weird Florida than the Naughty Nympho.

The committee printed more than two thousand copies, sending half to legislators, police officials, and Florida newspapers. A blurb on the back invited any "qualified person" to buy a copy for 25 cents, although it did not define who was "qualified."

The report sported an eye-catching purple cover, so it became known far and wide as "the Purple Pamphlet." The cover showed a photo of two shirtless men kissing, and inside were similarly lurid photos: a trussed-up teenage boy clad only in a G-string, two men having a sexual encounter via a hole in a bathroom stall's wall, and, worst of all, a series showing a preadolescent boy in various poses and stages of undress. The only thing missing was full frontal nudity.

The authors also included a glossary of homosexual terms that would have flummoxed Masters & Johnson—referring, for instance, to "pygmalionism," which it defined as "the sexual desire for a statue or statues." It was, as the director had promised, complete in its descriptions.

When word got out about the Purple Pamphlet, lots of allegedly "qualified" people around the country mailed quarters to Tallahassee, clamoring for a copy. The Dade County state attorney declared it obscene and threatened to prosecute anyone he caught selling it. The *New Republic* mocked the committee's hubris. *Life* called it "irresponsible." *Confidential* magazine hyped it with a story headlined, "Perverts Under the Palms."

Committee members tried to defend the report and its pornographic images, but they really couldn't. A year later, the Johns Committee winked out of existence, its work at last having become an embarrassment to Florida. It was such an embarrassment that the legislature kept its records locked away from public scrutiny until 1993—hidden in a closet, you might say.

In 1957, around the time the Johns Committee began shifting its attention from civil rights activists to gays and lesbians, a group of four gay men were meeting regularly, and discreetly, in Pensacola. They'd convene in a lovely old home owned by Ray and Henry Hillyer, who pretended to be brothers but were actually a couple.

The four had heard rumblings about a budding gay rights movement, about a group called the Mattachine Society, about books and magazines featuring fiction and photos that fit their interest. They wanted to order copies of these items but didn't want anyone to know, particularly the postal authorities.

They recruited a woman sympathetic to their plight to rent a Pensacola post office box. They picked a pseudonym for her that seemed unlikely to attract attention: "Emma Jones." One of Emma's "parents" later explained, " 'Emma' because it was such an awful name; 'Jones' because it was so common."

With the help of "Emma," the men ordered the books and magazines and 16mm movies. When Emma picked up her plain-brown packages once a month, nobody gave her a second glance.

The scheme worked so well that eventually the men decided to let Emma try something more daring. Every Fourth of July, the Hillyers played host to a small party at their home. In 1967, they sent out twenty-five invitations in Emma's name for a beach cookout. Fifty people showed up to party amid the privacy offered by sixty-foot dunes. The following year they did it again, this time drawing two hundred people, women as well as men, which was handy. If the cops showed up, the men and women could just pair off as if they were straight.

By 1971, the parties were attracting such a crowd that Emma and her creators decided to move the shindig indoors. They booked the once glamorous Hotel San Carlos, a sixty-year-old slice of Mediterranean Revival wedding cake in the center of downtown. They took over the seventh-floor ballroom to perform some of the most elaborate drag shows the South had ever seen. The first "Red, White & Blue Revue" featured a cast of twenty-six men and women. There were four ninety-minute shows, a different one for each night of the party. The cast rehearsed for two months to make sure everything was perfect.

The part of Miss Emma was played by a woman who appeared to have a fifty-two-inch bust. She wore a blue dress, white fringe, red fishnets, blue boots, and a crown, and she lip-synched "Indian Love Call" while perched atop a model of Mount Rushmore. A man dressed in a gold lamé Native American costume performed the male half of the duet. It brought down the house.

Emma Jones was done hiding behind the dunes. Now she and her cohorts were easily visible. Drag queens were riding in convertibles right down Pensacola's main drag. Where else would you expect drag queens to drive?

The Emma Jones convention—because that's what it had become—made the San Carlos and its employees lots of money. It inspired entrepreneurs to open Pensacola's first gay bars, with names like the Red Garter and the Yum Yum Tree. The bars' drag shows drew both gays and straights. This dismayed Emma Jones's creators, who feared a Bible Belt backlash.

Sure enough, a couple of years later, a Pensacola radio DJ joked on air that Pensacola was now the Gay Capital of the South. That ticked off the mayor, who ordered a police crackdown in the name of preserving Pensacola's family-friendly image. Sensing trouble, Emma Jones and Co. had already called off that year's party, but people showed up anyway, and some of them were caught up in the drag-ball dragnet.

This was the end. Emma had thrown her last party. The Yum Yum Tree burned down, and the ex-con owner was convicted of torching the place. Without the annual financial boost from Emma Jones's friends, the San Carlos closed in 1982.

Around the time the San Carlos shut down, a gay *Pensacola News Journal* reporter wrote a story about Emma Jones, revealing the ruse for the first time to many in the city's straight world. He received a ton of hate mail and angry calls—and not just from straight people.

"There were two or three calls I got from gay people in Pensacola who were really angry that I was writing about the whole Emma Jones phenomenon" the reporter, Craig Waters, told me. "They thought I was going to ruin a good thing. One caller even threatened to out me. I thought that was pretty funny—a gay reader outing a gay reporter for writing about gay events."

Yet around that time in the early 1980s, the parties started up again. They had returned to Pensacola Beach, this time on Memorial Day. It was as if Emma's spirit had summoned everyone back, determined to show Pensacola that it needed gays more than gays needed the city.

To make that point nationwide, though, required a visit not to the Yum Yum Tree but to the Florida Sunshine Tree.

Oranges are so intertwined with Florida's identity that you'd never know they aren't native. The fruit, brought here from Spain, is emblazoned on our license plates. The orange blossom is our official state flower, the orange our official state fruit. We have both a Citrus County and an Orange County. The University of Florida's football stadium is named for onetime citrus baron Ben Hill Griffin Jr. People call it "the Swamp," but a more accurate name would be "the Grove."

In 1967, the legislature named orange juice our official state beverage. A year later, the Florida Citrus Commission hired as its national spokeswoman a former beauty queen named Anita Bryant. She'd been discovered by Arthur Godfrey's talent scouts as a little girl, singing on TV in Tulsa. As Miss Oklahoma, Bryant had been second runner-up to Miss America in 1959, boosting her singing career. She collected gold records for such numbers as "'Til There Was You" and "Paper Roses." She toured with Bob Hope's USO shows, performed for the 1971 Super Bowl halftime program, and appeared at Billy Graham revivals at Madison Square Garden. She was so popular that in 1968 she sang at both political conventions—"Battle Hymn of the Republic" for the Democrats gathered in Chicago, "The Star-Spangled Banner" for the Republicans who caucused in Miami Beach.

On behalf of the Florida Citrus Commission, which paid her $100,000 a year, Bryant filmed a series of TV commercials that featured her singing about the joys of drinking OJ. She'd be standing in a grove belting out, "Come to the Florida Sunshine Tree! Florida sunshine—naturally!" Her catchphrase, used as the tagline of every commercial, was, "A day without orange juice is like a day without sunshine!"

Bryant and her husband, rock'n'roll disc jockey Bob Green, had been living in Dade County since 1960. They had a nice life, complete with a thirty-three-room waterfront mansion with its own waterfall and double Jacuzzi. But by the late '60s, South Florida was changing, amid signs that the counterculture, as it was called back then, was growing stronger.

In 1969, leather-clad rocker Jim Morrison—a Florida native, by the way—was busted by Miami cops for indecent exposure during a Doors concert. Three weeks later, thirty thousand people packed the Orange Bowl for a "Rally for Decency" headlined by Anita Bryant, TV star Jackie Gleason, and the venerable Kate Smith, who of course sang "God Bless America."

Throughout the 1970s, gay men moved to South Florida in droves, seeking both warm weather and freedom. Some who lived part time on Cape Cod bought winter homes in Key West, while others settled in as full-timers, opening businesses connected to the arts or the tourist trade. Even as Pensacola's gay community was going back into hiding, gay men in Key West and Miami figured out how to translate their economic power into political power.

In 1976, two gay South Florida residents, a former encyclopedia salesman and the owner of a national chain of gay bathhouses, formed the Dade County Coalition for the Humanistic Rights of Gays, trying to bring together the many factions that made up the gay population—from the disco party boys to the rough-trade biker club called the Thebans. Their coalition backed a slate of local and state candidates they thought would listen to their concerns. Thirty-five won. Most of them would have won anyway, but the coalition claimed victory.

The encyclopedia salesman was Solomon "Bob" Basker, a lean ex-cantor in his fifties who knew well the rhetoric of politics. He'd been active in left-wing causes up north but moved to Miami to be closer to his ex-wife and their children. Now he focused his activism on issues of importance to South Florida gays. He helped organize Miami's branch of the Metropolitan Community Church, the denomination primarily for gay believers started by the Rev. Troy Perry, who hailed from a family of North Florida moonshiners.

Basker worked with a University of Miami law professor to draft a Dade County ordinance banning discrimination against homosexuals in employment and housing. Then the coalition persuaded one of their successful county commission candidates to introduce it. To close the deal, Basker met with each of the commissioners, telling them that cities around the country were passing similar ordinances. He didn't mention that only two were in the South.

Amid an outcry by religious groups, the Dade County Commission approved the ordinance in January 1977 by a vote of 5–3, winning praise from the *Miami Herald*.

Anita Bryant had never been a political activist before, but the gay rights ordinance grabbed her attention like nothing else ever had. Her pastor encouraged her to get involved. She had a personal stake too. The commissioner who had sponsored the ordinance was married to Bryant's agent. Bryant had cut radio commercials endorsing the woman's candidacy. Now Bryant felt betrayed by her, and said so.

Bryant was among the crowd that showed up at the commission meeting to argue against the vote. After it passed, she called a meeting at her mansion of church members and political conservatives, and they formed a group called Save Our Children. What did children have to do with it? Bryant's pastor was worried that church-affiliated schools would be forced to hire gay teachers, which he was sure would lead to disaster. As Bryant put it, "Homosexuals can't reproduce, so they recruit."

Equating homosexuals with pedophiles sounded like an argument the Johns Committee would have gladly embraced. To Bryant, it was perfectly logical. By granting gays equal rights with straights, Bryant said in one forum, the county was "discriminating against my children's right to grow up in a healthy, decent community."

She needed ten thousand signatures on a petition to get a referendum vote on repealing the ordinance. In four weeks, she had sixty-four thousand.

The divide could not have been starker. On one side stood Dade's gay community—fractured, often at odds with each other, some of them serious activists determined to win equal rights, some interested in nothing more than having a good time. On the other side, Bryant: a well-coiffed wife and mother, a Sunday school teacher, a national figure, a woman of unquestioned virtue. As a pillar of moral rectitude, her pronouncements about evil exhibited a power that they would have lacked coming from some toothy Florida politician. She boasted that she spoke for "the normal majority."

She quickly acquired a group of allies who ranged from the local Catholic diocese—the irony of that became clear only in retrospect—to a Virginia-based evangelist named Jerry Falwell, who two years later would adapt Bryant's arguments as a basis for a new nationwide organization, the Moral Majority. She soon had professional pollsters and campaign consultants working for her too.

Bryant's husband warned her that she might lose bookings as a result of her advocacy, but Bryant didn't back down. She had been doing TV appearances since she was eight, and now she took to the airwaves to make her case not just to Dade voters but to the entire country. She appeared on Pat

Robertson's *700 Club* show and twice did a turn on Jim and Tammy Faye Bakker's TV program (the irony of which became obvious only in retrospect).

The gay coalition lacked Bryant's polish and connections, not to mention the professional organization backing her. A hotshot New York consultant brought in to help pushed a lot of the local folks aside or ignored their advice about how to reach out to the community they lived in. Meanwhile, a large contingent of lesbians quit the campaign because the snide comments they heard from the movement's male leaders about Bryant seemed sexist.

When the coalition tried to buy space in the *Herald* for a hard-hitting ad involving a swastika, the publisher said no. Meanwhile, Save Our Children was running TV ads featuring scenes from a San Francisco gay liberation parade—men in leather, men in dresses, men cavorting with other men. This, the ad said, is what gays want to turn our town into.

The coalition's natural base was Dade County's women, who felt far less threatened by gay men and more likely to know some as businesspeople. But Bryant's constant talk about children in peril turned many of the women voters against them. The *Herald* flipped positions and endorsed the repeal. Even Gov. Reubin Askew, a Democrat regarded as progressive on civil rights issues, said he would vote for Bryant's side if he lived in Miami.

Tensions rose. Phone threats poured into coalition headquarters. Someone pointed a shotgun at one coalition leader. Although Bryant claimed to belong to a religion of forgiveness, she had taken to referring to homosexuals as "human garbage" and blamed a California drought on that state's too-tolerant government.

Bryant feared gays would stage a violent attack on her family, so she hired guards for her home. One day a thick package arrived bearing a New York postmark. The police bomb squad blew it up, and was rewarded by a rain of confetti—the remains of some gay rights leaflets someone had mailed her.

In the end, Bryant proved to be a far better salesperson than Basker and his allies. In June 1977, Dade County's voters repealed the ordinance by 69 percent to 31 percent, a result so important it was announced on the national news by Walter Cronkite. The election results had Bryant "dancing a jig at her Miami Beach home," the *New York Times* reported. She vowed to take her crusade national, launching Anita Bryant Ministries, which offered deprogramming and halfway houses for gays wanting to go straight. The day after the vote, the legislature banned gays from adopting children.

Gay groups nationwide decided to repay Bryant by boycotting Florida orange juice. They demanded the Florida Citrus Commission fire her. Gay bars across the country dropped Florida OJ from their menus. They substituted California oranges in their screwdrivers, or they served a drink made with apple juice that they called "the Anita Bryant." Gay men strolled the streets of San Francisco in T-shirts that said SQUEEZE A FRUIT FOR ANITA. When Bryant made an appearance at an event in Iowa, someone hit her in the face with a pie.

Bryant's victory in Dade County had galvanized gay and lesbian activists all over the United States. In 1978, an openly gay member of the San Francisco Board of Supervisors gave an incendiary speech on the steps of City Hall that flipped Bryant's argument on its head.

"My name is Harvey Milk and I am here to recruit you," he began. His speech was a call to arms: "I ask my gay brothers and sisters to make a commitment to fight. For themselves. For their freedom. For their country . . . I am tired of the Anita Bryants twisting the language and the meaning of the Bible to fit their own distorted outlook."

Historians consider the Stonewall riots of 1969 as the start of the gay rights movement, but Anita Bryant's Miami fight is what put gay rights on the national political agenda and got people talking about the issue. Every battle over human rights needs a good villain—a Bull Connor. Bryant became the Bull Connor of gay rights, and thanks to her involvement, the subject of gay rights wound up on Cronkite's nightly news and the front page of the *New York Times*. Some historians now call Bryant the father of gay rights in America, which is exactly the level of irony characteristic of life in Florida.

The glow from Bryant's Dade County victory faded quickly. Her husband's prediction about contracts drying up proved to be correct. After her antigay campaign's shrill tone, she could no longer charm America the way she once had. A sewing machine company canceled plans for her to star in a sew-and-chat TV show. The Save the Children charity had lost contributions because of her and sued to block her from using the name. She lost her Florida Citrus Commission gig. She and Green divorced.

Bryant then gave an interview to *Ladies' Home Journal* in which she fell off her high horse and stayed down. Rather than being an exemplar of moral rectitude, she was a wreck.

Bryant revealed she'd been hooked on Valium, kicked that habit in 1978, then gotten hooked on sleeping pills and wine. Her broken marriage, she revealed, "was never much good to begin with." She responded to her ex-husband's allegations of infidelity by admitting, "I can't say that I'm totally innocent." As for gays, she said that "the church needs to be more . . . willing to see these people as human beings."

Bryant's confession gave the Dade County gay rights story a very Florida twist. She'd been a sham all along, shucking and jiving like any other huckster. Her divorce, and her honesty about it, cost her any remaining supporters. As Falwell's Moral Majority took her campaign nationwide, with smashing political success, she was left on the sidelines.

Despite the vote, South Florida continued attracting gay men and women who wanted to live more openly. Down the road from Miami and across the Seven-Mile Bridge, the gay voting bloc in Key West grew more powerful and focused. In 1979, a gay art gallery owner named Richard Heyman won a seat on the city council. In 1983, he was elected as the first openly gay mayor in the United States by building a coalition of gay businesspeople, historic preservation fans, growth management activists, and African American voters who felt disenfranchised. In 1987, he was reelected. Heyman's campaign slogan didn't call for anything radical, just "fair laws, fairly applied."

In 1991, gay activists held the first "Gay Days" at Walt Disney World, a one-day event that now lasts a week and draws 150,000 men and women from around the world. In 1998, Miami-Dade County reversed Bryant's win, passing a new human rights ordinance. By 2012, South Florida was so accepting of gays that the U.S. Census said Fort Lauderdale had the most gay couples in America. Court decisions struck down the state's ban on gay adoption. When Florida legislators tried reviving it in 2015, a Republican state senator from the Panhandle blocked the move, comparing it to discrimination against African Americans.

A 2015 court ruling also struck down the ban on gay marriage. Some Florida county clerks announced they would no longer perform any weddings at their courthouses, gay or straight, just to thwart gay couples from getting married there. Not Pensacola. Gay couples from Alabama and Louisiana drove to Pensacola to tie the knot, figuring they'd never get the chance in their own states. The court clerk welcomed them with open arms.

All these changes were made possible by the constant influx of newcomers to Florida, people who flocked to the state in search of a fresh start in sunnier circumstances. That's always been a big part of Florida's appeal: the chance to reinvent yourself, to create a whole new you.

Of course, this being Florida, the whole new you can sometimes run into a whole new set of problems, on top of the trouble that the old you brought along.

Patients watch television in their ward at Florida State Hospital in Chattahoochee, 1957. Not wanting to be there was considered evidence you belonged there. Photo courtesy of State Archives of Florida.

18

A Whole New You

"The longer I do my job," he said, "the more I realize humans lack good mirrors. It's so hard for anyone to show us how we look, and so hard for us to show anyone how we feel."
—*Paper Towns* by John Green, who grew up in Orlando

The first time I visited South Beach, Florida's glamour capital, I found myself on a soft and sweet Saturday evening walking down its main drag with some journalism colleagues, a mix of male and female reporters from other places. We strolled along chatting about this and that, a clump of rumpled working stiffs amid all the tanned and toned beautiful people hobnobbing at various open-air emporia.

One of our number didn't say much because he was too busy sightseeing. His head swiveled around as if his neck were a doorknob, his eyes darting this way and that. At one point, he stopped stock-still, thunderstruck. We kept walking and talking, and eventually he caught up with us.

"Did you *see* that?" he demanded.

None of us had witnessed whatever it was, and said so. He couldn't believe we had missed it, but then had trouble explaining what we'd missed.

"That woman back there, she—she was—she uh—" He sputtered for a minute, his hands fluttering in the air, then he shaped them as if he were palming a couple of basketballs held against his body. He stretched out his arms and held his cupped hands out about as far from his chest as he could reach.

"She had been so surgically enhanced she couldn't cut her own meat!" he said, finally finding the words. "She couldn't get her arms in tight enough to work the knife and fork. The guy with her had to cut her food up for her."

We all just nodded and kept walking because really, what could you say? Later, though, I wondered if my astonished colleague had inadvertently stumbled across a semicelebrity—a woman named Lacey Wildd, with the extra d implying her main identifying feature.

Her real name is Paula Thibert. She has appeared on the shows *My Strange Addiction* and *True Life* and even *Botched,* a program about plastic surgeries gone awry. She has gone under the knife thirty-six times so far, boosting here, tucking there, eventually looking like someone made a Jessica Rabbit balloon for Macy's Thanksgiving Day parade and then left the helium turned on too long.

Thibert has had her lips and hips and everything in between altered, but her main focus has been her breasts. They've been inflated to the point where they weigh twenty-one pounds each. She had to get a bralike structure made of pigskin inserted beneath the skin to prevent her from suffering physical injuries from carrying the weight. On one TV show, during Halloween, she shone a flashlight behind her breasts to show how they could glow like jack-o'-lanterns.

And yet it's not enough. Her chest quest, expressed on each show on which she appears, is to be bigger. She wants to have the biggest breasts in the world—which is, when you think about it, a very Floridian thing to aim for: a new life, with fame based on a bizarre achievement.

As I've mentioned before, Florida attracts a lot of people seeking second, third, fourth, or fifth chances. People are constantly moving here to change their lives. One of my friends complained that his sturdy Midwestern grandfather retired to Florida, ditched his sturdy Midwestern values, and joined a nudist colony, which tends to make visits a bit awkward. Also, you can't buy him a tie for Father's Day anymore.

Any Florida historian can reel off story after story of people who remade themselves here. There was Sidney Catts, the preacher who became a governor; Newton Perry, the former Navy SEAL who built a roadside attraction full of mermaids; Jack Rowland Murphy, who left behind studying the violin to become Murph the Surf, rider of waves and stealer of jewels.

My favorite example is Lilly Pulitzer, who married a rich newspaper publisher and then had a breakdown. Her shrink told her to find something to keep her busy, so she and a friend opened a stand to sell orange juice. The two women kept getting juice on their clothes, so Mrs. Pulitzer sketched out simple cotton dresses with colorful patterns to hide OJ stains. When her Palm Beach pals saw her creations, known as "Lillys," they had to have them too. That's how she became a fashion designer. In the 1960s, her work was exclusively for the well-to-do, the chic, like Jackie Kennedy. Now you can buy Lillys at Target.

Some visitors are so eager to start a new life that they fake their deaths. With all of our waterways and swamps, you can take your pick of places for a phony fatal plunge. We've had everyone from missing murderers ("Escaped Killer Caught After 37 Years") to elusive embezzlers ("Fugitive GA Banker Suspected of Growing Marijuana out of Fla. Home") show up here trying to make a major break with their past. Sure, they got caught—but who knows how many got away with it?

Many of the people here in Florida want more than just a do-over. What they want is a make-over. They want to go from plain Paula Thibert to traffic-stopping, can't-cut-her-meat Lacey Wildd.

And why not? In Florida, we've altered the landscape by filling in or draining wetlands, digging canals, and paving paradise to put up not just a parking lot but also some poorly built condos and a tacky strip mall. So why not alter the humans as well as the land?

Some people even try to do both. In 2002, police charged a fifty-five-year-old Boca Grande home builder with bilking a customer out of $300,000. The customer expected to get a seven-thousand-square-foot house. The builder planned to use that money for a sex-change operation. He would have gotten away with it, but he got into the middle of another couple's divorce case on the wife's side. The husband's private eye dug up the dirt.

We love our doctors in Florida. They're not just healers. They're also important economic engines. Until recently, the doctor who topped everyone else in the country for billings to Medicare was a Palm Beach County ophthalmologist named Salomon Melgen, who collected $21 million in 2012. Imagine what a trickle-down boon that was for all the luxury-car dealers and private jet maintenance workers! Unfortunately, Dr. Melgen's run at the top came to an end when he was indicted in 2015 for both Medicare fraud and bribing a Democratic senator from New Jersey.

Florida reveres its doctors so much that one of the two statues representing Florida in Statuary Hall in Washington is of an Apalachicola physician. Dr. John Gorrie, who was looking for a way to cool down his yellow fever and malaria patients, is credited with inventing a precursor of air-conditioning. He patented his system in 1851 and was promptly hailed by his contemporaries as a crank and a fraud. People lived in Florida before air-conditioning, but not many. It's hard to imagine anyone living here without Dr. Gorrie's invention now, especially around, oh, say, August 1.

Today, though, the Florida doctors we celebrate are trying to make their patients hotter, not cool them down. Plastic surgery is so popular in Florida that as of 2010, there was one plastic surgeon for every thirty-nine residents. That's the third most plastic surgeons per capita in the country, behind the District of Columbia and Maryland (who knew congresspeople needed that much touching up?).

These operations are supposed to be life improving. Sometimes they're also lifesaving. In 1993, a thirty-year-old stripper from Joe Redner's Mons Venus club in Tampa got into a squabble with her seventy-five-year-old sometime boyfriend. He pulled out a pistol and shot her in the left breast.

"My doctors say my implant saved me," the dancer said from her hospital bed. "They said if I didn't have that, I'd be dead. That is scary."

You could call it a fluke, except that in 2012, something similar happened. A forty-one-year-old woman in Melbourne who had spent $6,000 on an enhanced bosom got into a confrontation with her ex-fiancé's new girlfriend, and was stabbed several times in the left breast. Doctors said the implant had just enough saline in it to stop the knife from piercing her heart. Clearly, Florida's plastic surgeons are doing some highly creative work if they're incorporating Kevlar and chain mail into their implants.

One Florida plastic surgeon has done more than any other to spread the word about all the astonishing bodywork going on here. Dr. Michael Salzhauer, aka "Dr. Miami," posts clips on Snapchat of him chatting about his work during surgery, and before and after photos on Instagram. Despite the gruesome visuals, his broadcasts reach about 100,000 followers who are apparently fascinated by Brazilian butt lifts, with another 125,000 checking his Instagram posts. To him, such avid fandom makes perfect sense.

"In every aspect of our lives we try to do better. Build nicer houses, build nicer cars, become smarter," he said. "Why not have better bodies?"

Some of Florida's form-fixing doctors are so well known they draw patients from other states, a practice state officials have termed "medical tourism," which they would like to encourage. Wealthy folks who live elsewhere announce a Florida vacation, fly down, see the doctor for a touch-up, then return home after the scars heal and talk about how delightful and relaxing Florida was. Florida plastic surgeons are so eager to treat these folks that they're willing to not only make house calls at their mansions but even yacht calls.

The traveling customers get more than just treatment on the QT. They get treated by the top docs in the field. As one prominent surgeon indignantly told a Miami newspaper after he was sued for malpractice, "I'm known worldwide for my work on the buttocks."

Of course, not everyone who wants a little work done can easily afford the services of a worldwide expert on whatever body part needs buffing.

For the true Floridian, that's a challenge to be met with a little creativity. I am thinking here of the young woman from Pensacola who, in 2013, made headlines by standing by a busy road waving a sign that said NOT HOMELESS NEED BOOBS. She didn't tell reporters how much she raised panhandling in the Panhandle, just that people had been far more generous than she had expected.

Another approach is to fake it—to use a false front, as it were. That was the approach tried by a twenty-one-year-old Tampa woman who called herself Jasmine Tridevil. In September 2014, she announced that she had paid a plastic surgeon $20,000 to create a third breast, and had hired a camera crew to film her every move so she could convince MTV to make her a reality star.

Some media outlets took her word for what she said had happened and sent her story and photo spinning around the globe. Other reporters discovered that her real name was Alisha Jasmine Hessler, and that her luggage had been stolen from the Tampa airport the week before. A police report noted that when the suitcase was returned to her, inside was a "3 breast prosthesis."

Although she insisted her implant was as real as any implant can ever be, reporters couldn't help noticing that the Web site for Hessler's massage business featured this slogan: "Provider of internet hoaxes since 2014." Clearly her ambition had outpaced her expertise.

When it comes to prosthetics, why stop at faking just one body part? Why not fake the whole body? One night in 2006, a Wildwood carpenter named Chuck Ramos, his business idled by the recession, stumbled on a TV show about the woes of men who could not afford the $25,000 price of gender reassignment surgery. Some, in despair, committed suicide. Ramos saw a way to help them and make some money too. He created woman-shaped silicone suits that men can wear. He called them "FemSkin." The upper body is molded from a German woman's body, while the bottom is molded from a Brazilian woman's body. The suits cost between $1,000 and $2,000.

"FemSkins are very soft, strong and elastic," it says on femskin.com. "Tight and stretchy like pantyhose, they are silky smooth and will shape your body for a sexy female form."

"Form" is the key word there. The wearers don't really look like women. They look like blow-up dolls that the Blue Fairy has touched with her wand, so they come to life and walk (awkwardly) and talk (in a muffled voice). British TV produced a documentary about the phenomenon, calling it *Secrets of the Living Dolls.*

Chuck Ramos lived just long enough to see his suits start to sell, then died of liver cancer. The company he started is still in business, though. It's run now

by his three sons and by his wife. Her name is—are you ready for this?—
Barbie.

The Brazilian part of the FemSkin is the part that would be most popular
in South Florida, which is why it's home to the Fix-A-Flat butt-booster
brigade.

They offer cut-rate prices for inflated backsides. These derriere docs do it
by using illegal materials and avoiding regular office hours, licensing, and
taxes. They don't go in for surgery or hospitals. They set up in motel rooms
and plump up their clients' cheeks with injections of industrial grade silicone,
mineral oil, even the tire sealant material contained in Fix-A-Flat cans. Instead of stitches, they seal the wound with a dollop of Super Glue.

Illegal butt injections have sharply increased across the country, but they
have proved particularly popular in South Florida's bootycentric culture,
which has been celebrated in songs ranging from KC and the Sunshine Band's
"(Shake Shake Shake) Shake Your Booty" (1976) to Pitbull's "Culo" (2004).
Strippers looking for more junk in the trunk have been frequent customers/
victims of these illegal procedures, as have transgendered men, but housewives
and single ladies have taken their shots too.

The tops in bottom-boosters, for a while, was Oneal Ron Morris, a trans-
gender man whose own backside had been blown up to the point that Pitbull
would have declared that culo to be beyond tremendo. Morris, also known
as "Duchess," held pumping parties, where he injected several clients at once.
Later, after his clients developed welts, infections, and pneumonialike symptoms, they went to the cops.

Initially, Morris faced charges of practicing medicine without a license
and became something of a celebrity for his full-body arrest photo. He appeared on Telemundo's *Pa'lante con Cristina* show and got into a melee that
led to one woman hurling a syringe. Then, in 2012, Morris was charged with
manslaughter.

Police said Morris had charged a woman named Shatarka Nuby $2,000
for a series of injections between 2007 and 2010. The injections eventually
killed her, the medical examiner concluded. She died in federal prison while
serving time for identity theft. And why had Nuby committed identity theft?
To pay for new breast implants.

By 2015, Morris's various criminal cases still had not been resolved. In a
court hearing, he sounded weary of the whole thing, telling the judge, "I just
want to put it behind me."

If only Morris had been sticking needles into people at the other end! He could have charged more money, for one thing.

For years, the most ambitious shape-shifter in Florida medical circles was Dr. Fredric Brandt of Coral Gables, whose nicknames included "Dermatologist to the Stars," "the Baron of Botox," and "the Count of Collagen." His superstar patients included Madonna, talk show host Kelly Ripa, model Stephanie Seymour, actress Ellen Barkin, and enough New York magazine editors to fill a matinee showing of *The Devil Wore Prada.*

Unlike plastic surgeons, Brandt never used a scalpel for his living sculptures. Instead, not unlike Morris and the other toxic tush docs, he injected various substances to fill out and plump up the parts of his clients' faces that were sagging with age. Unlike the Fix-A-Flat docs, though, he used legal substances, such as Botox—a form of the bacterium *botulinum*—that paralyzes the facial nerves, and of course he had gotten his MD and license.

Patients declared Brandt to be an artist, carefully shaping their cheeks and jawlines, erasing wrinkles. What made him unusual among dermatologists was that—also like Morris—he experimented on himself first. He built the mask that he showed to the world, a mask that was impossibly smooth and about as expressive as the ones sold by FemSkin. It made him look like "a cross between a science experiment and a work of art," one of his friends wrote. And yet he'd tell everyone, "I think I look natural, don't you?"

To his patients he always seemed happy, sometimes singing show tunes as he worked ("Younger than Springtime" was a favorite). One magazine described him as having "a clownishly 'sinister' Dr. Evil–meets–Pee-wee Herman persona." He didn't wear drab medical scrubs. One day he'd wear the kind of outfit you might have seen Duran Duran dressed in for an '80s music video. The next day he'd have on a skirt over leather pants, or a plastic raincoat that he wore indoors.

The doctor's mask hid a darker side—depression. The *New York Times* ran a largely positive profile of him, which he liked until he read the 106 reader comments posted online, most expressing disdain or worse. One commenter said he looked like "an alien from another world . . . like *Star Trek.*" Such criticism left him dismayed and dejected.

Then, in 2015, a new TV show called *The Unbreakable Kimmy Schmidt* debuted on Netflix. Created by Tina Fey, the show's cast included a character named Dr. Grant who was clearly modeled on Brandt. Played by Martin Short, Dr. Grant had the same stringy white hair and artificially inflated profile. Dr. Grant's face was so plumped up he couldn't say his own name, pronouncing it "Dr. Pfafff."

Brandt was devastated by the depiction. In April 2015, someone found him hanging in his garage. Close friends said he'd been down for a while and the TV show just plunged him into a deeper despair. Still, his suicide stunned his fans. Who knew a dermatologist could be so thin-skinned?

Brandt's style may have been a tad, shall we say, fashion-forward, but his work was directly in the mainstream for Florida. In the state known for its phony Fountain of Youth, the anti-aging industry is bigger than anywhere else in the country, which meant Brandt based his clinic in the perfect spot.

"When he came into dermatology it was people treating sunspots and removing moles," *Allure* magazine editor Linda Wells told the *New York Times* after Brandt died. "Suddenly there were all these new substances and techniques that altered our relationship to age and aging, and he was at the absolute forefront of that."

Where better than retiree-rich Florida to build a business based on pointing to the normal signs of aging and calling it a disease you could treat? More than five hundred anti-aging clinics are doing a thriving business here, using names like Rejuvenation Center. They're handing out everything from steroids to human growth hormones, HGH for short.

A Florida doctor, William Abelove, was the first to join forces with a pharmaceutical company to hawk HGH—used to treat children with stunted growth—as a cure-all for old folks seeking more pep in their step. Abelove, like Dr. Brandt, used the stuff himself, which he claimed was the reason he could see a hundred patients a day at his Renaissance Longevity Center, even though he was in his seventies.

These clinics operate with little fear of state regulators showing up to shut them down. The regulators don't even care if the clinics are operated by people with criminal records—because hey, who better to help shape the new you than a bunch of people trying to cover up their pasts? Even if it was against the rules in Florida for anti-aging clinic owners to have criminal records, it wouldn't matter. What rules do exist are seldom enforced because the regulators are understaffed and underpaid, their budget slashed so deeply by Gov. Scott that more than two hundred were laid off.

That's why it took a whistle-blower slipping documents to the *Miami New Times* to uncover what was going on at a Coral Gables clinic called Biogenesis. The clinic was run by Tony Bosch, a cocaine addict with no medical license who pretended to be a doctor, right down to the white lab coat and phony medical degree on the wall.

Bosch, the son of a real doctor, gave injections of banned substances to more than a dozen Major League Baseball stars such as Miami-born Alex "A-Rod" Rodriguez of the New York Yankees, as well as pro wrestlers and boxers, pro tennis players, and NBA basketball players. At least eighteen high school players got performance-enhancing drugs too. Bosch went to prison for four years, and the judge said the sentence was so tough because of the kids whose lives he had messed with.

That was always the part of the story that stuck with me too. Those kids weren't showing up at the clinic alone. Their parents brought them in to get the shots. They weren't trying to make their kids look or feel younger, like the old folks. No, they wanted to give their kids an edge over other student athletes, even at the risk of ruining their health. They were, as one of my high school teachers used to say, sacrificing tomorrow on the altar of today. Two of the boys listed in Bosch's patient records were the sons of the University of Miami's pitching coach, who should definitely know better.

What no one could ever explain about all this was: Why? What were the parents thinking when they took their kids to see Bosch? What was their mental state? Were they insane?

If you live in Florida, you tend to spend a lot of time wondering about the mental state of people in the news . . . with good reason.

When I covered criminal courts in the 1990s, I soon noticed that a lot of the defendants had one thing in common. Tall or short, fat or thin, male or female, gay or straight, white, black, Hispanic, or Asian, the one unifying factor was that an awful lot of them seemed—not to get too technical about it—nuts.

I don't mean legally insane, unable to appreciate the criminal nature of their actions and thus unfit to stand trial. I mean they had been diagnosed as having a mental illness, such as being bipolar. But they never got the kind of treatment they needed to deal with the problem, and that affected their behavior. One of the reasons you read so many stories about people in Florida doing crazy things is that we do such a poor job of dealing with the mentally ill.

Alvin Rogers Jr. had been hospitalized nearly forty times for his mental illness, but never for long. The place he went, Personal Enrichment Through Mental Health Services, or PEMHS (pronounced "Pems"), was like an ER for people who needed long-term psychiatric treatment. The staff would keep him for a couple of days, talk to him a bit, hand him a prescription, and turn him loose.

By 1995, the twenty-five-year-old had reached a breaking point. Before his last visit to PEMHS, he'd been living on the street for twelve days, drinking alcohol and taking cocaine to try to quiet the voices he heard telling him to kill. The PEMHS doctor who talked to him didn't check the files on his previous visits because, she said later, it would have taken too long. She saw so many patients every day, she had forgotten that she'd treated Rogers before.

He stayed at PEMHS for three days, then told the doctor he felt fine. She turned him loose with another prescription he didn't fill. He was supposed to set up a follow-up appointment, but he never got around to that.

Instead, he went out and robbed two stores at gunpoint (yes, he got a gun, no questions asked). Then, on April 22, 1995, he stuck up a Church's Chicken drive-through and shot a bright, popular seventeen-year-old employee named Kimberly Leshore. A jury wanted to send him to death row, but the judge—a tough, no-nonsense general in the National Guard—overrode their decision. He sentenced Rogers to life in prison, knowing that's the one place where he would get long-term mental health care. He's been there ever since.

That's the way the system works in Florida for low-income people with mental problems. The largest warehouse for them in the state is Miami-Dade County's jail, where fourteen hundred inmates take psychiatric drugs. It's not a pretty place. In 2011, the U.S. Department of Justice conducted a sweeping investigation and declared, "Rather than being therapeutic, the [mental health] wing is chaotic, crowded, foul-smelling, depressing, and unacceptable for housing prisoners who are mentally ill or suicidal."

Mental health care at those jails costs taxpayers $80 million per year, which works out to about $218,400 a day. But heaven forbid anyone suggest spending that much taxpayer money on these folks *before* they commit a crime.

This is not a new attitude. In 1979, the state board that licensed psychologists rarely went after the quacks raking in dough from gullible patients. The board was up for what's called "sunset review," meaning that without legislative approval it would cease to exist. Legislative leaders who were fed up with the board's problems decided that instead of doing the hard work of reforming it, they would just pull the plug.

Thus, anyone willing to spend $10 on a county occupational license could claim to be a psychologist. Some people bought them as jokes—including the owner of a chameleon who claimed it was a "psychoanalyst and sex therapist." I bought one—an occupational license, that is, not a chameleon sex therapist—and took it back to my college newspaper in Alabama and tacked it up over my desk.

"Is that for real?" other students would ask, amazed.

"Absolutely!" I said. "That's how we roll in Florida!"

The legislature ultimately reinstated the board, but left it so weak that in 1991 the *St. Petersburg Times* reported that "someone who is completely untrained and unlicensed can hang out a shingle as a 'counselor' or 'therapist,' generic titles not covered under law, and do it legally."

Money is a major problem too. We're consistently ranked forty-ninth in the nation for funding of mental health programs, a fact which always makes me say, "Thank God for Texas!"

Don't look for the legislature to suddenly boost that funding anytime soon. Not long ago, the chairman of the Senate subcommittee on health and human services argued for cutting the amount even further because mentally ill people really just suffer from "a lack of willpower." He was recently chosen to be the next Senate president.

Lawmakers who huff and puff about being tough on crime never seem to see the connection to putting money in the state budget for preventing another Alvin Jones Jr. from hearing murderous voices. This was true even after a psychedelic mushroom aficionado named Marshall Ledbetter brought the issue home to the legislature in the most direct way possible—striking at the heart of the Tower of Power.

About 3:00 A.M. on Friday, June 14, 1991, after a long night of drinking, Ledbetter walked over to the Florida State Capitol building carrying a bottle of whiskey. He was a skinny guy with glasses, a quick wit, and serious problems with both sobriety and authority.

On this night, the night that would change his life, the FSU dropout wore a tie-dyed Jimi Hendrix T-shirt, acid-washed shorts, and flip-flops. He easily evaded the lone police officer patrolling the grounds and scouted around looking for the right spot for what he had in mind. He found what he was searching for around 4:00 A.M.

He wrapped the now empty liquor bottle in a towel and, after six tries, smashed a hole in one of the glass doors. Although the building had an elaborate computerized alarm system, no sirens blared. Ledbetter let himself in and became a one-man Occupy Tallahassee.

He found a pay phone and called 911 to report that he had taken over the Capitol. He wandered around the empty building for a while. He ditched his shorts and flip-flops, perhaps for more freedom of movement. On the fourth floor, he found the impressive office of the Senate sergeant at arms, where he made coffee, ate some Captain's Wafers, and found a stash of liquor and cigars. He shoved a couch in front of the door, then settled down to smoke a Hav-A-Tampa, sip some bourbon, and await the cops he was sure would come.

Ledbetter had a long wait. The cops who responded to his 911 call couldn't find the door he'd shattered. They thought his call was a prank. Nobody realized he was in the building until 7:00, when a cleaning lady discovered she couldn't get into the sergeant at arms's office. When she pushed at the blocked door, Ledbetter hurled a bottle at her, sending her scurrying.

What followed was an eight-hour standoff between a baffled SWAT team and a thoroughly looped Ledbetter. The cops spent two hours dialing the wrong number before they finally got through to him. They brought in an expensive Israeli-made bomb-detecting robot to check for booby traps. It failed to perform.

The high point of the confrontation came when Ledbetter sent out his list of "demands." He wanted to talk to a CNN news crew, as well as to Ice Cube of N.W.A., Flavor Flav of Public Enemy, and Jello Biafra of the Dead Kennedys. He wanted $100 worth of Chinese food from a particular restaurant. He also wanted "666 Dunkin' Donuts for my fine friends" on the police force.

The police were not amused, but everybody else sure was.

Ledbetter promised to give up if his list of demands was read aloud on CNN. The police recruited a local TV reporter named Mike Vasilinda to make a phony cable-news report that was shown only on the Capitol's in-house cable system. Vasilinda's fake broadcast convinced Ledbetter to surrender. He walked out half naked, carrying a bottle, puffing on a cigar. At the request of the nervous sergeant at arms, the cops grabbed the bottle before any reporters saw it. No liquor was supposed to be there.

Once in custody, Ledbetter was declared incompetent to stand trial and shipped off to the Florida State Hospital in Chattahoochee. This is the point where the story turns from the absurd to the tragic. Ledbetter escaped the mental hospital more than once, wrote odd letters, went back to his hometown of Winter Garden, and in 2003, put a shotgun in his mouth.

You might think having a mentally ill person seize control of the Capitol would convince legislators to do something about helping the mentally ill. You would be wrong.

What makes this doubly ironic is that the governor at the time was folksy former U.S. senator Lawton Chiles, aka "Walkin' Lawton," who had recently revealed he was being treated for depression with a new drug called Prozac.

"I think I was depressed about what was going on in the state," Chiles joked.

When I was growing up, we used to laugh about the place where Ledbetter was sent for treatment, the Florida State Hospital. We didn't call it that, of course. We called it by the name of the town, Chattahoochee. That seemed perfect, almost like "booby hatchery."

"That guy's nuts," we'd say. "He belongs in Chattahoochee!"

We had no idea what we were talking about. None of us had ever seen the place. We had no idea it had been built as a military arsenal in the 1830s, or that it had become Florida's first penitentiary in 1868. We just knew it was the place that you sent crazy folks. It seemed about as real as Santa's North Pole Workshop unless you knew someone who'd gone. My friend Barbara says she had an uncle who fried his brain with booze and was shipped off to Chattahoochee. She didn't see him again for years.

That kind of disappearing act, as it turns out, was all too common back then—until Kenneth Donaldson came along.

Donaldson had curly hair, blue eyes, an aquiline nose, and a deep and perpetual sense of having been wronged. In the 1940s, when he lived in New York and worked at a defense plant, he collapsed from exhaustion and checked himself into a hospital, hoping for some rest. The doctors gave him electroshock treatments twenty-eight times. That would mess up anyone, but it was common then.

By 1956, Donaldson was living in Pennsylvania and doing better. He wanted to visit his parents in Florida. He asked doctors to check him over, and they said he was fine. He headed south to spend a few months fixing things around their house and keeping them company.

He talked to them about how difficult it had been to find work after being a mental patient. He said he was writing a book about the people who had tried to ruin his life. The day he mailed it off to a publisher, he intended to leave town. He had a hotel job lined up.

His parents had other ideas.

Not long after New Year's 1957, two men knocked on the door, told him he was under arrest, then drove him to the Pinellas County Jail. He spent several days there, unsure what was going on. Finally someone explained his father had signed papers to have him committed. A pair of doctors stopped by his cell briefly. Then a judge visited his cell to tell him he was being sent to Chattahoochee.

Donaldson demanded an attorney and a hearing in open court. The attorney wasn't much help—he walked out halfway through the proceedings. The judge listened to Donaldson explain about the doctors who had checked him in Philadelphia, compared to the Florida doctors who had barely spoken to him. Then the judge delivered his verdict.

"You were in a mental institution once before, and your father doesn't think you're ready to go on to your next job," the judge said. "Therefore, for these two reasons, I'm sending you to Chattahoochee."

"But I'm not sick, Your Honor!"

"A few weeks up there—take some of that new medication—what's the name of it?—and you'll be back." With that, the judge rang for the jailers to take Donaldson away.

At the Florida State Hospital, Donaldson was diagnosed a paranoid schizophrenic. Rather than "a few weeks up there," he would not be released until July 31, 1971—more than fourteen years later.

Donaldson, a Christian Scientist, refused to take "that new medication" or any other medicine. He kept insisting he was not sick. To the Chattahoochee doctors, that was further evidence that he was mentally ill.

He warned them he was taking notes and planned to write a book someday about how they had treated him. To the doctors, that was another sign he was delusional.

He wrote anguished letters to the governor and other officials and mailed handwritten motions to various courts, trying to get out. To the doctors, that was additional proof of insanity.

"That's your illness, Donaldson," one doctor said. "You are so sick you won't admit it."

He spent most of his time locked in a room with about sixty other inmates. Some were criminals who had been declared incompetent to stand trial. Some were developmentally disabled. Some had serious mental problems that made them a threat to everyone else. Their beds were placed so close together that only a chair could fit between them.

A TV set blared all day long and, at night, some inmates suffered from screaming fits, waking everyone else in the ward. Donaldson said later that he suffered from "the fear, always the fear you have in your heart, I suppose, when you go to sleep that maybe somebody would jump on you during the night."

Living there for so long, under such conditions, would leave a man feeling numb, Donaldson said. The doctors would not set him free for any reason—not when friends offered him a place to stay if he was released, not when a halfway house agreed to let him move there, not even to attend the funerals of the parents who had committed him.

Donaldson repeatedly requested to be allowed access to the grounds outside the building. He was repeatedly turned down. He asked for occupational therapy. Same answer.

"Any healing done was done by one patient to another," he said later. "Just listening to another guy's troubles. Giving him some consolation."

Years passed. No matter what, Donaldson couldn't convince the doctors he was sane. The doctors couldn't convince him to take any medication. Because of the stalemate, he received no treatment whatsoever. Perhaps that was for the best, though. The principal doctor overseeing Donaldson's case was certified as an obstetrician.

One day Donaldson noticed an opinion piece in the *New York Times* that argued that mental patients have a constitutional right to adequate treatment. Otherwise the involuntarily committed were nothing but prisoners and thus were being deprived of liberty without due process. Donaldson wrote a letter to the author, Dr. Morton Birnbaum, and Birnbaum wrote back.

Birnbaum traveled to Chattahoochee to meet with Donaldson and became his champion. He helped Donaldson connect with the American Civil Liberties Union to sue not just Florida State Hospital but also the doctors who'd been in charge of his care. Before the case went to trial in Tallahassee federal court, the Chattahoochee doctors suddenly found a reason to set Donaldson free.

"My lawyer said it was a miraculous cure," he quipped.

It didn't help the doctors' case. On the stand, they sounded utterly clueless. They admitted Donaldson was not violent, even though the threat of violence was the only valid reason for keeping someone locked up for so long. They contended he really was getting treatment, something they called "milieu treatment." Pushed to explain that, they said it meant the time he spent hanging around in the ward with other inmates and talking to them, that was his therapy. It was hardly therapeutic.

The medical records were particularly damning. In Donaldson's first year in Chattahoochee, one doctor made a note in his file that his illness appeared to be "in remission." But after that, nothing happened. Why didn't he ever follow up on that? Why not declare him cured and turn him loose?

"When you have nine hundred patients, you do that," the doctor testified, apparently meaning, "Drop the ball."

The jury found for Donaldson, awarding him $20,000 in damages. They acquitted three doctors, but not the two in charge. Those two appealed to the U.S. Supreme Court, which voted 9–0 for Donaldson.

But this is where the story takes a Florida twist. Donaldson's attorney had been arguing that he had a right to treatment. That had been Birnbaum's position, and thus it became Donaldson's too. But the Supreme Court didn't address that issue at all.

Instead, the justices focused on what they called "a single, relatively simple, but nonetheless important question concerning every man's constitutional right to liberty." The court ruled that "a finding of 'mental illness' alone cannot justify a state's locking a person up against his will and keeping him indefinitely in simple custodial confinement." There must be some finding that the patient is a danger to him- or herself or to others for the state to have a good reason for locking him up.

The ACLU still calls *Donaldson* the most significant court decision on mental health in U.S. history, even though it didn't quite turn out the way their client hoped. As for Donaldson, he was delighted to be out in the world again. And as he'd promised his doctors, he wrote a book about his captivity. It wasn't a bestseller, but it was enough to give him a reason to tour the country, telling his story and pushing for reforms so that no one else would ever have to go through what he did.

He even came back and visited Florida—but not for long.

Not as long as his first visit, anyway.

A family stops by a Florida welcome sign to check their map, 1947. Perhaps they were debating which body part the state most resembles. Photo courtesy of State Archives of Florida.

Epilogue: The Unified Theory of Florida

Brothers and sisters, this morning I intend to explain the unexplainable, to find out the indefinable, to ponder over the imponderable, and to unscrew the inscrutable.

—*GOD'S TROMBONES* BY JAMES WELDON JOHNSON, WRITER, LAWYER, COMPOSER, EDUCATOR, DIPLOMAT, AND CIVIL RIGHTS ACTIVIST FROM JACKSONVILLE

Every weekday afternoon I drive to the school my younger son attends to pick him up. Waiting for the kids to be turned loose, I stand in a line with the khaki-clad dads and activewear-adorned moms, many of them focused on their phones. One day while I was waiting, I overheard the woman behind me say into her phone, "Well, it *was* his condominium, and he *did* let them set up a meth lab in it, and now the neighbors all want his head on a platter. Apparently it's a bad idea to put a meth lab in a condo. It can blow up or something. But I'm sure he won't make that mistake again." I snuck a glance back. She looked just like everyone else.

Once my son is free to leave, we jump in our van to drive home. Along the way, we pass first through a middle-class subdivision full of nice brick and concrete homes built atop poorly filled wetlands that flood on a regular basis. It's not uncommon after a hard rain to spot piles of wet carpet and soaked furniture sitting by the curb. Yet people stick it out there, even as their sunken living rooms get *really* sunken.

Then we drive across a small bridge into a ritzier neighborhood, where the houses are much grander and the lawns all neatly clipped. The developer who built it in the 1920s wanted to convey "unimagined splendors and unwonted joys." Thus, each intersection is marked by concrete statues of lions, tigers, panthers, and gryphons. Over the decades, many of the statues have been stolen or vandalized. The survivors are decorated with big ribbons for Christmas.

This is the neighborhood where a divorced couple set up an unusual child custody arrangement. They took turns living in the same house so the kids would never feel as if they were being shuttled back and forth. The setup wasn't easy on the adults, but it worked well—right up until the man flipped out, killing his ex and himself and their two dogs.

Next we pass the ornate 1920s country club that gives this upscale neighborhood its shape and heritage. In addition to the stone panthers, the golf course is occupied by real wildlife—raccoons, possums, alligators, and, according to two fishermen who took a grainy cell phone video, an eight-foot Burmese python somewhere off the twelfth hole. Trappers failed to capture the snake, so it's probably still out there. And laying eggs.

Past the golf course we cross another bridge, this one stretching over a body of water called Coffee Pot Bayou, and follow a road that curves around its shoreline. We sometimes see dolphins and manatees slicing through the waves, and ospreys soaring overhead clutching a freshly caught fish. We also see well-toned people walking, jogging, riding bikes, and pushing strollers. Meanwhile, sun-fried guys stand on the seawall throwing cast nets or hanging a fishing pole over the placid water, and leaving behind litter that annoys the upscale homeowners.

In the middle of the bayou lies a thicket of mangroves known as Bird Island. It's a popular roost for herons, egrets, roseate spoonbills, and pelicans. A few years back, some fool wanted to build a condo atop that spit of land. A man who insists on remaining anonymous bought the island and donated it to a trust to keep it natural forever. I think about that every time I stop to buy gas at one of the island savior's convenience stores.

Now we're in the neighborhood known for having the most desirable address in the city, although all the big Victorian-style houses sit on lots so tiny they're in spitting distance of their neighbors. This is also where the Case of the Naked Nanny occurred. The less said about that one, the better.

Then we zip through downtown, first passing the upside-down pyramid known as the Pier, where the ship used in the *SpongeBob SquarePants Movie* was once anchored. While there it was also used in the filming of a pirate-themed porn movie, to the chagrin of city officials who did not realize what they'd approved.

Next we catch just a brief glimpse of the apartment building where a runaway blimp crashed ("It bounced all the way down the face of the building," a witness said. "It was baboom baboom, bam bam bam, and then, 'CRASH!' "). A few blocks away is the apartment complex where a desk clerk mistook a woman's body for a mannequin from an April Fool's joke and tossed it in a Dumpster. When he found out he had thrown away the mortal remains of a ninety-six-year-old woman who had jumped from the sixteenth floor, he was stunned.

"I swear to God," he said, "the face looked like a rubber mask."

Soon we're scooting through a small waterfront college campus where the marine science complex is named for a politician who, as a legislator, served on the Johns Committee, and later, as a congressman, fathered a child out of wedlock. With his secretary. While he was still married to his first wife.

Then we zoom over a humpbacked bridge that spans tiny Salt Creek. Everyone calls this bridge "Thrill Hill" because if you hit the top going about 40 mph, the people in the backseat will go flying up in the air. A couple we know kept their toddler from throwing a tantrum by crossing it twenty times one afternoon.

On one side of Thrill Hill stands the Salvation Army social services building, where we often see homeless folks in tattered clothing catching a nap on the lawn or arguing on the bus benches. On the other side, wrapped in a tall iron fence, is a yacht renovation and storage business that's full of expensive craft with names like *Salacious*. Salt Creek literally stands in for Florida's income gap.

Then we're on the home stretch, rumbling over uneven brick streets, past Craftsman bungalows and '50s concrete block homes, and then taking a turn by our neighborhood's waterfront park. Sometimes people train their dogs for agility contests there. Sometimes people string a clothesline between the palms and practice tightrope walking. The whole park is taken over by dozens of kite-boarders every time the wind gusts above 10 mph. Usually we see a mullet or two—the fish kind—leaping out of the water, but sometimes we also see the kite-boarders leaping up, twisting back and forth, doing stunts. Once we saw one of their enormous kites caught in a tree and wound up discussing how that would have delighted Charlie Brown.

We cruise past members of the SuperAmish commune out for a stroll in their bonnets and gingham dresses and the lot where the people who owned the emus used to live before their house was condemned and torn down. At last we roll to a stop in front of our own charming little 1920s home which, we learned after buying it, was previously occupied by a guy who was briefly a suspect in a triple homicide.

If you collect Florida stories, as I do, you find them everywhere you go.

I think some people believe that because most Florida homes have no basements—the water table is too high—therefore nothing in Florida can be hidden. That's not true at all. Florida stories—stories of dopey behavior and deep irony—hide everywhere. You just have to keep an ear out for them.

Why does Florida produce so much weird news? I've laid out the combination of factors in some detail already, but here they are summed up in Al Neuharth's favorite style of writing.

- **Our weather.** The Sunshine State's subtropical climate has attracted everyone from circus freaks to CIA spooks looking for a warm place to chill out. With no snow to keep them cooped up indoors, Floridians and tourists are out creating mischief and mayhem all year long, running into roving alligators or some other unusual creature basking in the warmth. And when the weather gets really hot, tempers tend to flare and people reach for any weapon, producing such headlines as "Man Escapes on Lawnmower from Intoxicated, Machete-Wielding Man." Our warm weather is also a good excuse for removing as much of our clothing as possible—just ask the Fort Pierce woman who was caught driving at night in her undies and explained to the cops she did it "because it's real, real, real, real real real, real hot."

- **Our geography.** My friend Caryn—herself a transplant from Noo Yawk—always says, "Florida is the drainpipe of America." Florida has often served as the end of the line for anyone fleeing a past, not to mention all the people fleeing winter. But once you're here, you're funneled into a fairly narrow space, a peninsula between the Atlantic and the Gulf of Mexico, where most of the people stick close to the coastline or cluster around Theme Park Central in the middle. Put twenty million residents and nearly one hundred million tourists in such a narrow space and you're bound to generate conflict over whose turn it is at the drive-thru or whether oak trees or palms should line the streets. Adding fuel to this fire is the discovery that Florida is full of perils to life and limb, ranging from sand spurs to hurricanes, sinkholes, and shark bites.

- **Our shifting landscape.** It's not just the sinkholes that make our lives shaky and uncertain. We change the view so often and so rapidly it's hard to find anything solid to cling to. In 2015, a study found that cities have a "memory," thanks to longtime citizens. The study found that most American cities have a memory that goes back twenty-five years, but traumatic events such as the Depression can generate memories that affect cities longer. I would argue, though, that Florida citizens have to deal with this kind of "trauma" on a regular basis because of the rapid cycles of economic development and disaster, by the constant reworking of the road system, by the loss of forests and swamps to pavement and sprawl. Nothing is constant but change, which helps explain the grab-for-the-gusto attitude.

- **Our history.** "More than any other force, the frontier shaped Florida for most of its history," historian Gary Mormino says. "Frontier values—fierce individualism, gun violence, a weak state government, and rapacious attitudes toward the environment—defined and continue to define Florida." To that I would add our collective ignorance of our history. For natives, that's because of a failure of the educational system. For the two-thirds of the population who came here from elsewhere, that's the result of caring more about their previous home than the one they're in now.

- **Our government.** As Mormino mentioned, we've always been resistant to government interference in our pursuit of scams—excuse me, happiness. As a result, our public officials have frequently seemed more interested in how they can cash in on their positions than in actually doing their jobs. Remember they're the ones who make sure our funding for mental health programs ranks forty-ninth among the states. But hey, at least they're entertaining.

- **Our people.** You'll find every race and nationality in Florida, every age group, not to mention every social stratum from obscene wealth to abject poverty. Take a cross section of our population and you're just as likely to wind up with a deposed South American dictator as you are to get spring break bros or professional mermaids or Jamaican sugar harvesters or Hooters waitstaff. Yet, as Miami documentary filmmaker Billy Corben noted, a common misconception about Florida is that it's a melting pot. Actually, he said, "We are more akin to a TV dinner, where sometimes the peas spill over into the mashed potatoes." In a neighborhood full of transient strangers, it's easy for irritation to become outrage, leading to stories like: "A dispute between Jacksonville neighbors over grass clippings involved one man armed with two small knives versus one with a machete and five Rottweilers." The only thing that joins us all together is a common illusion.

- **Our big lie.** We tell a lot of lies in Florida: "Ten dollars down and ten dollars a month" and "The rules are different here," to name a couple. Many of those lies we tell not only to outsiders but to ourselves as well. They all carry the same message: "Florida is a risk-free good time, so come on down and bring your money! There is no tomorrow, only today!" We do this because our economy depends on hauling in more suckers to keep the game going. If the flow stops, the game stops—and then the consequences start falling on us like anvils on a cartoon coyote. Here's a true statement, from Alex Sink, former bank president and failed gubernatorial candidate: "Florida has always been susceptible to the Wild West mentality. If it's too good to be true, we're going to be involved in it."

- **Our greed.** Everything in Florida is up for sale. Everything is geared toward sucking the maximum amount of dollars out of anyone who wanders through the door looking for Harry Potter tickets or a good deal on a water view. If you think there can be no consequences for your actions, then you are inclined to maximize your right-now profits even if it means siphoning off your water supply or knocking down the dunes that will save you from the next hurricane. That mind-set leads people to overreach as they grab for the gold ring, like the woman who made millions working a phony refund scam and then boasted on Facebook she had become the Queen of IRS Tax Fraud. We lead the nation in mortgage fraud, identity theft, and tax fraud. We're also the only place in the world where a polo mogul tried to adopt his girlfriend so the couple could dip into his children's trust fund.

- **Our wildlife.** We've got quite a menagerie here in Florida, between the native animals like manatees and the nonnatives like Burmese pythons. Thus we wind up with stories like the one about the guy who, while taking out the trash, discovered he was being stalked by an Argentine tegu, or the one about the woman who discovered a bear had broken into her house to eat her Easter candy, or the one about the guy in Key Largo who stopped a crocodile from chomping his bulldog by snapping a towel at it.

- **Our open records.** Thanks to Emory "Red" Cross, Florida has long
enjoyed a tradition of open records, which means a lot of the weird
stuff that the cops see winds up available to reporters looking for something to make their readers' jaws drop. Thus, when a woman claiming
to be a vampire attacked a man outside a vacant Hooters, that made
the papers. And when a pet kangaroo and goat got loose, and it turned
out they had escaped from rapper Vanilla Ice, it made the papers.
Thus, too, when a Vero Beach woman called the cops to report that her
ex-girlfriend was at that moment "decapitating" all her sex toys—well,
that's in the uncensored police reports as well. Just remember, though,
that the crime reports are only a conduit to making these events into
news. It's not like there are tons of oddball stories going on in, say,
Wyoming, that you don't hear about because of the public records laws.

It is true, though, that not all of the weird Florida stories grab the headlines. Some of the best ones might never make the papers. An encounter with
an oceanographer reminded me of this.

I was writing about the fifth anniversary of the BP oil spill, so I wanted to
interview a scientist who had been studying the effects of the oil's chemicals
on certain fish. He had had knee surgery and was recuperating at home. I
drove over to his house in the little town of Gulfport, which in the grand
Florida tradition is not in fact a port, or on the Gulf of Mexico, but is instead
a quiet village on Boca Ciega Bay.

His home was a marvel. On two-acres-plus of lush landscaping he had a
delightful Bauhaus-on-the-beach modernist abode designed by an architect
named Paul Rudolph. When he invited me in, I could see the interior had
been tastefully decorated from stem to stern. Beyond the glass doors lay a ter-
rific view across the sparkling waves.

We sat on couches in his living room and I took notes while he talked
about his research and used phrases like "chemical signatures." When we were
done, I stood up to leave and complimented him on having such a lovely home,
and he ducked his head a bit and smiled and said, "Welllllll . . ."

I pricked up my ears, because a drawn-out "welllll" is often the first word
in a real humdinger of a Florida story.

The house, he explained, used to be occupied by a hoarder. Floor to ceil-
ing, it was full of garbage. Clearing it all out filled up seven Dumpsters.

"Wow," I said, trying to hide my disappointment. I had expected more—
some twist to the narrative, a thick irony. But he wasn't done.

The family that had previously lived in the house consisted of a father, mother, and son, he explained. But when the son became a teenager, the boy began selling drugs. The father, disgusted, kicked him out.

When the father died, though, the mother let the son back in. She wasn't just okay with him selling drugs, the oceanographer said. She had some ideas to improve the business. She ended up taking it over and expanding it.

"She became the Godmother of Gulfport," he said. I nodded, smiling. This was more like it.

But then the Godmother died too, he said, and so the son took charge once more. He continued selling drugs, and continued living in his parents' house, but now he started accumulating all the trash that would eventually fill up the place. Meanwhile, the son didn't alert the government that Mom was dead, so her Social Security checks kept right on showing up in the mailbox, and he kept on spending the money.

Finally, after eight years, the feds nailed him for fraud and sent him to prison, and the bank took the garbage-filled house and made it available for a reasonable price. The oceanographer and his wife and son bought the place and tackled the mess.

Amid the garbage, he said, were some surprises.

"We found drugs. We found guns. Annnnd"—here he put in a wholly appropriate dramatic pause—"we found a Mickey Mantle rookie baseball card that paid for the entire cost of the cleanup."

There, that was the payoff.

At first they had been tempted to keep the Mantle card, he said, but the O. Henry symmetry of the whole thing was too much to ignore. The card in the garbage would pay for removing the garbage, but only if they sold the card. So they did.

Granted, there are no roving gators, nobody waving swords, nobody getting naked. Yet in a way this is the perfect Florida story, the story that epitomizes my state. You've got drugs and guns and fraud and family strife and garbage—and in all the garbage, an entirely unexpected treasure that makes it all worthwhile.

But you've got to hunt for it.

Florida can fool you. Amid the constant flow of weird Florida stories, people see this state as nothing but a house full of drugs, guns, and garbage. They don't see the treasure. Or sometimes, in pursuit of the treasure, they overlook the garbage.

In his book *Up for Grabs,* John Rothchild recounts how he and his wife and child moved out of decadent and depraved Miami Beach hoping to re-build their lives in bucolic Everglades City. They were intent on getting back to the land, getting beyond the rococo artifice, finding what was real.

They bought a lot, he writes, "and prepared to build a genuine Florida house, with no air-conditioning, porches on two sides, paddle fans, open to nature's breezes, and with a view of the Banana River. It was here, engaged in back-to-the-land activities such as making sea grape wine . . . that we learned we were homesteading on a failed golf course."

Every square foot of Everglades City, they soon learned, had been created by diverting the river and doing a lot of dredge-and-fill work. It was about as natural as a shopping mall.

People come to Florida, as Harriet Beecher Stowe noted, with their heads and hearts full of expectations. Aasif Mandvi, a correspondent on *The Daily Show,* moved from England to Florida when he was sixteen. When his father announced the move, Aasif was convinced his family would be living in "a sun-drenched beach paradise" where "my life would be underscored by the gentle harmonies of surf-rock, my girlfriend would look like Miss Teen USA, and my best friend would be a dolphin." Instead he wound up in a landlocked Tampa suburb, going to a school where the uniform tended to be "cut-off shorts, T-shirts, and a mullet."

What you hear and see about Florida is rarely the whole story. The Chamber of Commerce ads focus on the beauty of Florida, which definitely exists, but they don't mention the hurricanes and sinkholes. Similarly, when Jon Stewart ranted that Florida is a "giant cockroach-choking, hazard-infested, Hooters-dining, reptile-abusing, Everglades-draining, election-ruining, stripper-motorboating, ball-sweat-scented, genitalia-shaped, 24-hour mugshot factory," he was right—but his description was not complete. That's not the Florida that gave us "Her Deepness" Sylvia Earle or computer inventor John Atanasoff or NASCAR progenitor Bill France.

No matter how many thousands of people find the @_FloridaMan tweets amusing, those wacky tales of crime and mayhem ("Florida Man Shows Up to Rob Bank Drunk, In a Taxi") don't tell you anything about Florida Men like Ochopee nature photographer Clyde Butcher, the Ansel Adams of the Everglades; or Jack Rudloe, founder of the Gulf Specimen Marine Laboratory in the Panhandle town of Panacea, which has shown tens of thousands of schoolchildren just how cool biology can be; or Miami resident Donald J. Sobol, who, starting in 1963, wrote twenty-nine books for kids featuring boy detective Encyclopedia Brown.

All of the Encyclopedia Brown books are set in an idealized Florida beach town that's about as different from Miami as you can get. I like to picture the late Mr. Sobol sitting in his home in the mornings, eating breakfast while reading in the *Herald* about all the mayhem going on around him: the cocaine gangs shooting up the Dadeland Mall, cops getting busted for taking bribes, and so forth. Then he folds the paper neatly, clears away the dishes, sits down at his Smith-Corona and tap-tap-taps out another story about his Sherlock in tennis shoes solving a crime thanks to some arcane but pertinent fact about numismatics.

Encyclopedia Brown is a Florida Man, miniaturized. He embodies our state's best values in his love of the outdoors, his sharp eye for a con job, and his inventiveness in dealing with a problem that's stumped everyone else.

Jeb Bush and Marco Rubio embody other Florida values: our love of big talk and disdain for contrarian facts, our reliance on surface flash and name recognition and buddy-buddy favor swapping, our sweaty desperation to make a buck and overcome or even ignore the past. It's in our DNA and theirs too.

I would argue that the conditions that give birth to all the weird news we're known for are the same conditions that led to the works of Sobol and Rudloe and Butcher and Bush and Rubio. Those same conditions and attitudes are what have allowed Florida to influence the rest of America.

If not for two crooked Florida cops and an insomniac, we wouldn't have cameras in America's courtrooms. Without the 1920s Florida land boom going bust, Billy Graham would not have gone to a Bible college at a bankrupt country club and become a preacher. If not for our alligators, Spanish bayonets, and disease-bearing mosquitoes, John Muir might never have figured out that not everything in nature is made for us to exploit.

Our wacky tabloid writers, our homophobic singing sensations, our gun-rights activists, and Native American casino kingpins—these have all made their marks on American society. They changed the culture and political discourse everywhere, sometimes without intending to, often without anyone acknowledging that the change was produced by Florida and could have happened nowhere else.

The next time you read some wacky news out of Florida and are tempted to say, "Only in Florida!"—sure, go ahead and say it. It's true. But bear in mind that there's a lot more going on down here than just that. There's treasure amid the garbage.

If you live here already, or are planning a move here, I encourage you to embrace our weirdness, to celebrate our funky, fun state, to dig into our history, grab hold of our culture with both hands, and take a big old whiff of the sin, scandal, and screwball silliness.

I am a big fan of Florida letting its freak flag fly high, because that's who we are. We may have once been stolid Midwesterners, close-mouthed New

Englanders, laid-back Californians, uptight New Yorkers—but now we're Florida Men and Florida Women, with all that that implies.

You want peace and quiet? Go to one of those boring rectangular states like Nebraska. You want to greet every day's news with a raised brow and widening eyes? Then come on down to the Sunshine State . . .

. . . and bring your cash and credit cards.

We're waiting for you!

Select Bibliography

Chepesiuk, Ron. *Gangsters of Miami: True Tales of Mobsters, Gamblers, Hit Men, Con Men and Gang Bangers from the Magic City.* Fort Lee, NJ: Barricade Books, 2010.

Clark, James C. *A Concise History of Florida.* Charleston, SC: History Press, 2014.

Denham, James M. *"A Rogue's Paradise": Crime and Punishment in Antebellum Florida, 1821–1861.* Tuscaloosa: University of Alabama Press, 1997.

Gannon, Michael, ed. *The History of Florida.* Gainesville: University Press of Florida, 2013.

Grunwald, Michael. *The Swamp: The Everglades, Florida, and the Politics of Paradise.* New York: Simon & Schuster, 2006.

Jackson, Harvey M., III. *The Rise and Decline of the Redneck Riviera: An Insider's History of the Florida-Alabama Coast.* Athens: University of Georgia Press, 2011.

Kerstein, Robert. *Key West on the Edge: Reinventing the Conch Republic.* Gainesville: University Press of Florida, 2012.

Nolan, David. *Fifty Feet in Paradise: The Booming of Florida.* San Diego, CA: Harcourt, 1984.

Reyes, Paul. *Exiles in Eden: Life Among the Ruins of Florida's Great Recession.* New York: Henry Holt, 2010.

Wynne, Nick, and Joseph Knetsch. *Florida in the Great Depression: Desperation and Defiance.* Charleston, SC: History Press, 2012.

Index

Page numbers in **bold** font indicate photographs.

31901059918781